JEWISH WRITING IN THE CONTEMPORARY WORLD

Series Editor:

Sander L. Gilman, University of Illinois at Chicago

Contemporary

Jewish Writing

in South Africa

An Anthology

Edited by Claudia Bathsheba Braude

University of Nebraska Press : Lincoln & London

Acknowledgments for the use
of copyrighted material appear
on pages 167–68, which constitute
an extension of the copyright
page. Copyright © 2001 by the
University of Nebraska Press.
All rights reserved. Manufactured
in the United States of America.

∞

Library of Congress Cataloging-in-Publication Data
Contemporary Jewish writing in South Africa: an anthology /
edited by Claudia Bathsheba Braude.
p. cm. — (Jewish writing in the contemporary world)
Includes bibliographical references.
ISBN 0-8032-1270-4 (cloth: alkaline paper) 1. South African
literature (English) – Jewish authors. 2. Jews – South Africa –
Literary collections. 3. South Africa – Literary collections.
I. Braude, Claudia Bathsheba, 1967– II. Series.
PR9364.5.J48 C66 2001 820.88084724 – dc21 2001027553

Dedicated in loving memory
of my father, Barney Braude,
grandmother Sophie Braude,
and grandfather Faive Braude

Contents

Claudia Bathsheba Braude

Introduction

After the release of Nelson Mandela from prison, the South African Truth and Reconciliation Commission (TRC) was perhaps the most significant public symbol of the country's break from apartheid. Exploring hidden and suppressed aspects of South African history as one step toward the healing of a brutalized nation, the TRC's assessment of the impact of apartheid created space throughout South African society to reengage with memory and identity formed and promoted before and during the apartheid years (1948–94). Changes in South Africa's political landscape with the end of Afrikaans nationalist rule have been accompanied by attempts to grapple with silences constructed and perpetuated in the name of apartheid. The centrality to the TRC process of the question of apartheid's status, like Nazism, as a crime against humanity had particular resonances for South African Jewish history and memory. Engaging debates about history, race, and ethnicity in newly post-apartheid South Africa, this introduction and the selections that follow trace the construction of memory and racial identity in South African Jewish literary and cultural history.

While Jews were classified as 'white' in apartheid's white supremacist environment that divided people into different racial and cultural groups, for long periods of South African history both before and after the introduction of apartheid they were not seen and consequently did not see themselves in this way. Jews did not automatically fit into 'European' and 'white' social and legal frameworks. Nor were they ever completely marginalized as 'non-European,' 'colored,' or 'black.' This ambivalent racial in-betweenness produced anxieties about Jewish racial status and belonging within the white power base. Given the Afrikaans nationalist pro-Nazism encountered a decade before the introduction of apartheid, including the direct influence of Nazism and Nazi officials on apartheid's ideology and ideologues, this ambivalence significantly informed the subsequent development of South African Jewish social, psychological, and cultural organization. Fearful of the potential for state-sponsored anti-Semitism, the establishment Jewish community sought to demonstrate Jewish whiteness and loyalty to white concerns in order to secure a place of belonging for Jews under the apartheid government. The cordial relations sought with the government resulted in distortion, and even loss, of memory of Afrikaans nationalist pro-Nazism and ultimately in the internalization of apartheid discourse within mainstream Jewish identity. In contrast with and distanced from the establishment Jewish community, many leftist Jews refused to conform to the white nation being engineered through apartheid. Opposing racism in general, necessarily including anti-Semitism, their political identity was motivated by and retained a different kind of memory.

These divergent mnemonic and political responses to the fears and insecurities resulting from a history of racial stigmatization—on a spectrum from collusion with racism and apartheid to involvement in the struggle for a nonracial society—produced different writerly strategies. The construction and use of memory and forgetting of specific aspects of South African and European racial history run throughout the development of South African Jewish literature and consciousness like a line of gold beneath the city of Johannesburg. For the purposes of this anthology, South African Jewish literature is defined as writing that reflects this memory and forgetting in a series of complex ways. This is 'Jewish' fiction not because its authors are biologically Jewish but because it illuminates a specific convergence of issues around race, identity, memory, and history. Writers represented here respond to and are informed by their often contradictory confrontation with Jewish racial status and social position in South Africa. They reflect the specificities of historical circumstances of South African Jewish life under apartheid, and particularly the insecurities arising from the fear of National Party (NP) links with Nazism. In other words, this is 'Jewish' writing to the extent that it reflects on experiences in South African history and society in ways that would not be possible by other writers who were not themselves similarly positioned, or even by the same writers in different interpretive contexts.

It is hoped that this introduction and the selections in this anthology will restore memory to a racial history that is largely forgotten in both popular and critical perception. Including both current and some older writing, this anthology is contemporary in representing not only writing *of* the time but also writing speaking *to* the time. Tracing these paths of Jewish memory has been made increasingly possible by contemporary changes in South Africa's political landscape. Together with the demise of Afrikaans nationalist rule, the achievement of a constitution that ensures nonracism and political equality for all South Africans has brought older writing into new focus. It is now possible to assess the long-term impact of apartheid on Jewish identity, culture, and literature.

This introduction focuses less on the literary features of the selections than do other volumes in this series. Such focus, no doubt, will follow, as the still largely unrecognized body of writing that is South African Jewish literature is increasingly represented in university libraries and is read and studied. Instead, I have chosen to engage certain key historiographical and political issues in order to open up this writing to readers and scholars in South Africa and internationally. Key features of the fiction come into focus only when one pays close attention to the political landscape in which it evolved. Responding to South African racial history and textuality, this writing is explicitly South African. It reflects far more about life under apartheid than about an essential diaspora Jewish experience that some believe to be potentially evident in any other geographical or sociopolitical context. Methodologies that seek to demonstrate essential continuities among all Jews worldwide have functioned in the South African context to conceal the influences of apartheid ideology and social organization and have thereby promoted the apartheid illusion that South African Jews, Judaism, culture, and identity were a 'separate,' 'group' affair, distinct from other equally discrete 'groups' and 'communities.'

This writing is less continuous with constructions of other diasporic Jewish identities than with other South African constructions. Juxtaposing the writers anthologized here in a 'Jewish' context refers back to South African literary production generally. Restoring memory to the racial history of Jews in South Africa and to their fears of racial in-betweenness brings into focus apartheid's construction of a white nation. This necessitates an interrogation of the relation between 'Jewish' and other subjective positionings. For instance, contextualizing parts of the writing of Nobel Laureate Nadine Gordimer (b. 1923) not only as, inter alia, 'white' and 'female' but also as 'Jewish' problematizes and complements aspects of South African literary history. Reading writers traditionally received as 'white' who, in fact, deal in varying ways with doubts regarding their racial status within white supremacist society problematizes conventional literary wisdom. Restoration of memory to Jewish consciousness of not fitting comfortably into the 'white nation' explodes racial categories of 'white,' 'black,' 'Jew,' and other and reveals the constructedness of that 'white' tradition. In the process, it interfaces with developments of a nonracial South African literary tradition.

It is hoped that this exploration of the specificities of South African Jewish history will add to the complex tapestry of post-Holocaust Jewish life in the diaspora and to the growing literature on political uses of memory of the Holocaust. Memory of racial ambivalence, southern African pro-Nazism, and the Nazi Holocaust had political objectives and consequences. Jewish amnesia of NP pro-Nazism interfaced with the political needs of the apartheid state. Given international post-Nuremberg judgments regarding Nazism, the NP's promotion of apartheid's respectability within the international community demanded similar public amnesia of the Nazi influence on Afrikaans nationalism. The resulting historical and mnemonic distortions are clearly reflected in Jewish fictional and historiographical texts. Thus examination of the relation between identity, memory, and race in South African Jewish literature is useful for understanding broader South African trends. This examination of how apartheid and Afrikaans nationalist racism (including its anti-Semitism) influenced South African Jewish consciousness is intended to feed into the developing history of apartheid's impact on South African society as a whole. Restoring Jewish memory to enduring, if invisible, Jewish fears of the influence of Nazism on Afrikaans nationalism parallels and becomes part of restoring memory about the impact of Nazism on apartheid ideology. It enhances understanding of the history of South African racism. Specifically, the illumination of this hidden South African

Jewish history provides a useful model through which to examine contemporary variations of attempts, including those in the TRC context, to inhibit memory of the nature and extent of apartheid's criminality.

Preparing for Freedom

The early days of 1990 witnessed a significant cultural debate about post-apartheid culture in South Africa. Albie Sachs (b. 1935), then the exiled legal expert of the African National Congress (ANC) and now a judge on the Constitutional Court, published 'Preparing Ourselves for Freedom' (De Kok and Press 1990) on the role of culture both in the struggle against apartheid and in a changing South Africa. Originally presented to an ANC in-house seminar on the implications for culture of the legal department's Constitutional Guidelines, the paper was widely circulated inside the country, where it sparked a major debate about the role of art and culture in the construction of new South African identities.[1] The timing of both the piece and the ensuing debate was no accident. It reflected a political climate about to change gear significantly. Nelson Mandela was released from twenty-seven years of incarceration a short couple of months after the paper appeared, and the ANC and other political parties, including the South African Communist Party (SACP), were unbanned after several decades.

Sachs encapsulated the Guidelines' thrust as reconciling political equality in a nonracial democracy with ensuring the country's cultural and linguistic diversity (1990a). Carefully differentiating between legal sameness and cultural difference, he argued that from a legal point of view the struggle against apartheid was a struggle both against separateness and to be the same but that it assumed a different shape in the realm of culture and identity. Sameness and identity related to different things: 'Sameness refers to one's status as citizen, voter, litigant, scholar, patient or employee. In this capacity, one's appearance, origin and gender are totally irrelevant. Identity relates to personality, culture, tastes, beliefs and ways of seeing and doing things. Here we struggle for the right to be different,' he said (161). The quest for national unity was not a 'call for a homogenized South Africa made up of identikit citizens' (179).

Rather, it involved acknowledging and taking pride in the cultural variety of South Africa's people (179–80). According to Sachs,

> Apartheid philosophy . . . denied any common humanity, and insisted that people be compartmentalized into groups forcibly kept apart. In rejecting apartheid . . . we do not plan to build a non-racial yuppiedom which people may enter only by shedding and suppressing the cultural heritage of their specific communities. We will have Zulu South Africans and Afrikaner South Africans and Indian South Africans and Jewish South Africans and Venda South Africans and Cape Muslim South Africans. . . . Each cultural tributary contributes towards and increases the majesty of the river of South African-ness. While each of us has a particularly intimate relationship with one or other cultural matrix, this does not mean that we are locked into a series of cultural 'own affairs' ghettos. (180)

Sachs's affirmation of cultural differences marked a decisive shift in debates about the nature of post-apartheid culture and identity. It was new in an anti-apartheid context. Fearing that an affirmation of ethnicity would indirectly legitimize the apartheid regime's manipulation of ethnic and race categories in its entrenchment of white domination, people involved in anti-apartheid work deemphasized and silenced issues of identity. 'We were acting essentially as committed South Africans and not as Jews,' said trade unionist Taffy Adler (Suttner 1997, 13). Pauline Podbrey (b. 1923) agreed. 'Nobody [in the South African Communist Party] ever discussed their Jewishness or brought it forward as an issue, and it was quite irrelevant to the politics of the day' (52). Born in Lithuania, Podbrey came to South Africa in 1933. She was active in the SACP and married the prominent Indian trade unionist and Communist Party leader H. A. Naidoo.

Against this background, it is not surprising that much of the writing and self-expression by Jews who actively opposed apartheid obscures Jewish identity or culture. Comparing Gordimer's treatment of Jewishness with that of American Jewish writers such as Saul Bellow, the literary critic Michael Wade discerned an 'unusually powerful mechanism of concealment in a body of work whose telos is to reveal' (1993, 156). In The Jail Diary of Albie Sachs (1990b), Sachs's account of detention in a South African prison in

1963, he similarly underplayed the Jewish cultural heritage he subsequently affirmed in 'Preparing Ourselves for Freedom.' But it is no coincidence that he first noticed the shape of his nose—that classic indicator of perceived Jewish difference—while in police custody.[2] Imprisoned with little to do, he embarked on a voyage of self-discovery: 'Some of the discoveries are amusing. My nose for example is askew, veering, like my views, quite markedly to the left. When did that happen? Perhaps at my birth. Funny that in all my twenty-eight years I have never noticed it before' (40). Sachs was incarcerated in an environment in which his leftist, oppositional politics was equated with his Jewishness. Associating Jews with Communism and the 'Swart gevaar' ('Black peril') (Shimoni 1980, 135), upholders of the apartheid regime regarded Sachs as the Communist conspirator out to destroy Afrikaans self-determination and the civilized Western values on which it purported to be based. One of the few references in Jail Diary to his Jewishness is in Sachs's description of being harassed by the security lackeys of the apartheid state. Searching his flat before his arrest, the lieutenant 'made remarks from time to time to let me know that he was very aware that he was an Afrikaner and I a Jew' (1990b, 28). A devout Bible-thumping station commander subsequently explicitly sees Sachs as 'a Jew and a communist and an agitator' whom he nonetheless may not hate (137). 'Doesn't the Bible say I should love my enemy?' he asks (137). Inspired by a story of a longtime atheist Jew who ultimately becomes Christian, he desires to convert Sachs (135–36). This pointed awareness of his Jewishness heightened Sachs's sensitivity to how he was (literally) seen. Thus he too believes that his politics are visible in his very physiognomy—both his nose and his views veer to the left. The accompanying absence in the Jail Diary of real treatment of this perception or of reference to his Jewishness is particularly striking when contrasted with his recent writing.

Sachs's position in 'Preparing Ourselves for Freedom' marked a comfort with acknowledging diverse cultural heritages that was simultaneously post-apartheid and postmodern. It also marked a decisive point in the body of writing that can be called South African Jewish literature. An autobiographical version of the cultural implications of the Constitutional Guidelines is to be found in The Soft Vengeance of a Freedom Fighter (Sachs 1991). Soft Vengeance is Sachs's account of recovery from extensive injury caused by a bomb planted by South African agents while he was in exile in Maputo, Mozambique, in 1988. The extract published here from *Soft Vengeance* is taken from the book's opening. In the first few pages Sachs represented as 'Jewish' his narrative account of the way he handled coming to terms with and surviving the explosion. His narrative involved the use of the Jewish joke about Himie Cohen falling off a bus. The joke is characterized by dark, survival humor, 'from the days when we Jews still told jokes to ward off the pains of oppression and humiliation' (10–11). In the course of the book, Sachs recounts telling the joke to several people, including a group of journalists who looked at him 'as though the bomb has affected my head a little' (26). This led Sachs to muse that 'jokes do not translate easily' (26). His ex-South African Communist, Jewish psychiatrist with whom he shared 'a certain common cultural background' already knew the joke (60), but the father of a fellow ANC comrade who was killed by agents of the apartheid regime remained unmoved by it. It was in the mirth of another ANC member, Jacob Zuma,[3] that the joke finally found its resting place in the context that lent Sachs self-definition:

> *Often when African comrades are telling a story I feel very 'white' and inhibited, lacking in laughter and impatient to hear the story's end, as if what matters is the piece of factual information being conveyed and not the savour of the telling and the rich personal interactions involved in the narrative. Yet today I know that I will relate the story well, African-style, no hurry, emphasis on the concrete little episodes that illuminate the multi-faceted relationships involved. . . . I will enjoy doing the narration and Zuma will get pleasure from egging me on to even richer and more comic concreteness, counterpointing my reportage with a melodic accompaniment of rising and falling laughter.* (116)

Through the process of storytelling Sachs overcame his 'whiteness' to become 'African.' This did not, however, prevent him from feeling Jewish. Speaking subsequently to a Jewish audience, he described the significance of this integration of Jewish and African humor. 'Some months later I recalled the moment to my ANC colleague Jacob Zuma. His Zulu laughter and my Jewish humour blended so easily that I took it as a symbol of the unity we were achieving in the ANC, a unity which drew its strength from the fact that we came into the organization as we were, bringing with us and sharing rather than leaving behind and negating our different cultural ways,' he said (1993a, 13). In Sachs's recounting of the episode, Zuma's own experience of the hardships that came with fighting apartheid in exile provided an experiential grid that made the Yiddish joke meaningful. According to Sachs, the specificity of the Jewish cultural and historical experience was transcended, speaking to Zuma's experience, as a Zulu-speaking South African, of oppression and suffering in exile fighting against apartheid. Written in a similar period, Sachs's reference to his Jewish cultural background echoed his earlier, legal affirmation of diverse cultural heritages in a post-apartheid society. Replacing the absence of discussion of his Jewishness in his Jail Diary, Sachs included his Jewish culture among the tributaries that would contribute toward a unified South Africanness.

Between Two Worlds

The significance of the post-apartheid shift, encapsulated in Sachs's cultural, legal, political, and autobiographical output, from silence and suppression of Jewish cultural heritage to its acknowledgment and affirmation is heightened by turning back a generation to that of his father, Solly Sachs. Born in Kamaai, Lithuania, Solly Sachs was one of thousands of Eastern European Jewish immigrants who, between 1881 and 1914, sought to replace political oppression and poverty in Eastern Europe with the economic opportunity offered by the discovery of mineral wealth in South Africa. The South African Jewish community, numbering 120,000 at its height and (after significant emigration and Israeli immigration) today numbering an estimated 85,000, is descended in large part from these Lithuanian immigrants.[4] Together with his mother and brother Bernard, Sachs came at the beginning of 1914 to meet his father and elder siblings, who had preceded their arrival by several years and were already settled in Johannesburg. While earlier Jewish life had centered around the Kimberley diamond fields in the Cape, the focus shifted after the South African War at the turn of the century to Johannesburg's gold fields. The aspirations, traditions, and activities of

Jewish immigrants in their new society combined with the development of mining and general industrialization of South Africa. The history of the Johannesburg Jewish community, like that of the Sachs family, is intimately intertwined with the history of the early mining town.

Many of these immigrant Jews were regarded as unassimilable into European South African society. Jews were popularly perceived to be non-Western and consequently not 'white.' Eastern European Jews (pejoratively labeled 'Peruvians') (Shain 1994, 27), said one newspaper correspondent, 'made the name of the white man stink in the nostrils of all men' (30). Jews were paralleled with blacks, Indians, and coloreds. The *Owl*, the Cape Town weekly newspaper, said that 'the fact is Cape Town at the present time is full of those Polish Jew hawkers who live in dirtier style than Kafirs. . . . Respectable Europeans should order these people from their doors. That is the only way to put them down. Let these people do manual work' (32). Perceived as undesirable, Eastern European Jews were made to feel inferior and uncivilized. Even at school, Solly and Bernard Sachs were confronted with anti-Semitism. Considered to be dirty and to speak with strange, guttural accents, they 'were on the whole regarded as an unwelcome foreign intrusion,' the kind who were 'prone to collect insurance from bogus fires' (Bernard Sachs, 1949, 104). Once, when the brothers were unable to contribute to the war effort, their teacher declared they were 'no credit to the school, or to the country which has given you protection' (Bernard Sachs, 1959, 48). She was articulating popular sentiment. According to his brother Bernard, for Solly Sachs the very word 'civilisation' was a source of pain. It 'made Solly feel bitter' (47). In accordance with Queen's English, 'he had once spelt it with a "z" instead of an "s", and Miss Johnstone had brought her bamboo stick down viciously on his hand,' he said (47).

Referring to the ambiguous racial status of Eastern European Jewish immigrants, a 1905 editorial in the *South African Jewish Chronicle*, the first Anglo-Jewish newspaper, said that Jews would be the first to be affected by 'the levelling process going on between white and coloured' since 'the Russo-Jewish immigrants [are] the most prominent section of those who stand on the *border-line between white and coloured*. The raw Russian Jew is, of all Europeans, the one who has the least of the European and the most of the oriental about him.'[5] That Jews were themselves aware of the ambiguity of their racial status is further reflected in Yiddish fiction. In his short story 'Gold and Diamonds' Richard Feldman (1897–1968), a prolific writer in English and Yiddish, describes the hardship experienced by one new immigrant, come across to make his fortune to save the rest of his family left behind in the old country. 'The most terrifying week of his life had been the first week, alone in a new land, without a language, without friends, without a trade.' With no one to turn to, he goes in search of any available work. 'It made no difference what sort of work. Surely they would accept him for work done by blacks—he was no worse than a black,' he says.[6] Only two of Feldman's stories deal with uniquely Jewish experiences.[7] According to the Yiddish scholar Joseph Sherman, Feldman endeavored to meet and engage black South Africans working on mines and farms, and his short stories consequently represent black South African life for the first time in Yiddish literature.[8]

Thirty years later a Russian Jewish immigrant unwittingly diagnosed the Jewish condition of living on the borderline, of being caught between two worlds. Wulf Sachs (1893–1949) was the first practicing psychoanalyst in South Africa. Not related to Solly Sachs, he was an active socialist and Zionist. In Black Hamlet (1937), Wulf Sachs described his psychoanalytic encounters with John Chavafambira, an herbalist living in Johannesburg. Believing that 'the manifestations of insanity, in its form, content, origin and causation, are identical in both natives and Europeans' (71), Sachs sought to demonstrate the universality of psychological drives irrespective of race. According to historian Saul Dubow, his view contrasted with the prevailing colonial belief that people's mental structures and illnesses were racially determined (12). Significantly, his assertion that Europeans, Africans, and others all shared common drives applied as much to himself as to Chavafambira. As an Eastern European Jew, he was as unlikely as Chavafambira to be classed as 'European.' The comic side of Sachs's claim to have changed Chavafambira's narrative into 'normal, as opposed to the broken though fluent English in which it was told to me' (75) comes into play with the journalist and editor Edgar Bernstein's posthumous tribute to Sachs. 'So many lawyers, doctors, merchants, think they can write novels: without the training they would not disregard in their own avocations, attempt the highest form of literary art,' he wrote, '[but] I hadn't read more than twenty pages before I was moved to wonder. *Across his then still faulty English* this man was capturing life' (Bernstein 1962, 182). Like that of Chavafambira, Sachs's flawed English and all it represented were stigmatized as inferior.

Sachs had immigrated to South Africa from Russia in 1922.[9] At this time, the immigration legislation, including a clause that allowed the exclusion of immigrants on economic grounds, was used to reduce Jewish immigration (Shimoni 1980, 89). A question about race on the declaration form filled in by passengers disembarking in South Africa unambiguously indicates that Jews, like Indians and Africans, were considered non-European: 'Race (European, Hebrew, Asiatic or African)' (90). Sachs's description of the cure he sought for Chavafambira suggests that *Black Hamlet* invisibly treated his own anxieties about Jews being marginalized as non-European. Sachs diagnosed Chavafambira as living a psychological 'double life,' torn between his rural African and urban Europeanized worlds, norms, and values (1996, 235). He argued that Chavafambira was unable to reconcile the competing and conflicting moral and religious codes and lifestyles and thereby to secure his place in urban modernity. Sachs accompanied Chavafambira back to the latter's home in then Northern Rhodesia in an effort to get him to confront the traditional life he had physically left but continued to carry with him in Johannesburg. Sachs described inadvertently contributing to Chavafambira's confusion one morning by offering him 'some ham from my [breakfast] provisions' (311). Although Chavafambira had previously eaten ham with Sachs, 'the horrified stare of those present reminded him of the pig-meat taboo of the family' (311). Sachs projected the pig-meat taboo away from his own (Jewish) breakfast tray onto Chavafambira's. In so doing, he deliberately represented himself as having no internal conflict between his Jewish world in which the consumption of ham is a taboo as rigorous as in Chavafambira's and the European world to which he aspired. He inscribed himself as European through his description of Chavafambira's inability to do the same. His anxiety regarding his Jewishness translated into a fundamental tension in his representation of Chavafambira. Writing in English, the language and point of reference of 'real' 'Europeans,' Sachs reinscribed Chavafambira's racial identity as 'other' while shaking off and silencing his own. He did so in order to belong to the dominant European group.[10] While explicitly seeking to counter racism, he implicitly and unconsciously affirmed it by projecting his own racial insecurities onto another man whom he knew to be similarly stereotyped.

Like that of Wulf Sachs, communal South African Jewish social, cultural, and political output took shape in response to the anxieties provoked by the doubts about Jewish assimilability that were at the heart of immigration laws and by the popular perceptions that informed them. The history, for instance, of the South African Jewish Board of Deputies (SAJBD) is inextricably linked to the status of Jews as potential immigrants. The SAJBD was established as the body concerned with and responsible for representing the interests of the Jewish community to the Afrikaans and English core groups. From the outset it defined its role in specific terms that would have long-term consequences. As early as 1910, the SAJBD positioned itself as a nonpolitical organization and promoted a policy of non-involvement in political issues except where they impinged on the rights and interests of Jews. It consistently argued that Jewish political behavior was no different from that of other South Africans and there was no specifically Jewish response to South African politics. Intervention in political matters was deemed appropriate only where Jews were negatively and directly affected. Two of the SAJBD's founders, advocate and parliamentarian Morris Alexander and editor David Goldblatt, succeeded in getting the Cape 1902 Immigrant Restriction Act amended. That act required immigrants, including Indians and Jews, to fill in the necessary forms in the characters of a European language, a test with potentially adverse consequences for would-be Jewish immigrants. In 1911, the SAJBD opposed a new immigration bill designed to inhibit Indian immigration and to exclude certain groups of undesirable 'white' immigrants. It too, included a threatening language test. Fearing its impact on Jewish immigrants, Jewish communal leaders opposed the bill's potentially negative consequences for Jewish immigration rather than the bill itself. They accepted the anti-Indian motivation of the immigration laws while contesting their potentially negative impact on Jewish immigrants. Responding to the uncertainties of Jewish racial status by distancing themselves from the parallel plight of Indian immigrants with whom they were pejoratively associated, the SAJBD implicitly hoped that Jews would be securely classified as European.

Literary Anxiety About Racial Status

The writing and career of the South African novelist, political commentator, and biographer Sarah Gertrude Millin (1888–1968) is at the heart of a literary tradition dealing with the anxiety experienced by many South African Jews concerning their racial status and place within white society. In many ways it established the terms that were to be accepted or denied, either implicitly or explicitly. Millin's enduring concern with the minority status of Jews in their host societies was described by Edgar Bernstein as being stronger than that of anyone else he knew. She modeled her self-perception on the biblical figure of Esther, who, while resident in the house of the Persian King Ahasuerus, successfully intervened in the politics of the day to protect the Jews. In her radio play *The Jewess Esther*, Millin expressed her belief that 'the story [has] a striking modern parallel.' Monitoring local and international politics, she was closely in touch with political developments and enjoyed direct access to key political players. These included Jan Smuts, South African prime minister from 1919 to 1924 and deputy prime minister from 1933 to 1939.

Contrary to popular assumptions informing, among others, South African academic and prize-winning novelist J. M. Coetzee's ahistorical reading of Millin, who claimed that her 'ideas on blood and race change little between 1920 and 1950,' consideration of and regard for chronology and context are crucial.[11] Spanning a period of half a century, her writing reveals various treatments of her anxiety about Jewish belonging. Assuming different forms over the course of the half-century in which she wrote, it responded to changes in South African and international political conditions. Dealing in complex ways with the place of Jews in the context of South African racial politics, her writing serves as a mirror of both

South African Jewish identity over fifty years (including close to
two decades after the introduction of apartheid) and of positions
adopted by the establishment Jewish leadership concerned with
protecting Jewish minority interests. *God's Stepchildren*, her international best-selling novel and a central text in South Africa literary
history, traces miscegenation through four generations of a family
of 'mixed blood.' First published in 1926, it is conventionally read
to epitomize South African racist expression. Considered to be a
chief literary apologist for apartheid and white supremacy, Millin
is read as being 'above all a white South African' (Rubin 1977, 11).
Her fiction, autobiographical narratives, and war diaries, however,
present a personality far less sure of her place in South African
society. It is precisely in her writing about miscegenation that Millin
revealed the nature and extent of her anxiety about perceptions of
Jews as not being white and therefore of being racially unaccept-
able. Millin was herself acutely aware of and sensitive to being seen
as racially different from members of the white power base. She
was once described as having 'the frizzy black hair, the flashing
black eyes, and the golden brown skin of the typical African' (Millin
1941a, 191). Years later, she refuted the description, saying, 'I have
light blue eyes, dark brown hair, and the skin that goes with such
eyes and hair, but I suppose the reviewer thought this too unin-
teresting and preferred to describe me as a *coloured person*' (191;
emphasis added).

Millin's fear of being perceived as 'colored' and of the attendant
social and economic discrimination is evident in significant places
in her earlier writing. This is especially true in *The Coming of the Lord*
(1928). Returning from years of medical training, Saul Nathan (the
son of Old Nathan, the Jewish trader) reintegrates into the small,
rural town of Gibeon. He knows himself, as a Jew, to face a 'peculiar' test: 'he is under suspicion [while being], on the face of it,
more capable of absorption than the member of any other excluded
race' (96). Millin represents Saul as being caught between two
worlds, as being 'two men': 'one of him lived among the people in
the big world, and had their interests and conventions, even their
thoughts and traditions and standards and prejudices. And the
other lived in a little ghetto, and suffered and enjoyed with his own,
and looked on at the big world, and himself in it, with shame and

amusement and satisfaction and sorrow and contempt.' 'That,'
writes Millin, 'really doubled his life' (96).

Everyone implicated in the prevailing racial hierarchy recognized
the Jew's ambiguous position in it. Tetyana, the Edinburgh-trained
African doctor, 'would have preferred it if it had not been a Jew
[who was the first doctor to sit down and talk to him], for a Jew had
not the same standing as another European' (108).

Millin establishes an identification between Saul and Tetyana,
between Jew and African. Both the words 'Jew' and 'Kaffir' '[were]
regarded as an insult,' she writes (98–99). Alienated from their
communities of origin as a consequence of their education and
from the rest of the society on account of their racial origins, both
men suffer from loneliness (110). This identification underpins the
development of their friendship. Knowing what it means to be
marginalized, Saul understands Tetyana and, as a result, treats him
sympathetically (109). Tetyana, in turn, offers to show Saul the
Heights, where the two thousand African followers of Aaron, a
religious leader, wait for heavenly redemption from their oppression as black colonial subjects. Transgressing the social norm by
walking with Tetyana in the streets, Saul is 'self-conscious' (112)
but succeeds nonetheless in overcoming the 'whole world of social
distinction' involved in such an act. While unable to 'forget the
colour of their skins,' the two men try 'to act as if it were not a
remarkable thing that they should have any sort of community'
(113). Never eliding the social and racial barriers between them,
Millin, in complex ways, affirms their human and professional
community. Subsequently assisting Tetyana in an operation on the
Heights, Saul becomes embroiled in the conflict between Aaron
and the government, which has come to forcibly remove Aaron's
community. While free to leave, Saul chooses to stay to help Tetyana
with the people who he and Tetyana know will be wounded in the
conflict. ' "If there's to be work, I can't leave you here alone, [says
Saul]." "They're my people," [says Tetyana]. "They're human beings," [Saul replies]' (291). Rushing to assist the wounded Aaron,
Saul's affirmation of a common humanity that transcends racial
barriers costs him his life. Raging against his son's fate, Old
Nathan finally succumbs to the views of the town's white supremacists who conspired to get rid of Aaron's community: 'it was [Old

Nathan's] most awful regret that it had been for black savages [that] Saul had given his life' (303). But Millin represents another, humanitarian way of looking at Saul's death:

> In the moment of his dying, Aaron had seen a bigger thing than that for which he had waited. He had looked for a God to come. And a man had come. Not in a holy passion for mankind—since it was not in humans to love one another; but in a terrible passion for duty because it was in them to love what was right. And here was the real triumph of humanity: that it had found a greater love than this rewarded love that could make a man lay down his life for his friend. Without hope, in bitter resentment, a man could lay down his life for one who was not his friend. These little mean and shabby beings, walking their precarious way to they knew not what, they had it in them to teach godliness even to God.

Central to her treatment of the conflicts of colonial Jewish identity in The Coming of the Lord was Millin's affirmation of Saul's choice to transcend socially determined racial boundaries in order to help a fellow man. In affirming Saul and Aaron's shared humanity, Millin, like Wulf Sachs, countered the prevailing colonial views of the day.

In light of this affirmation, it is possible to read Millin's God's Stepchildren (which was published two years before The Coming of the Lord) as presenting a far more nuanced understanding of questions regarding South African racial dynamics than is the case when it is read in isolation. Elmira, her protagonist, was the product of mixed racial heritage, caught between two worlds. While successfully passing as white, she constantly acted to conceal the 'darkness' of her blood. Elmira knew that her place of belonging within her white school environment would be compromised should the truth about her mother be known. The book was ostensibly based on a memory from Millin's schooldays of a friend's embarrassment concerning her 'colored' mother. But the narrative also related to a different aspect of Millin's life. Millin's parents were Yiddish-speaking Eastern European immigrants, neither of whom spoke any English when they fled Lithuanian pogroms for South Africa (Rubin 1977, 12). Like Elmira, Millin knew that knowledge of her parents could threaten her sense of her social belonging. She knew that association with 'undesirable' Eastern European immigrants could have shaken her ability to pass in 'real' white society. Like Elmira (and Saul in *The Coming of the Lord*), Millin would have lived a 'double life': 'At school she was one thing; and at home, when she came there twice a year for the holidays, she was another' (Millin 1986, 141). Millin's characterization of Elmira's anxiety was a product, arguably, of her own relationship with her parents and their background. But she did not succeed entirely in obliterating her involvement in the racial concerns she attributed to and projected at Elmira: 'And although, at school . . . [Elmira] actually got to the stage of putting on a few little airs and of looking down on other children for this or that—although she even went to the length of joining in the universal condemnation of one little girl because her father was in prison, another little girl because her father was a butcher, and *a few more little girls because they were Jewish*—there was always at her heart a frightened pain' (141–42; emphasis added).

As a Jew, Millin would herself have received Elmira's and others' condemnation. The wound of this racist treatment (not dissimilar to that experienced by Solly Sachs at the hands of his teacher) runs throughout her treatment of prejudice in *God's Stepchildren*. Attempting like Wulf Sachs to divert such prejudicial perceptions away from Jews, Millin displaced it onto 'coloreds.' Her characterization of Elmira served as a foil for her own experience and fear of not being accepted as white. Writing in the English language her parents never mastered, in *God's Stepchildren* Millin concealed from her readers the anxieties attached to the 'darkness' of her Jewishness. Rather than expressing 'the prevailing white South African feeling about miscegenation' (Rubin 1977, 34), her writing implicitly expressed a specifically Jewish anxiety about the status of Jews in an environment in which they were considered undesirable. Her warning against miscegenation was motivated more by her fear that the white South African society to which her parents had fled for refuge from Eastern European anti-Semitism would expel them from its midst than it was by her whiteness. By adopting and mimicking prevailing white views on miscegenation in her writing, she sought to demonstrate loyalty to and thereby unambiguous belonging within white South African society. Involving a strong initial identification with people who were marginalized on account of their race, including 'coloreds' trying to pass as white, Millin ultimately used racism as a smoke screen to deflect attention from her own dubious racial status. Her fear of being seen as different from the whites with whom she mixed and desired to be a part informed much of her literary production, including her later defense of apartheid and white supremacy.

An unexpected continuity exists between Millin and Gordimer, two writers seemingly positioned at opposite ends of South African literary history. Gordimer attributes the beginning of her writing career, inter alia, to her attempt as a child to sort out the confusion resulting from the social hierarchies and racisms of the small mining town of Springs where she grew up. 'On the way [to school] I passed store keepers, themselves East European immigrants kept lowest in the ranks of the Anglo-Colonial social scale for whites in the mining town, roughly abusing those whom colonial society ranked lowest of all, discounted less than human—the black miners who were the store's customers,' she said in her Nobel Literature Prize acceptance speech (1992, 7–8). Here, she implicitly describes Jewish nonacceptability in 'real' white society. She explores Jewish in-betweenness in 'My Father Leaves Home,' a short story first published in Jump (1991). In the story, on arrival in a small mining town in South Africa the Eastern European immigrant father established his newfound identity in relation to and in between the white mining officials and black miners. While identifying with the black miners, who, like him, 'were migrants from their homes' and 'had only a few words of the language' (62), he simultaneously occupied a space of white command:

> While he picked up English he also picked up the terse jargon of English and their languages the miners were taught so that work orders could be understood. Fanagalo: 'Do this, do it like this'. A vocabulary of command. So straight away he knew that if he was poor and alien at least he was white, he spoke his broken phrases from the rank of the commanders to the commanded: the first indication of who he was, now. (62)

The child narrator observes the fear the father can instill in blacks in his shop: 'He shouted at the black man on the other side of the counter who swept the floor and ran errands, and he threw the man's weekly pay grudgingly at him. I saw there was someone my father had made afraid of him. A child understands fear, and the hurt and hate it brings' (66).[12] At the same time, she is also aware that he is associated with them. She witnesses his failure to integrate fully into white colonial society: 'In the quarrels between husband and wife, she saw them [his Eastern European family] as ignorant and dirty; she must have read something somewhere that served as a taunt: you slept like animals round a stove, stinking of garlic, you bathed once a week. The children knew how low it was to be unwashed. And whipped into anger, he knew the lowest category of all in her country, this country. *You speak to me as if I was a kaffir,*' he said (64). Here, Gordimer represents the pejorative associations attached to the father's Eastern European background. As a Jewish immigrant who was excluded from the category of European, which was synonymous with white, he, like blacks, was seen as racially inferior and dirty. Gordimer has indicated the autobiographical origins of 'My Father Leaves Home' (Suttner 1997, 110). Indeed, aspects of the story are reminiscent of details she recounts from her childhood:

> *My father thought that he had married above his station. My mother came from a Jewish background, but they had been in England for generations. . . . Now my father came from a typical little shtetl. . . . Somehow or other he met my mother. [She was educated] and was middle class and he was not. He came from a very poor background. . . . He always felt timid talking about his background because she always sneered at him. 'Where you came from people slept on the stove to keep warm.'* (Suttner 1997, 108–9)

Like Millin, Gordimer grew up knowing the social stigma involved in being associated with Eastern European Jews. For Gordimer, however, whose Anglo-Jewish mother was better able to integrate into the upper ranks of English-speaking colonial society, it was only one parent who threatened belonging in white, European society. Her autobiographical representation of her parents in 'My Father Leaves Home' testifies to her mother's attempt to avoid the racial stigma of her own Jewishness by projecting unassimilability at the more obviously visible Eastern European Jew. Contemptuous of her Yiddish-speaking husband, her mother distanced herself from him. Indeed, Gordimer says of her own childhood that her 'father's background was never discussed. It was indeed despised. My sister and I were brought up to think that these poor things sitting in some village in Russia [his family] were not even worth thinking about' (Suttner 1997, 109). Where Elmira in *God's Stepchildren* concealed her colored mother, the children in 'My Father Leaves Home' silenced their father's past. They did not speak his language, they did not accompany him to synagogue on Yom Kippur, they knew nothing about the family he left behind—'feeble flame: who were they?' (Gordimer 1991, 64)—nor even the name of his village—'I didn't ask him about his village. He never told me; or I didn't listen' (66).

Derisory representations of Jews of her father's class and background are present in Gordimer's early short stories. In 'The Umbilical Cord' in *Face to Face* (1949), a short story, Leo, the son of a Jewish general store owner, contemptuously regards his parents and their world, both of which he hopes to escape by entry into a profession. Thus, 'he stood breaking a match in his fingers, watching her as if she were not his mother' (27) and 'how distasteful it all was to him' (30). The contempt is echoed in 'The Defeated' in *The Soft Voice of the Serpent* (1953), where Gordimer describes the Jewish Mrs. Saiyetowitz as having not only 'the short, stunted yet heavy bones of generations of oppression in the ghettos of Europe' (198) but also 'the blunt ugliness of a toad' (198). Leo's contempt is repeated by the story's female narrator, the childhood friend of Miriam, Mrs. Saiyetowitz's daughter. The two girls' lives initially ran a similar course: 'Miriam Saiyetowitz and I had dropped like two leaves, side by side into the same current, and had been carried downstream together' (187). The story of the two girls is autobiographically derived, representing dual aspects of Gordimer's childhood identity. 'She was the powerful young Jewess. Beside her, I felt pale in my Scotch gingery-fairness' (185). In an article that appeared in the *New Yorker* in 1954, Gordimer said her mother preferred 'the Scots ladies of the town' to their Jewish counterparts.[13] Similarly, as a young adult, the narrator in 'The Defeated' distances herself from Miriam's Jewishness. '*Race and creed had never meant very much to Miriam and me*, but at the University she shifted naturally toward the young Jews who were passing easily and enthusiasti-

cally, with their people's extraordinary aptitude for creative and sci-
entific work, through Medical School,' she says (186; emphases
added). Disinterested in identifying in terms of 'race' or 'creed,' the
narrator sheds commonality with Miriam and her background.
Whatever they might once have had in common, their lives part
permanently: 'Now the current met a swirl of dead logs, reeds, and
the force of other waters, and broke up, divided its drive and its one
direction. The leaves floated clear; divergent from one another'
(187). This divergence characterizes the writing strategy Gordimer
evolved to avoid being associated with 'their people,' the Eastern
European Jews to whom she, through her father, is linked. Gordimer projected the conflict related to her own Jewish identity onto
her fictional Jewish characters.

Like Millin, it was through her writing in English that Gordimer
succeeded in obscuring her Jewishness and in securely locating
herself within the dominant European group to which her mother
aspired. However, the political consequences of the projection of a
troubling racial identity are diametrically opposite to Millin's. That
Gordimer's unambiguous location as white did not involve any
similar support of white supremacy is clear, for example, in My
Son's Story (1990). Written around the same time as 'My Father
Leaves Home,' the novel reveals many similar themes and concerns. It tells the story of a writer, William, who comes to understand his father, Sonny, by writing about his life: 'What he did—my
father—made me a writer' (277). The novel represents Sonny's
'colored' experience of being divided from and caught in between
whites and blacks: 'Halfway between: the schoolteacher lived and
taught and carried out his uplifting projects in the community with
the municipal council seated under its coat-of-arms on the one side
of the veld, and the real blacks—more, many more of them than the
whites, "coloureds" and Indians counted together—on the other'
(21). William describes the projection of 'real' blackness at others
that was involved in attempts by many 'colored' South Africans to
gain acceptance into white society:

> If you wanted to claim a self that, by right, ought to be accepted by the
> town, you had another self with an equal right—one that was a
> malediction, not to be thought of—to be claimed by them. With that
> strain of pigment went more interdictions, a passbook to be produced

tremblingly before policemen, dirtier work, even poorer places to live and die in. Better to keep them at a distance, not recognize any feature in them. And yet they were useful; the self that recognized something of itself in the franchised of the town inherited along with that resemblance the town's assumption that blacks were there to do things you didn't want to do, that were beneath your station; for nothing was beneath theirs. (22)

These power relations between whites, 'coloreds,' and blacks echo Gordimer's autobiographical descriptions and fictional representations of her father's ambiguous place in the Anglo-colonial racial and social hierarchy. The colored protagonist in My Son's Story can be read, at one level, as a foil to treat Gordimer's own Jewish anxiety of belonging. Gordimer explicitly represents Jews and 'coloreds' as sharing common racial features. Thus Sonny recognizes a part of himself in his lawyer, Metkin, whose Jewishness is crudely indicated: 'he looked like a rabbi,' says Gordimer (158). Looking at him, Sonny saw 'eyes black as his own, the eyes of old races' (158). Like Millin, Gordimer worked through her Jewish anxiety by representing the real dilemmas of 'colored' South Africans, a group more obviously caught between whites and blacks. In My Son's Story, Sonny was able to resolve the discomfort of racial in-betweenness by moving away from religion to involvement in non-racial politics. Having to abandon his career as a teacher as a consequence of his increasing political activities, he comes to be 'one of the best speakers' of the nonracial liberation movement (97). In the process, he succeeds in traversing the distance that separated him from 'real' blacks: 'No-one could say Sonny wasn't black enough to be a spokesman of the people, either in terms of his skin or his actions!' (112). Speaking on the same platform as a white anti-conscription activist at the memorial service for nine comrades killed by the police, he affirms the nonracism they died to help bring about: 'They will never live in the unitary, non-racial, democratic country our struggle is going to create. They have died without freedom; but they have died for freedom. Our freedom. We have heard from a young comrade who is not up there on the hill [with the police] pointing a gun at us, although he is white. The presence of our white comrades from the city here today is surely proof that the nine died also for their freedom' (113–14).

Nonracism stands here as the cure for the malaise of mixed race. The nonracist denial of racial difference that has characterized Gordimer's writing functioned, at one level, to secure a place of belonging for all, including Jews, along with Indians, 'coloreds,' and Africans. While primarily concerned with securing equality for black South Africans, her writing is silently concerned with her own equality, as the daughter of a man marginalized as non-European. Her earlier anxieties about Jewish racial status are concealed within the writing that helped to focus world attention on the acute racial dilemmas of black South Africans. Her involvement in the anti-apartheid struggle for a nonracial society can be read in part as a cure for the anxieties concerning Jewish racial status that are manifest in her writing.

Gordimer's unarticulated and complex treatment of anti-Semitism through her promotion of nonracism was consistent with the political activity of Jews who fought anti-Semitism along with all forms of racial prejudice. Some, for instance, had previously responded to the discriminatory paralleling of Jews and Indians in immigration law by affirming the association and by criticizing the official Jewish response. Comparing treatment of Indians in South Africa with anti-Semitism in czarist Russia, Henry Polak (an English Jew who arrived in South Africa in 1903) expressed anger toward those Jews who 'either in ignorance or by design . . . have lent themselves to, or at least not openly dissociated themselves from, racial persecution' (Shimoni 1980, 83). Polak worked closely with Mahatma Gandhi, who formulated his philosophy of *Satyagraha* during his years in South Africa. Other Jewish immigrants imported radical workers' ideologies and political traditions formed in the context of Russian opposition to the czar. Formed in 1918, the Zionist Poalei Zion (Workers of Zion) analyzed racism along socialist lines and promoted a racially united workers' struggle. The anti-Zionist Yiddisher Arbeter Club (Jewish Workers Club), founded in 1929, was affiliated to the Communist Party. Its members, including Solly Sachs, believed that the South African working class consisted of 'integrated black and white segments' (Adler 1979, 84). Their anti-Zionism was motivated, in part, by their insistence on the impossibility of a solution to anti-Semitism under the capitalist order. They chose to fight anti-Semitism through socialism rather than through cooperation with either white supremacy or Jewish nationalism. South African Jewish socialists became pioneering figures in the South African trade union movement. Opposing economic and racial inequality, they worked to create a society that was not premised on notions of racial superiority. Though not fighting specifically on behalf of Jews, they were undoubtedly concerned about the Jewish condition.

Rise of White Supremacy

Existing perceptions of Jews as being non-European and undesirable had direct political and legislative consequences in the 1930s. This period witnessed the rise of pro-Nazism in South Africa. Existing anti-Semitic perceptions combined with the influence of German National Socialism on Afrikaans nationalism to move anti-Jewish sentiment into a central position in South African politics. The beginning of 1930 saw a radical change in the conditions of Jewish immigration into South Africa. The Nationalist Labor government headed by Barry Hertzog, leader of the National Party, together with Daniel Malan, minister of the interior, proposed a bill to restrict immigration. The 1930 Immigration Quota Act restricted access to immigrants from all countries other than Britain, the British Commonwealth, the United States, and the countries of western Europe. Significantly, this included Germany. Without referring directly to Jews, the act was generally understood as intending to stifle Eastern European Jewish immigration (Furlong 1991, 49). Malan admitted that 'we definitely had the tremendous influx of Jews in mind at that time' (Shimoni 1980, 100). Hertzog came close to acknowledging the anti-Jewish bias involved when he referred to a 'fifth national group' separate from 'the natives, the Indians, the Coloured people and the Europeans' (99). Jews were seen as a separate and unwelcome nation and as a threat to the national character and unity of these 'four great national classes' (99). Malan considered Jews to be 'an undigested and unabsorbed and unabsorbable minority' (98). He claimed that 'the Jews oppose discrimination because they fear discrimination against them. In South Africa this means miscegenation' (Furlong 1991, 65). Reducing Jewish immigration would help to maintain the purity of Western civilization in South Africa, said Malan, because the 'civilisation of Eastern Europe is to a very large extent a different one from the civilisation of Western Europe' (Shimoni 1980, 98). Jews were clearly regarded as a different, non-European, and therefore inferior race.

The influence of the ideas and political ethos of Nazi Germany on Afrikaans nationalism at a time when apartheid ideology was taking shape and subsequent to the demise of the Third Reich has been downplayed in much South African historiography.[14] Tracing the relationship between mainstream Afrikaner nationalism and fascism and the influence of German National Socialism on the NP, the historian Patrick Furlong, however, argued that the rise of fascism had a 'fundamental and lasting impact on mainstream Afrikaner nationalism' (8). A generation of leading nationalists was influenced by contact with Nazi Germany. Piet Meyer, longtime head of the South African Broadcasting Corporation (the apartheid state broadcaster) and chair of the secret and militantly pro-Afrikaner nationalist Afrikaner Broederbond, was an ardent pro-Nazi. In 1934, he was invited to lead a student group to Europe, to learn about National Socialism (80). He excitedly learned to ski in the Alps with Rudolf Hess, Hitler's chief of staff (80). As recently as 1984, he expressed enthusiasm at having seen Hitler from a distance.[15] His colleague Hendrik van den Bergh, head of the Bureau of State Security, the feared apartheid security intelligence outfit, had been interned in 1942 by Jan Smuts for subversive extreme right-wing pro-Nazi activities (144).

Similarly, J. F. Janse van Rensburg, the leader of the extreme right-wing Ossewabrandwag, promoted National Socialism as a solution for Afrikaans nationalist aspirations. (In an extract from his unpublished graphic novel, the political cartoonist Dov Fedler [b. 1940] depicts the incident in 1942 when the Ossewabrandwag planted a bomb in the Mayfair synagogue, next door to the Fedlers' home.) Leading Afrikaans nationalists even suggested that they would not oppose a request from Germany to return the territory of South West Africa, the vast former German colony administered by the Union under a League of Nations mandate since the end of the First World War (now Namibia) (Kentridge 1959, 275). Organizational structures of the National Socialist German Workers' Party (the Nazi Party) in South Africa and South West Africa were a strong site of fascist influence. This influence was unequaled elsewhere in British colonial territory (Furlong 1991, 20). Responding to information that the Germans were planning a putsch in South West Africa, South Africa sent police reinforcements there (132–33). Had such a putsch succeeded, Germany would have had an excellent submarine base at Walvis Bay, accessible to both South Atlantic Allied convoys and the South African coast (121). Morris Kentridge (1881–1964), the Jewish parliamentarian who led the fight against anti-Semitic agitation during the Hitler years,[16] indicated the 'very grave danger of South West Africa being handed over to the Reich' (1959, 270), where 'she could establish a large air base . . . capable of bombing and smashing up Johannesburg in a few hours' (257). The influence of Nazi activity among the German-speaking people of South West Africa compelled Pretoria to ban the Nazi Party in the territory in 1934. Nazi officials believed they had a 'South African Sister Movement' (Furlong 1991, 24) in the Greyshirts, the most important of the ultraright 'shirt' movements that emerged in South Africa shortly after Hitler's accession to power in Germany in 1933 (20). The Greyshirts adopted the style and philosophy of National Socialism (25), adorning uniforms, banners, and the title page of its mouthpiece Die Waarheid with the swastika (73). The Nazis considered its leader, Louis Weichardt, 'an honest fanatical Nazi' and consulted him on South West African affairs (24). South Africa was flooded with anti-Semitic propaganda from Germany (26), and Johannesburg streets were filled with Afrikaans anti-Semitic posters. Jews, Communism, interracial sex, and 'antinationalism' were constantly linked in the Afrikaans nationalist imagination.

Millin closely followed developments in Nazi Germany as well as the growth of pro-Nazism in South and Southern Africa. Her war diaries[17] testify to her profound awareness and distrust of the German presence in South West Africa and to the possibility that the Germans were planning to use South West Africa as a port of attack on South Africa.[18] In revising her book The South Africans (1926) for republication in 1934, Millin expressed her concern about the influence of Nazism on Afrikaans South Africans. These concerns were echoed in South Africa (Millin 1941b):

About the time of the submission of the German nation to Hitler, a small
political party had arisen among the Boers that, looking for some means
of enlargement, had discovered in Hitler's racial diversion a policy well
suited to its needs and the country's peculiar conditions. It remembered
about the German blood in the Dutch and began to model itself on
Nazism. It incorporated Shirt and Swastika bodies. It was anti-British,
anti-Indian, anti-native, anti-Jew—particularly anti-Jew. It expressed
pride in its own descent from refugees by hounding, in its days of better
fortune, other refugees. (13)

Millin was partly referring to the contestation regarding Jewish immigration. Although Malan had expected the 1930 Quota Act to restrict Jewish immigration completely, it reached a peak in 1936 with increased immigration from Germany, a country considered unrestricted by the act. Anti-Jewish opposition became more vocal. The Greyshirts demanded that German Jewish immigration be blocked. The sentiment was repeated nationwide. Malan argued that 'an organized Jewish *geldmag* [money power]' was promoting the immigration (Shimoni 1980, 116). The government responded by imposing a cash deposit of a hundred pounds on all would-be German Jewish immigrants (117). The London-based Council for German Jewry chartered a ship, the *Stuttgart*, to transport as many German Jewish refugees as possible before the new restriction came into effect. The South African prime minister was lobbied to prevent the ship's landing, and the Greyshirts organized a mass protest meeting in Cape Town. A meeting at the Afrikaans Stellenbosch University attended by fifteen hundred people, prominently including Hendrik Verwoerd, who later became prime minister and the architect of apartheid, passed a unanimous resolution appealing to the government 'to put a stop to this organized [unrestricted and undesired Jewish] mass immigration by means of legislation and other measures' (118). Speaking at another public protest meeting against Jewish immigration, Malan said, 'The poor White problem in South Africa cannot be solved unless the Jewish problem is solved first' (119). Seen by Afrikaans nationalists as nonwhite and a threat to the white nation, Jews were considered a significant problem. The working-class Pretoria suburb of Hercules submitted a draft resolution to the National Party Transvaal provincial congress of 1936 to the effect that 'no Jew, Colored or Asiatic may become a member of the Party' (Furlong 1991, 56). At an NP congress in 1936, Malan demanded that German Jewish immigration be halted and proposed measures that would result in unequal treatment for South African Jews. Jews were banned from the NP in the Transvaal in 1937 (37). Malan's concern with the so-called Jewish threat to the economic advancement of the Afrikaner nation resulted in his proposal, based on the demands of the NP's 1936 congress, of a new immigration bill to Parliament in January 1937. According to Kentridge, Malan's 1937 resolution and his accompanying speech to Parliament 'showed clearly that whilst prior to that he disclaimed any attempt at discriminating against the Jews as Jews, he now unashamedly claimed that it was inevitable to name the Jewish race. The reason for that was, he said, "because South Africa has a Jewish problem"' (Kentridge 1959, 249). Malan's proposal was superseded by the Smuts government's sudden introduction of the Aliens Bill on 13 January 1937, which repealed the 1930 Quota Act. While framed in universal terms, the main effect of the Aliens Act was to stem German Jewish immigration (Shimoni 1980, 144). Consistent with her self-appointed role as Esther in the House of the King, Millin tried to influence Smuts and other world leaders for the benefit of South African and German Jews. She unsuccessfully appealed to Smuts to deal with the Greyshirts and to allow German Jewish refugees into South Africa. Feeling the potential for her own victimization at the hand of South African pro-Nazis, Millin identified with the fate of the Austrian Jewish writer Stefan Zweig, who, 'weary of his homeless wandering,' she said (1946, 156), committed suicide in 1942. Millin said of Zweig and his brother Arnold that 'they never wrote tragedies as great as those they endured' (156). She was fearful that her own life could also become a tragedy greater than those she had written about miscegenation.

The insecurity increased as anti-Semitism became an essential element of Malan's Purified National Party. Between 1937 and 1939 mainstream nationalist politics became overtly anti-Semitic. The National Party cooperated closely with the Shirt movements. In 1939, Malan declared that 'the Jewish problem . . . hangs like a dark cloud over South Africa' (Furlong 1991, 68). Echoing the anti-Semitic propaganda broadcast in Afrikaans by the Europe-based

Nazi Zeesen Radio Service, which constantly sought 'to tie Smuts to the Jewish community' (134), Malan and others blamed Jews along with the British for obstacles to Afrikaans national self-determination. He believed Jews directly threatened Afrikaner nationalist aspirations. 'Behind organised South African Jewry stands the organised Jewry of the world. They have so robbed the population of its heritage that the Afrikander resides in the land of his fathers, but no longer possesses it,' he said (68). Afrikaans nationalist anti-British sentiment, a hangover from the Anglo-Boer War, translated into support for Hitler. Seeking independence from Britain, Afrikaans nationalists identified with Germany. Referring to the Treaty of Versailles, Hertzog clearly expressed the nature of this identification: 'I know what it is to be humiliated and trodden . . . so that you feel that a state has been reached when you can no longer bear the humiliation. . . . *With what justification can one ask me and South Africa to take part in a war because Hitler and the German nation will no longer suffer . . . humiliation? No, you have to excuse me when I say that you have no right to expect such an action from me*' (123–24; emphasis added).

Malan and Hertzog were among those who voted against South African support for the Allies in the war against Germany. South Africa went to war against Germany by a vote of eighty to sixty-seven (126). The vote destroyed Smuts's and Hertzog's fusion government. Smuts's declaration of war was denounced by J. G. Strijdom (then Transvaal leader of the Purified National Party) as an attempt to satisfy 'English Jews' (132). In 1940, Malan and Hertzog formed a new united Afrikaner political organization, the Herenigde Nasionale of Volksparty, the Reunited National or Volk Party. It was more commonly known simply as the National Party. The views regarding Nazism of some prominent members of the NP were unambiguous. Verwoerd's open support for the Nazis was the subject of a libel action. Judge Philip Millin, Sarah Gertrude Millin's husband, found that Verwoerd supported Nazism and had willingly made *Die Transvaler*, the newspaper he edited, a tool of Nazi propaganda.[19] Malan clearly indicated the desire, should Afrikaner nationalists come into power, to introduce a policy that incorporated Nazism. 'Perhaps eighty to eighty-five per cent of the New Order (National Socialism) has been taken up in the Nationalist Party programme, which the Party will carry out in letter and in spirit when it comes to power,' he said in 1941 (Mzimela 1980, 104). 'German National Socialism strives for race purity,' said J. G. Strijdom. 'That philosophy is certainly the nearest to our National-Christian philosophy in South Africa,' he said (104). John Vorster was clearest of all: 'We stand for Christian Nationalism which is an ally of National Socialism. You can call this antidemocratic principle dictatorship if you wish. In Italy it is called Fascism, in Germany National Socialism, and in South Africa, Christian Nationalism,' he said (105).[20]

Knowledge of Nazism and fear of its possibility in close range on the streets of Johannesburg invisibly inform Barney Simon's (1932–95) story of 'Our War,' first published in 1974 and included in this anthology.[21] A founding director of the Market Theatre in Johannesburg, Simon was a key figure in South African anti-apartheid theater history. 'Our War' expresses the sustained impact on South African Jewish literary imagination of this fear. 'During the war we would hear from my mother about her sisters [in Lithuania]. Obviously with Hitler there became a terrible silence from there,' he said.[22] His mother's attempt to bring a niece from Lithuania to safety in South Africa was foiled by the changed immigration laws. 'Nobody knew what had happened to . . . my beautiful cousins who one had heard so much about and who you thought were coming out and then didn't. They died in the gas chambers,' said Simon. In an interview shortly before his death, Simon described the influence of the destruction of Lithuanian Jewry on his work in theater (Suttner 1997, 120). Simon, whose parents were born in Lithuania, recalled the visit of a rabbi to his parents' synagogue in Johannesburg and his description of the slaughter of Lithuanian Jews in the Vilna ghetto (120). The sight of all the Lithuanian Jews in the synagogue wailing on hearing of 'bayoneting and rapes and beheadings and God knows what' greatly influenced Simon, then a small child. 'I will never forget looking up in the middle of all this chaos in the synagogue—that terrible wail—and seeing my mother beating herself,' he said (121). That memory related, he said, 'to my life, my family, and theatre' (120). He internalized the knowledge of events in Europe. Describing a city and country under siege, populated with wounded, missing or dead people, 'Our War' is silently inscribed with knowledge of events in Europe, as well as with memory of the fear attached to the possibility of a German power within striking distance of Johannesburg.

On winning the 1948 national elections, the NP muted its anti-Semitic rhetoric. In a meeting with a delegation from the SAJBD, Malan (then prime minister) denied that his party was anti-Semitic. Franz Auerbach (b. 1923), himself a child refugee from Germany, mildly suggests the possibility that 'the National Party changed because after Auschwitz it wasn't that fashionable to be seen to be anti-Semitic' (Suttner 1997, 556). With the collapse and exposure of Nazism (by now internationally judged a crime against humanity), further anti-Semitism would have undermined the new image Malan sought to project. Locally and internationally, the NP's credibility had little to gain from acknowledgment and public memory of the influence of Nazism on Afrikaner nationalism. Instead of the discriminatory action anticipated by many, Malan included Jews in his definition of pluralistic white South African society. Jews were now to be included among 'white' South Africans.[23] Inviting all whites to unite against the black threat to white civilization he perceived in South Africa, even Ossewabrandwag leader J. F. Janse van Rensburg replaced his former adherence to the principles of National Socialism with inclusion of Jews in his definition of 'white': 'There come times when you can undertake common action with your English-speaking or Catholic (or Jewish) neighbours in the interests of all Whites,' he said in December 1948 (Shimoni 1980, 211). Nonetheless, Jews could not but be alarmed by the NP's election success. Knowledge of the Nazi Holocaust in Europe and memory of the NP's promises of a Nazi-type regime in South Africa shaped Jewish political responses to apartheid. Across the political spectrum, Jews dealt with the knowledge and trauma of the Holocaust by seeking invisibility in the South African context. The quest for invisibility assumed politically divergent and even contradictory shape.

Jews Become White: Amnesia and Cordial Relations

Welcoming the shift in NP policy toward Jews, the SAJBD and the establishment Jewish community sought to create and promote a cordial relationship between the Jewish community and the new government in order, as they saw it, to avoid the possibility of activating state-sponsored Afrikaans nationalist anti-Semitism.[24] They sought to win approval by demonstrating loyalty to the government. The impediment to the desired cordial relationship that was presented by the NP's pro-Nazi and anti-Semitic history was partly dealt with by an active process of historical revisionism. The textual results are discernible in The Jews of South Africa: A History (1955), coedited by Louis Hotz and Gustav Saron. Saron served as secretary of the SAJBD from 1936 to his appointment as general secretary in 1940, in which capacity he served till 1974, including the period in which he produced the book (Feldberg 1965, 376). Although in the preface he denied it was an official publication of the SAJBD, the book reflected the organization's operating assumptions. Indeed, the board supported Saron in writing the book, and on occasion he presented it as an official gift from the SAJBD.[25] Seeking to establish a firm history of affinity between Jews and Afrikaners as a basis for the desired relationship of cordiality, he reread the position of Jews among the Uitlanders who opposed Boer rule in the Transvaal at the end of the nineteenth century. Active political, civic, and educational discrimination was practiced against Jews and Catholics in the Boer Republic. Only Protestant Christians were able to serve in the civil service, and government educational subsidies were granted only to Dutch-medium Protestant schools, which Jewish children were not allowed to attend. Rabbi J. H. Hertz, then minister of the Witwatersrand Old Hebrew Congregation, was prominent among the Uitlanders calling for the removal of all religious disabilities. He was consequently deported from the Transvaal. While acknowledging 'the special religious disabilities which Jews as a group were subject to' (181), Saron argued, however, that 'the Jews had little or no cause to complain of the general treatment which they received in the Transvaal Republic' (181) and that 'these disabilities were not regarded as symptoms of anti-Jewish discrimination but as flowing from the Calvinistic foundations of the Boer Republic' (185). Seeking to affirm the possibility of Jewish loyalty within the ranks of the Afrikaners, he similarly deemphasized the views and activities of Jews who had been critical of the regime and highlighted Jewish support for the Boer administration: 'It is clear that the general attitudes of the

Boer towards the Jew was a wholesome and friendly one, and that
the Jews appreciated the freedom which they enjoyed,' he said
(183). It was significant, said Saron, that organized efforts by Jews
and Catholics to have the disabilities removed 'did not meet with
unqualified support from Jews' (186). He further said that 'to Jews
away from the scene of the conflict [the South African War], the
religious disabilities suffered under the Kruger regime do not seem
to have been important in determining attitudes. . . . Leading Jewish personalities in Europe were outspokenly pro-Boer' (210). He
countered previous emphasis on Jewish support for the British during the Anglo-Boer War. For complex reasons relating to the position of Jews in England, the Jewish Chronicle highlighted the dispro-
portionate extent of Jewish participation in the war effort, listing
the names and publishing photographs of Jewish soldiers fighting
for the British. Acknowledging the 'detailed reports' pertaining to
Jewish soldiers fighting in South Africa (211), Saron proceeded:

> Interestingly enough, the very fervour of [the Jewish Chronicle's]
> advocacy and of its insistence on the religious disabilities suffered by the
> Jews in the Transvaal Republic led to a controversy. A number of former
> Transvaal Jews, now resident in England, wrote to the paper at length,
> pointing out that the religious disabilities did not count much with the
> average Jew in the Transvaal, and stressing that 'there was no political
> or social crusade against the poor down-trodden Israelite; they were
> permitted as much freedom as anyone else . . . it would be ungrateful for
> us to pass over this generosity without recognition, and especially in
> these days.' (211–12)

Saron concluded the chapter by extensively quoting the views of
Rev. David Wasserzug, a Jewish minister from England, on his
departure from South Africa after four years in the Transvaal (1897–
1901): 'It was the mission of the Israelites to sow the seeds, not of
discord but of concord and good feeling. It was part of their mission to promote a better feeling between Briton and Boer' (212). He
referred to research done by Rabbi Louis Rabinowitz, which 'en-
abled him to trace the names of some 198 Jews who fought on the
Boer side' (208). Dissatisfied even with this research, Saron suggested that 'in the nature of things, the list cannot be complete'
(208). While Jewish involvement on the side of the Boers was not

insignificant, says David Saks, editor of *Jewish Affairs*, 'one senses that the writers were trying a little too hard to make their point that Jews too fought bravely.'[26] Saron indicated that critical Jewish thinkers in England, including notably Solomon Shechter, 'did not hesitate to join the band of critics of the war policy' (Saron 1955, 211). At pains to represent 'the cordial relations that were established between the early Jewish immigrants and the Boers,' 'especially because of the common bond of the Bible' (182), Saron extensively quoted views expressed by Hertzog nearly three decades after the war. 'Both were deeply imbued with the spirit of South African nationalism; no wonder then, that during the Boer War, among the most faithful and most trusted men on commando, there was almost everywhere to be found a Jew in the ranks of the Afrikaners,' said Hertzog (208). Thus, ignoring the deeply entrenched anti-Jewish sentiment that existed in the half-century before the introduction of apartheid and replacing the highly troubled relation of the two decades preceding the NP's election success, Saron promoted a tradition of a healthy, respectful relationship between Jews and Afrikaners. He further dismissed the NP's pro-Nazism by arguing that 'the real meaning of Nazism and of its doctrines and aims was misunderstood or ignored by many,' presumably including its leaders and members (383).

The Jews in South Africa concludes with Saron positing a positive relation between Jews and the apartheid tenet of cultural pluralism. Affirming apartheid as positive for Judaism and Jewish life in South Africa, he described it as a cure for 'the problem of assimilation' (398). 'The general cultural and political climate in South Africa, which emphasizes the separateness of the various racial and cultural groups of the population, favours the perpetuation of a Jewish group existence,' he said (398). Interpreting Jewish history as contributing to cultural pluralism—'Perhaps the Jews, through their centuries-long existence, may help [to show] that it is possible to combine fidelity to their own group and heritage with respect for the cultural aspirations of other groups, wholehearted loyalty to South Africa, and concern for the welfare of all its peoples' (399)—he expressed satisfaction that Malan, shortly before, had promoted the same relationship between 'national unity and . . . the role of [the] Jews' (399). Not everyone agreed. Considering Malan's views

to be both 'nasty and insulting,' the Hungarian-born rabbi Andre
Ungar commented on the way the Jewish press had interpreted
them as having 'an appearance of profound, philosophical phil-
osemitism' (Ungar 1959, 31). The publication of *The Jews in South
Africa* marked Jewish acceptance and self-acceptance as white, including the appropriation by Jewish communal leadership of the
terms and discourse of apartheid. As such, it stands as a seminal
moment in South African Jewish life. Acceptance of Jews as 'white'
required a profound suppression of memory, on the part of both
Afrikaans nationalists and Jews, of the general fear of being seen
as nonwhite and specifically of the NP's anti-Semitism and pro-
Nazism. Jews did not want to remember their fear or to be reminded of their vulnerability, and in a post-Nuremberg world, the
NP wanted its links with the Third Reich forgotten.

A key feature of the SAJBD's fear-driven attempts to demonstrate
loyalty to the Afrikaner nationalist government and to avoid being
seen as distant from its interests was its promotion of communal
political acquiescence with apartheid. Jews, it was felt, should not
'compromise' their own 'group interests' or safety by opposing the
ruling powers. The organization reaffirmed its existing policy of
political noninvolvement as a justification for the refusal to oppose
apartheid. This is not to say that all members of the board approved
of apartheid or that the board did not call for just social relations.
But though it condemned injustice, it did not use the word 'apartheid' until 1986.[27] When David Mann, then national chairman of
the SAJBD, told then prime minister Vorster that the board disap-
proved of his government's discriminatory policies, his criticism
was contained by the context—he was speaking at a banquet given
in Vorster's honor.[28] A clear anti-apartheid message emerged from
the SAJBD only in 1985, when it passed a resolution explicitly reject-
ing apartheid, by which time 'it was relatively easy and uncontrover-
sial for the Board' to do so.[29]

The consequences for South African Jewish consciousness and
identity of the line promoted by the SAJBD are best seen in the
writing of Sarah Gertrude Millin. Like that of Saron, her opposition
to the NP changed to active support. In spite of her earlier commitment to Smuts's leadership as well as her fear of and anger
toward the pro-Nazism of members of the new government, by the

mid-1950s her criticisms of the nationalists had given way to a defense of them. Hers would perhaps have been a personal as well as collective imperative in light of her husband (by then deceased) having called Verwoerd a Nazi. She promoted white supremacy in *The Wizard Bird* (1962) and provided a historical justification for it in her unpublished manuscript 'Time No Longer.' With the end of Smuts's rule, Millin no longer enjoyed access to political leadership. She nevertheless continued to try to secure what she saw as South African Jewish interests by retaining the favor of the ruling forces through demonstrations of Jewish loyalty to the apartheid cause. In 1960, her presence at a conference of PEN, the international writers' guild, marked the beginning of her active role as a defender of apartheid to the outside world (Rubin 1977, 263). Responding with fury to the novelist and playwright Lewis Sowden's attack on apartheid, she publicly expressed her support for the NP. When she was refused permission to respond to Sowden, Millin immediately quit both the conference and PEN. One wonders if she would have reacted as vehemently had Sowden not been a Jewish writer of some visibility (he was married to Dora Sowden, a prominent Jewish journalist and cultural critic who had contributed several chapters to *The Jews in South Africa*) and if Millin was not motivated by a displaced and fear-driven desire to demonstrate Jewish loyalty to apartheid to counter Sowden's criticism. Contrary to accepted wisdom in South African literary history, it was not in spite but *because* of her awareness of Hitler's activities and of Nazism and of Afrikaans nationalist sympathies for such that she adopted the ideology of apartheid as her own. Millin supported white supremacy and Afrikaans nationalism precisely because of her fear of Nazism and of Afrikaans nationalist pro-Nazism. That Millin, as Gordimer, who was present at the PEN conference, indicated, 'ended her long life as a passionate defender of apartheid' is the consequence of her sense of place and displacement as a Jew in South Africa. It was the direct result of her fear that those who had been pro-Nazi not too long previously would regard Jews as nonwhite and treat them accordingly. She sought at all costs to ensure that her 'white' cover would not be blown and that she would not be victimized like Zweig as a Jew or like Elmira in *God's Stepchildren* as the product of 'mixed blood.'

By the time of the publication of *White Africans Are Also People* (1966), Millin's unashamed defense of apartheid and white supremacy necessitated rewriting the history of Afrikaans nationalist pro-Nazism. Her reading of Afrikaans-Jewish relations diverged significantly from her earlier account. It did so along the same revisionist lines mapped by Saron:

> The Boers . . . saw themselves escaping into the desert as the Jews from Egypt. . . . And it thus came about that when, in the eighteen-sixties, Jews fled to South Africa, as to America, from the pales and pogroms of Russia and Poland, a thing happened to them never before known in their history: they were received by the people of a country as long-lost brothers. In the days of the Nazis Jews again fled from persecution to South Africa. But now South Africa, like all the world, feared an influx of the too many Jews who feared for their lives. In South Africa, besides, were people who, remembering the Boer War, supported those who stood against the British. They also therefore began to have German thoughts about Jews and, forsaking the ways of their fathers, they rejected the fugitives from the Nazis and were offensive to the Jews in their midst: concerning which they are today ashamed: doing their best to uphold them, and also Israel. And particularly when they see Israel struggling for survival against the Arabs as they against the Africans, something of the feeling for Jews of the Old Testament and Voortrekker days returns to them. (47–48; emphasis added)

The pro-Nazism that had occupied Millin's attention for the better part of a decade became a fleeting mention sandwiched between periods of great sympathy and support for Jews as 'long-lost brothers.' This distortion of memory was an essential ingredient in the development of military connections between South Africa and Israel during the apartheid years. One of the architects of the military collaboration, described by a senior figure in the South African arms industry[30] as a 'strategic alliance between two pariah nations,' was none other than the Nazi-supporting Hendrik van den Bergh.[31] Military collaboration was justified through the promotion of ideological affinities between the two countries.[32]

Two pieces in this anthology particularly reflect the unique paradoxes and contradictions of post-Holocaust South African Jewish consciousness evolving in a white supremacist environment in

which Jews did not bear the brunt of racism. Both Nehemiah
Levinsky (1901–57), in his short story 'In the Shadow of Nuremberg,' published in Yiddish in 1959, and Dov Fedler, in 'This One's
Gonna Killya,' an extract from 'Gagman,' grapple with the com-
plexities accompanying Jewish involvement in white South African
society when they had previously been victims of a related form of
racism. Levinsky explicitly commented on the collapse of memory
involved in the internalization of white supremacist racism. Jews
had themselves become 'infected with the Nuremberg madness.'
'Haven't you yourself suffered enough from this nonsense?' asked
Helen, the new wife of German Jewish refugee Hanns, who some
suspect to be 'colored.' Levinsky's criticism, written in Yiddish for
fellow South African Jews, was not muted by the fear of possible
Afrikaans and other scrutiny.

Nearly four decades later, Fedler (whose stepmother survived the
Dachau concentration camp where her first husband and son of
Fedler's age were killed) similarly treats the shift from being subjects of racial discrimination to becoming part of the white ruling
power base. Gagman, the novel's protagonist, is a joke personified.
He survives imprisonment in a Nazi concentration camp by enter-
taining the camp commandant. Assuming the commandant's personality ('I felt myself become him'), Gagman knows his enemy
through humor. 'I had colluded with the enemy by making him
laugh,' he says. Gagman succeeds in fleeing 'from the grave of
Europe in search of a new life in the New World.' Like many Jews in
South Africa in the 1930s and 1940s, he experiences anxiety about
the safety offered in the new country: 'But even as I walked the
streets in this land of freedom, I knew that I had escaped nothing.
The shadows of the past still haunted me.' Adopting a survival
strategy, Gagman disguises his visibility by pretending to be one of
the native-born free men. Fedler's description of the subterfuge
reads like a summation of Saron's and Millin's revised South African Jewish consciousness: 'I would still have to play a role rather
than be myself. I would have to pretend to be a free man. If I
allowed myself to be perceived as a stranger in the land, my pursuers would soon ferret me out. . . . Instead of stooping, I would
strut. Yes, that was it—I must strut. I must be perceived as a bold

man, a man of substance.' Fedler displaced his own understanding of South Africa as home onto another geographical and imaginative location, that of the fictional world of American superhero characters. 'I lifted my eyes above the huddled masses and sought out another role model. Immediately, I was caught by the perpendicular line of his spine—Hominus Erectus,' says Gagman of Superman, whom he follows into a meeting of American superheroes. 'I wanted so much to become part of this gathering. Instinctively I knew that I had stumbled on an opportunity to create a new identity for myself,' he says. Gagman represents the South African Jew who recognized the chance to create a new identity no longer stigmatized as inferior or uncivilized. Instead, it offered the possibility of becoming part of the ruling white supremacists, of the Supermen. In Fedler's words, Jews wanted to avoid being perceived as strangers in the land so as to avoid being ferreted out. He marked the construction of South African Jewish acceptance of newly acquired white identity and the attendant unspoken anxieties of being discovered to be fake.

Similarly, while Maja Kriel makes no explicit reference to Jewish history, memory, or identity in her short story 'Number 1-4642443-0,' she implicitly compares the respective identification documents Jews and blacks were forced to carry in Germany and South Africa. The white, suburban woman, oblivous to the life of Amos Selepe, the man she employs to tend her garden, thinks of him in racially stereotypical, including overly sexual, terms: 'Lying in bed in the morning, she could see him through the lace curtains, moving about the garden. . . . The bed became warmer and more comfortable when she saw him outside through the curtains.' Angered when she observes two women leaving his room one day, she represents him using terminology familiar from Nazi representation of Jews:

> He was still in his room, belonging to its darkness and dirt, while the two girls had disappeared into the streets still carrying his smell. So this is what was happening in the yard? While the front overlooked trees and shrubberies with scented herbs and honeysuckle creepers trailing around the doors and windows to allow perfume to drift into the house, the back was polluted with vice and vermin; every wretch could find her way to his door. (emphasis added)

Lilian Simon's story 'God Help Us,' in this anthology, depicts the long-term political consequences of the pursuit of cordial relations with the apartheid regime. The narrator cannot act against the racist police brutality she witnesses. Her political paralysis results partly from her immigrant father's discouragement throughout her childhood against making a scene. She grew up in proximity to a hub of apartheid social engineering, an office that issued the pass books carried by all black South Africans and that regulated access to 'whites only' areas. Now it was blacks, not Jews, whose movements were controlled by racist legislation. Her mother's less than gentle treatment of her black domestic workers involved the successful internalization of the accompanying white attitudes. 'My mother was always shouting at the servants. She shouted because they mixed up the milk and meat utensils in her kosher kitchen, because they came late for work, and simply because she was in a bad mood,' she says. Guarding the constraints of Jewish dietary laws, she simultaneously protects her privileged position in apartheid's racial hierarchy.

Sandra Braude's (b. 1938) short story 'Behind God's Back' represents the ahistorical rabbinic Judaism that, under the watchful eye of the secular leadership, became increasingly characteristic of much South African Jewish religious practice. South African Jewish theology became articulated through the prism of apartheid ideology. Responding to official discouragement from involvement in South African political arenas, rabbinic Judaism was gradually interpreted after 1948 as more engaged with spiritual salvation than with the pursuit of social justice, as it had previously been.[33] The SAJBD's denial that there could be a communal response to apartheid resulted in the incremental interpretation of Judaism as having no message for South African politics. Jewish theology became increasingly interpreted as ahistorical and apolitical. The pulpit, in spite of recent protestations to the contrary, was infrequently used to inspire Jews to oppose the injustices of apartheid.[34] While a handful of rabbis actively opposed apartheid, rabbinic Judaism, particularly, was rarely interpreted in a meaningful way in the context of the South African struggle for freedom and liberation.[35] The narrative of 'Behind God's Back,' sandwiched between Saturday morning synagogue activities, spans the week in April 1993 of the assassination of South African Communist Party leader Chris Hani (a turning point in the negotiated settlement between the then ruling Afrikaans nationalist government and the ANC liberation movement) and the week of Passover (the festival of liberation celebrating the escape of Jews from Egyptian bondage). The Sabbath is presented in the story as an ahistorical 'island in time,' providing 'a haven of peace' from the 'trouble in the world' from which it is removed for those waiting messianic redemption. In the story, silence on issues of political concern involves speaking about something else, as it frequently did under apartheid. The process of sermonizing involves a strong displacement mechanism. Although the rabbi claims to 'have something very important to say,' no reference is made to the fact or significance of Hani's murder or to the march under way several streets from the synagogue. The silence is particularly resonant given the time of the Jewish year and the significance of freedom to the festival of Passover. The rabbi speaks instead about Yom Ha-Shoah, the day commemorating the Holocaust and, specifically, the Warsaw Uprising. He berates members of his community who intend to participate in this memorial. Who told members of the uprising to take up arms and fight? he asks. 'Is this what God wanted? If God saw fit to cut off so many Jews, perhaps there was a reason for His doing so. . . . But I tell you this, that God did not want His people to act like the animal that slew them. If Hitler, may his name be blotted out, was the instrument of destruction, then maybe there was a reason for it,' he preaches. This quietist interpretation of Jewish history involves a peculiar view of remembering the victims of Nazism, indicating that even had they had the chance to resist they should have gone willingly to their deaths. This assertion becomes coherent when read as displacement—the rabbi rejects resistance against Nazism because he rejects armed struggle against apartheid. Memory of the Holocaust functions, in this instance, to divert attention from the political reality in South Africa, even while informed by it in such a way as to make a mockery of that memory.

Self-preservation in the form of political noninvolvement would come to have far less to do with Jewish fears of potential anti-Semitism than with the benefits of white life in South Africa. According to Shimoni, 'The stakes involved in this perception of self-preservation were . . . not persecution and matters of life and death, although the record of anti-Semitism in the two decades preceding 1948 left little cause for sanguinity. They were simply the preservation of full rights for Jews as White citizens of South Africa and the unhindered free existence of a Jewish communal life in which Zionism occupied a place of centrality' (276). Recently contemplating the reticence of the Jewish community to speak out against apartheid, the anti-apartheid activist Max Coleman echoed this view. 'Jewish sensitivity to injustice seem[ed] to have been overcome by their privileges,' he said (Suttner 1997, 204). 'They became white South Africans rather than Jews, who had been close to discrimination and persecution. Once the previous generation had settled down comfortably in South Africa, the Jewish community became accustomed to the way of life and accepted the division of the races very comfortably. Of course, they were on the right side of the fence and it was a comfortable life,' said Coleman (204).

Opposition to Apartheid

Jewish responses to apartheid were not monolithic. In contrast with the official stance of the organized community, many Jews refused to conform to the white nation being engineered under Afrikaans nationalist rule through the implementation of apartheid. Opposition took different forms. While internalizing the cultural and social norms of apartheid society, many mainstream Jews voted against the NP. Jews were conspicuous in the Progressive Party and were overrepresented in the liberal parliamentary opposition. Most prominent of these was Helen Suzman, who, during thirty-six years in Parliament, opposed apartheid laws and drew attention to their resulting injustices. Many expressed their opposition by emigrating, particularly after the 1960 Sharpeville massacre. Of those in South Africa, many joined various protest groups such as the Black Sash. The Union of Jewish Women organized social upliftment projects. Some synagogues organized soup kitchens and adult education classes. Jews were also overrepresented among the whites in sections of the mass anti-apartheid movement such as the End Conscription Campaign. At the same time, the leadership's equivocal stance was never seriously challenged, and the commu-

nity tacitly accepted a bystander role.[36] Reluctance by Jewish leaders
to involve the community more directly in anti-apartheid activities
led, in 1985, to the emergence of the United Democratic Front-
aligned Jews for Justice (JJ) in Cape Town and Jews for Social Justice
(JSJ) in Johannesburg.[37] Both organizations 'sought to enlighten
Jews about South African realities, to build bridges to black community organisations, and to participate actively in changing South
African society.'[38]

The combination of memory of anti-Semitism, knowledge of the
Holocaust, and fear of the influence of Nazism on Afrikaans nationalism, however, produced an altogether different political direction, namely active and radical opposition to the apartheid government and its policies. Many Jews were actively involved in the
anti-apartheid movement. Some were prominent in its leadership.
According to the exiled writer and editor Ronald Segal (b. 1932),
who accompanied ANC chief Oliver Tambo (1917–93) out of South
Africa into exile in March 1960 the day after the Sharpeville massacre, which brought in its wake the banning of the ANC and the
SACP and other restrictions that were not lifted until 1990,[39] South
African Jews were unable to forget the experience of the 1930s
(1963, 18), a time when the nationalist parliamentary opposition
'brayed their hatred of the Jews' (28). Describing the fear arising
from South African pro-Nazism, he said that 'the constant threat
that the neo-Nazi element within Afrikanerdom would whip up
anti-Semitism into popular violence has left scabs on the group
consciousness which no number of current reassurances can peel'
(18). Segal's 'loathing of white rule' (28) was informed by memory
of parliamentary debate when NP politicians 'sullenly rejoic[ed] at
the fury unleashed by Hitler against Europe's Jews and consol[ed]
their powerlessness with the prospect of the fury that they would
unleash one day soon against their own [Jews]' (28). It resulted in
affirmation of and commitment to the nonracial liberation movement. 'In a society of race rule, Jewry must logically be menaced by
racial repression and racial resistance alike. Only a South Africa
finally blind to race can give to Jewry the security that it pretends to
itself it is purchasing by its silence,' Segal wrote (19).

If Afrikaner pro-Nazism left its mark on South African Jewish
consciousness, so too did the Holocaust itself. The desire of many

Jews in the anti-apartheid movement for a society free of discrimination was marked by memory and experience of anti-Semitism in
general and pro-Nazism and Nazism in particular. 'I still haven't
got over it,' said Pauline Podbrey in an interview (Suttner 1997, 58).
'The experience of our families in Eastern Europe is something that
I have lived with every day in some way or other. . . . It's something
that my generation will have to die with, this consciousness of the
Holocaust. . . . My daughters are very much aware of the Holocaust.
But I don't think in as subjective a way as I am. . . . It's not a living
sore in their body as it is in me,' she said (58–59).

According to Albie Sachs, knowledge of this history of oppression resulted in 'a sensitivity to suffering, to discrimination' (361–
62) and 'contributed to the feeling that you didn't belong to the
master race' (361). Similarly, the anticonscription activist David
Bruce was motivated, in part, by knowledge that members of his
mother's family were killed in the Holocaust. 'I am conscious that it
was my own family that suffered in the Holocaust' (172). 'My family
equated the racism of the apartheid system with anti-Semitism. I
saw the comparison between what happened to Jews in Nazi Germany and what was happening to blacks in South Africa,' said
Bruce (171). 'For me to be able to condemn what happened in
Germany, I had to be able to say that in the same circumstances I
wouldn't do the same thing,' he said (177). The comparison drawn
by Bruce was not without legal basis. 'If you look at the Nuremberg
Laws, and at the techniques that the Nazis used initially to margin-
alise Jewish communities, they were very similar to the techniques
used by the [Afrikaner] Nationalists,' said Arthur Chaskelson, a
judge on post-apartheid South Africa's first Constitutional Court
(330). Cornerstones of apartheid legislation echoed Nazi law, including inter alia the outlawing of sexual intercourse and marriage
between race groups.

The struggle for nonracism suggested a solution to the traumas
that resulted from knowledge of Nazism. Segal, Podbrey, Sachs,
Bruce, and many others pursued a society in which no one, including Jews, would be seen as different, inferior, or uncivilized and in
which all people would be safe from racist violence and stigmatization. At the same time they silenced their Jewish identity in their
political lives and literary production. This silence included, para-

doxically, the impact on their lives and consciousness of knowledge of Nazism. In her autobiography, which recounts her lifelong fight against racism and class domination, Podbrey (1993), for instance, avoided explicit acknowledgment of the sustained and traumatic memory of Nazism. Even when describing her profound awareness of Nazism, she explicitly denied the relevance of Jewishness for her political involvement. There is a strong tension between her life devoted to ending oppression against the backdrop of a Jewish immigrant family's flight from Eastern Europe and scarred by racial hatred and the sometimes explicit denial of any Jewish overlay to her political activities.

While consistent with the general nonracist denial of ethnic, religious, and cultural difference between South Africans, this suppression of Jewishness had another dimension. Jewish identity, the source of the trauma, could be forgotten. By displacing Jewish fears, anxieties, and memories onto the political pursuit of non-racism, the 'living sore' described by Podbrey could become tolerable. She and others pursued nonracism as a way to prevent anti-Semitism and the trauma associated with it.

The leaders of the establishment Jewish community ostracized Jews who were active in the anti-apartheid movement. Their prominent political activity was strongly problematic to the leadership of the SAJBD. In 1959, then chief rabbi Louis Rabinowitz made clear the dynamic whereby the activities of politically outspoken Jews were marginalized beyond communal acceptance: 'There are some Jews in the community who do attempt to do something [to oppose apartheid],' he said, 'and when, as a result, they fall foul of the powers that be the defence put up by the Jewish community is to prove that these are Jews only by name, that they do not belong to any synagogue' (Shimoni 1980, 283–84). Written off as Jews, they were written out of Jewish consciousness under apartheid and the history produced in that period. While ostensibly having nothing in common with the establishment Jewish community's pursuit of cordial relations with the apartheid regime, the two divergent responses to Afrikaans nationalism—acceptance of whiteness and rejection of all forms of racism—were both motivated to a large extent by the common desire to secure a society in which Jews would feel safe.

Public acknowledgment of the memory of a consciousness of parallels between apartheid and Nazism informing some Jewish opposition to apartheid increasingly occurred in and itself informed a period that witnessed a heated public debate on the topic. In complex and contradictory ways, Jewish memory and the Holocaust were brought to bear on the processes of transition from apartheid to democracy. The debate was initiated by the publication of the first book on the TRC, *Reconciliation Through Truth* (Asmal, Asmal, and Roberts 1996), in which Kader Asmal, a cabinet minister, declared that 'there is a striking overlap between early Nazi German solutions to the Jewish Problem and apartheid's ways of dealing with the Black Threat' (132). 'Apartheid . . . amounted, under international law, to a form of genocide,' he said, even while acknowledging that there was no South African equivalent of 'the systematic process of hi-tech Nazi exterminations' (132). 'There were no gas chambers; but there can be genocide without gas chambers, which is what many apartheid dumping grounds achieved' (133). Seeking clear memory of apartheid's fundamental criminality, he insisted on acknowledgment of apartheid's status like Nazism as a crime against humanity. In the process, he cut to the heart of the TRC process, which, born in an era of negotiation, was agreed to as a political compromise. Rather than pursuing perpetrators of crimes against humanity, as had been anticipated in the 1970s, when ANC intelligence operatives assembled dockets for future Nuremberg-type trials,[40] a truth commission[41] providing amnesty for 'gross violations of human rights' committed on both sides of the political struggle was established.[42] The compromises were made in the name of nation-building and peace, to try to placate the right wing and thereby avoid further violent conflict.[43] They involved a legal equation between those who fought to maintain and those who sought to destroy apartheid.[44] South Africa's first democratically elected government hoped that, in spite of the country's obligation to prosecute perpetrators of crimes against humanity, the international community would respect its decision. Locally, many South Africans took the amnesty process to mean that each side was equally justified and that the atrocities committed in the name of apartheid were no worse than the acts of armed struggle against it. In contrast, Asmal differentiated between the two.

He sought memory of apartheid's fundamental criminality, even though perpetrators of apartheid were able to apply for amnesty. Albie Sachs concurred. Emphasizing the necessity of accurate historical memory and truth for genuine psychological healing, he similarly differentiated between the criminality of the apartheid regime and the gross human rights violations perpetrated within the liberation movements (Sachs 1993b).

Not everyone agreed with the historical and legal parallels drawn between apartheid and Nazism. Among these was the writer, editor, and poet Lionel Abrahams (b. 1928). Abrahams shaped the development of two generations of South African literary history by conducting literary workshops and by publishing, among other things, several South African classics, including the poet Wally Serote's *Yakal'inkomo* (1972). He grappled with language and culture under apartheid. Though his literary production over several decades was consistently informed by critical awareness of the impact of apartheid rule on the literary soul of the nation—'a government so guilty-minded that it resorts to gagging and detention-without-trial puts a strange price and pressure on the use of words. It inhibits everyone at the verbal source' (1988, 205)—Abrahams believed that authentic communication in interpersonal relationships was far more important than political processes in enabling people to transcend racial boundaries.

Presenting the South African Institute of Race Relations (SAIRR) annual Hoernlé lecture in 1995, Abrahams spoke about, inter alia, the effects of politics in South African literary studies, language, and culture in a politically transformed environment (1996). He spoke about the pursuit of truth, the TRC, and contemporary comparisons made between apartheid and Nazism. He referred to his response three decades before to comparisons between the apartheid state and Nazi Germany made by the renowned anti-apartheid theologian Rev. Beyers Naude (18). In that context, he described the comparison as 'false,' 'sensational,' 'useless,' and 'paralysing' (1988, 153). Nazism was, he said, 'synonymous with a unique horror because of Hitler's war for domination of the world and more especially because of the systematic killing out of Jews, Slavs and Gypsies.' 'The case of Nazi Germany is not available for comparison, but ought to be regarded as standing outside normal history,' he said (147). 'South Africa, with its ubiquitous colour bar, its systematised economic exploitation of the black population, its police and bureaucratic cruelties, etcetera, is replete with wickedness. But the German evils are not within the scope or intention of the South African government. The German evils stand apart, I hope forever,' he said (158). Abrahams did not reject the Nazi analogy in order to defend apartheid. 'Even if the Nazi enormities are out of the question here, our leaders all too often act in accord with the Nazi temper of prurient joy in power,' he said (153). Actively remembering the history—'many of the Nationalists were admirers and supporters of the Nazis' (170)—he said that 'we have much of fascism in our government' (148). Uncomfortable with the possibility that he would be understood by some 'to be siding with the Nationalists, trying to strike an effective weapon from the hands of their opponents' (148), he experienced 'surprising difficulty' explaining his objection (147). Indeed, his objection to the Nazi analogy was motivated, to varying extents, by two different concerns.

First, he was interested in Jewish history and suffering. While not specifically evoking Jewish concerns with accurate memory of the Holocaust, Abrahams's rejection in 1995 of what he considered the insensitive reduction of the Holocaust for political gain in the post-apartheid context (19)—'does a high politico-moral purpose excuse reducing the Nazi holocaust to a rhetorical mustard pot?' (19)—echoed his concern with anti-Semitic dismissals of Jewish history. This concern dated back to the period of his childhood. In *The Celibacy of Felix Greenspan* (1986), a series of linked autobiographical short stories (including 'Cut Glass' in this volume), the schoolboy Felix gets into a verbal fight with Willem Prinsloo, an Afrikaans boy who calls him 'Jewboy' (53). Together with the other big boys at the Senior Home for boys with various disabilities, Willem teased Felix because of his severe physical disabilities and 'despised him because he was Jewish' (52). 'What have you got against Hitler, pipsqueak?' asks Willem, overhearing Felix shout 'down with Hitler.' ' "He's the worst man in the world," said Felix. "Ag, kak, man!" Willem growled. "Come on, what have you got against him?" "Well, he wants to kill all of the Jewish people." "That's just propaganda," said Willem. "Anyway, what did he ever do to you?" "He's

killed lots of my people already. . . . I think he's got some of my
father's relations," ' writes Abrahams (52). Through Willem, Abrahams presents a quintessential form of South African Holocaust
reductionism: 'Do you know what the English did in the Anglo-
Boer War? They killed thousands of Boer women and children. . . .
So, don't you talk kak when you don't know about something. I say
down with England up with Hitler!' said Willem (53). Abrahams's
representation of the denial of Hitler's annihilation of the Jews that
accompanied Willem's Afrikaner nationalist sentiment was set
against the backdrop of the politics of the 1930s and 1940s. Like his
friend Barney Simon's 'Our War,' it was clearly informed by the
impact of events in Europe on Abrahams's own life, family, and
consciousness.

If as a Jew, Abrahams was concerned that Jewish pain should
neither be trivialized nor forgotten in the service of any cause (including Afrikaner nationalism or in the struggle against apartheid),
as a poet, literary critic, editor, publisher, and teacher, he considered the equation between South Africa and Nazi Germany to be
unhelpful in reaching an imaginative understanding that could
awaken beneficiaries of apartheid to its harsh realities (147). Responding to Naudé, he said it was 'a political expedient, a sim-
plification, an emotive conjuring trick, a lie' (147):

> It is of no consequence whether our actual abuses, oppressions and
> injustices are to be paralleled in the history of Hitler's Germany: we have
> to confront them recognising their own intrinsic evil. Our situation is
> one of challenge to our moral and creative powers: there are calls here on
> our courage, our wit and intelligence, our generosity, our capacity to
> discover and utter the truth, perhaps chiefly on our imagination. . . . I
> don't believe it is possible by . . . means [of the analogy] to generate the
> energy for the things that have to be done. On the contrary, it can only
> obscure our vision and obstruct our necessary action. (147)

Abrahams said he found support for his attitude in the praise of war
poets, in a different context, for 'their determination to be sane, to
be articulate and intelligible, and scrupulous with the language'
(148). He sought a similarly careful use of language to avoid the
imaginative traps of racist thinking (154). Abrahams, who opposed

armed struggle against the apartheid regime, also believed such language would help to avoid violence as a response and remedy to apartheid. 'A situation which truly paralleled that of Nazi Germany, even at an incipient stage, would present as the only possible courses of action: exile, despair (in the form of surrender or cultivated blindness) or violence,' he said (147). Three decades later, at the SAIRR, Abrahams said that not only did the Nazi analogy render public life 'unauthentic' (1996, 18); in helping to justify violence in the struggle against apartheid, it also 'helped to cause some of the serious ills that still afflict and threaten us' (18).

The historian Hermann Giliomee echoed aspects of Abrahams's position in his presidential address to the SAIRR four months later (1996). The analogy between apartheid and Nazism was 'propaganda in a war in which the higher moral ground was decisive,' he said (9). Dismissing as popularist those who remembered the links between Nazi and Afrikaans nationalist ideology, he discerned a 'political subtext' behind 'all the frantic efforts to prove that the NP and the Afrikaner Broederbond were influenced by the Nazi party' and argued that contemporary reminders of Nazi influence on apartheid were politically rather than historically motivated. They served, he said, as an excuse for 'revolutionary violence' and as 'propaganda designed to muddy the waters, and to provide a moral shield for . . . [revolutionary] actions' (9). Emphasizing the horrors of Nazism, Giliomee dismissed the United Nations General Assembly's 1973 declaration that apartheid, like Nazism, was a crime against humanity. 'The concept of "crimes against humanity" was developed by the Nuremberg Tribunal in the context of the Nazi atrocities committed during World War II,' he said. 'Such crimes were defined by the tribunal as including "extermination, enslavement and deportation." They connote crimes of unspeakable horror—such as the extermination of six million Jews and the incarceration of conquered civilian populations in Nazi concentration camps where they were subjected to starvation, forced labour, brutal abuse, and medical experimentation' (8). He argued that the UN declaration was motivated by nondemocratic countries, almost all of which 'were either dominated or heavily under the influence of the Soviets' (9), whose own human rights record was dubious.[45]

Significantly, former state president F. W. de Klerk's participation in the TRC process on behalf of the NP and his justification for his own refusal to apply for amnesty relied extensively on the relativist denial that apartheid, like Nazism, was a crime against humanity. He too dismissed the UN declaration that apartheid was a crime against humanity as 'little more than a mobilisation exercise by the African National Congress and its totalitarian and Third World supporters' (De Klerk 1996, 1). Distancing himself from responsibility for crimes against humanity, he denied that he or his party had participated in or authorized any illegal action and praised the achievements of what he described as the 'apartheid years.'

Though Giliomee ostensibly shared Abrahams's liberal agenda, his apologetic denials of apartheid's fundamental criminality underpinned an entirely different project, namely the pursuit of minority and cultural rights for Afrikaners. He argued that the challenge to liberalism was to support consistently all national claims since they applied to all nations and not only those that 'suffered severe discrimination in the past' (31). Speaking subsequently at a Jewish Board of Deputies seminar on 'the transformation of South Africa and its significance for the South African Jewish community,'[46] he said that 'liberals outside ANC ranks have generally speaking not concerned themselves much with the issues of the cultural rights of Afrikaners. Liberals tend to side with underdogs, like discriminated-against minorities. They find it difficult to accept that if a claim is sound, one cannot restrict the application on the grounds that the claimant has an unsavoury recent history or because it is wealthy' (1999, 28). Giliomee argued that 'the Afrikaners' search . . . is also that of the Jews and of every ethnic group that wants to escape the bleak cultural uniformity that is inexorably bearing down upon us' (34). In so doing, he positioned himself in opposition to the views, for instance, of Albie Sachs.[47]

In commenting on the TRC, others avoided a competing relationship between Jewish and black history and suffering. For instance, opening a workshop on Jewish perspectives on justice and forgiveness in South Africa, Geoff Sifrin said that when Jews engage the TRC process 'there is a parallel sub-text running in their psyches, which has to do with the Holocaust and the Nuremberg Trials of Nazi leaders which followed it, as well as all the other aspects of the

complicated relationship between Jews and Germans over the past
fifty years since the end of World War Two. While no simple comparison between the Holocaust and apartheid can be made, either
in nature or scale, nevertheless there are certain similarities in the
events, in the roles of perpetrators, victims, and bystanders, and in
the attempts to deal with the aftermath.'[48] The question of reparations to victims was one such aspect. Franz Auerbach (who had
been on the short list for a position on the TRC) suggested that the
German word for reparation to victims of Nazism, Wiedergut-
machung, making good again, captured the spirit of the TRC process.[49] In 'Letters from Doreen' by Tony Eprile (whose mother, like
Auerbach, was a German Jewish refugee to South Africa), this history interfaces with the author's recollections of his South African
childhood. Eprile left South Africa as a child with his politically
active parents. Writing in North America, he remembers 'home'
from the site of exile. The autobiographical Mark, the story's protagonist, attempts to come to terms with his South African past.
Recollections of Doreen, his black 'nanny,' who was central to his
white South African childhood, are filtered through his awareness
of the irreversible wounds history can inflict. 'There are some things
that can not be made good again. They become part of the past, and the
world is forever changed by them,' he said, implicitly referring to
German reparations (emphasis added). Eprile's treatment of his
South African childhood in partial relation to his mother's German
Jewish background provides a trenchant comment on the challenges posed by the legacy of apartheid in contemporary post-
apartheid South African society. Similarly, Auerbach brought critical insights from the German Jewish experience to bear on some of
these challenges:

> When [Jews] hear about the revelation of the cruelties of an oppressive
> system based firmly on racial discrimination by law then we must
> acknowledge: WE HAVE BEEN THERE. We know that the past leaves
> wounds and memories, both personal and collective. . . . We . . . know
> something about the pain of people who do not know when and where
> their loved ones died, or even where they were buried. And we know that
> people who have gone through a process of de-humanisation, where
> their dignity was systematically crushed, will bear the scars of that for

*the rest of their lives—anyone who has had contact with Holocaust
survivors at the personal level will know that.*[50]

The living sores that resulted from experience and knowledge of
Nazism which had previously been silenced in the pursuit, by some,
of cordial relations with the apartheid regime and, by others, of a
nonracial just society directly informed engagement (itself at times
contested) with the life of the post-apartheid nation.

Visibility

The emergence of a new direction in the telling of South African
Jewish history coincided with the highly visible TRC process of
exploring and publicly representing traumatic histories. Rose Zwi
(b. 1928) and Dan Jacobson (b. 1929), two of the most seminal of
South African Jewish writers, who, over decades, have themselves
explored and represented different aspects of South African Jewish
consciousness and culture, embarked on autobiographical jour-
neys in search of silenced, traumatic aspects of their own pasts.
Although both emigrated from South Africa (Jacobson to England
in 1954 and Zwi to Australia in 1988), they have continued to write
about South Africa. In *Heshel's Kingdom* (1998), Jacobson travels to
Varniai, the Lithuanian town in which his family lived before his
grandfather's death in 1919. His death, says Jacobson, was a gift,
resulting as it did in his grandmother's departure for South Africa.
She consequently avoided the fate of the vast majority of Lithuania's
Jewish population, 220,000 of whom were killed in 1941 by Nazis
and their local collaborators. Among these was Zwi's uncle Leib,
the subject of *Last Walk in Naryshkin Park* (1998).

Through Ruth, the autobiographical child of Lithuanian immigrants in *Another Year in Africa*, Zwi's first novel, published in 1980,
Zwi gave fictional form to memory of her childhood nightmares.
Set in the Johannesburg suburbs of Mayfair and Doornfontein, the
novel explores the lives of Jewish immigrants during the late 1930s.
Ruth's nightmares were permeated by adult conversations about
Lithuanian pogroms, deportations, and destruction. Zwi actively
sought to escape the difficult memories. 'After the war I had taken a
deliberate decision to cut myself off from the past, from the *shtetl*,
from the centuries of oppression and suffering,' she wrote (Zwi

1998, 56). She ceased asking about her father's postwar correspondence with Leib's wife, Leah. Documenting her 1993 meeting in Lithuania with Leah and Leah's daughter Frieda, *Last Walk in Naryshkin Park* replaces the resulting silences. Even though she wrote in Australia, Zwi's encounter with both the importance and the limitations of memory and history adopt the language and logic of the TRC. Aspects of her book refer implicitly to contemporary South African confrontations with apartheid history. During her research, Zwi befriended an American, Catholic, Lithuanian-born woman, whom she calls only Bronye. Confronted by the Lithuanian war crimes tribunal, Bronye explores the erasures of Lithuanian collaboration with Nazism in the production of a sanitized Lithuanian history. Establishing a solid friendship, the women transcend historical oppositions between 'Jew' and 'Lithuania.' 'Neither of us believes in collective guilt,' says Zwi (1997, 116). 'To ask questions is not to slander a nation. An entire nation cannot be blamed for the evil actions of some of its people' (233). Such words could arguably refer also to dealing with the legacy of apartheid. So too could her comments on the then newly independent Lithuanian government's rehabilitation of Lithuanians who had previously been convicted of war crimes: 'It reflects badly on the nation . . . when convicted mass murderers are released from jail, rehabilitated and given pensions' (233). Thus if Jewish memory was brought to bear on the examination of the past under way in the TRC, so too did the TRC influence South African Jewish memory in this period.

The space to explore suppressed memories and traumatic histories that accompanied changes in the post-apartheid political environment also informs the adapted extract here from satirist Pieter-Dirk Uys's (b. 1945) *A Part Hate a Part Love: The Legend of Evita Bezuidenhout* (1994). During apartheid, Uys used the persona of his creation, Evita Bezuidenhout, to circumvent political censorship and thereby publicly to deconstruct the logic of apartheid. Uys located Evita, the socialite wife of an imaginary apartheid diplomat who was posted to the imaginary apartheid homeland, Bapetikosweti, at the center of Afrikaans nationalist history. Flitting between theaters, publishing houses, television stations, and recently even Parliament, Evita is an instantly recognizable personality on the national stage. The cultural critic Marjorie Garber argues that part of the cultural significance of cross-dressing lies in its disruption not only of gender categories but of all other binary opposites. Apparently distinct categories such as black/white, Jew/Christian, and master/servant are crossed, and an alternative 'third term' becomes possible.[51] Exposing the absurdities of apartheid, in part by undermining gender binaries, the character of Evita simultaneously suggested the possibility of hybridizing other seemingly mutually exclusive identities that were fundamental to apartheid.

Having grown up thinking of himself as 'a hundred percent Afrikaner,' Uys confronted belated knowledge of a very different past (Herber 1979, 93). Through his writing, he responds to his discovery, in his mid-twenties and after his mother's death, that she was a German Jew who had escaped Nazi Berlin. Arriving in South Africa in 1938, both his mother and her brother married into established Afrikaans families. Her Jewish past remained a secret. 'She and her brother were damned sure they were not going to be caught again,' said Uys wryly.[52] In his contribution to this volume, he describes how, at the age of eleven, he caught a glimpse of this past when he met his mother's friend Freda. Visiting from Germany, she described telling 'terrible shocking jokes about terrible unspeakable things' as a way of coping with the conditions she and other Jews had experienced in the concentration camps she had survived. Uys's work is invisibly imbued with this terrible humor produced from the German Jewish past which his mother escaped. Evita says factual, not funny things 'because apartheid is the most unamusing thing in the world, coming a close second to the grim experience of Auschwitz. The day that Jews can produce a musical about the death camps and call it *What a Gas* is the day that apartheid can venture a little "knock-knock" joke,' says Uys. The site of the 'third' occupied by Evita intimated the possibility of crossing the divide between Jew and Afrikaner to claim and reconcile Afrikaans and Jewish aspects of Uys's history and identity. In the 1980s, Uys alias Evita received letters from people who, believing her to be real, promised to support her in her legal efforts to control what they considered to be the third-rate satirist Pieter-Dirk Uys, who made such cruel fun of her. Spurred on by such letters, Uys invented a third-person character called Pieter-Dirk Uys and wrote Evita's biography, *A Part Hate a Part Love*, in that voice. For the piece in this volume, Uys adapted extracts from the biography of the fictional woman and interspersed them with his own biographical voice. He explicitly juxtaposes his autobiographical voice and the Evita narrative. By introducing his mother's till-now silent narrative in this context, the extent to which the impact of her German Jewish past and its recuperated memory inform Uys's satirical representation of and commentary on the history of apartheid becomes apparent. In the process of overcoming the silences of his mother's past, Uys engaged anew with the fear that motivated them.

The exploration in the TRC period of histories that had been obscured during apartheid also explicitly occurred in the realm of Jewish memory. Consistent with the post-apartheid shift from suppression to affirmation of his Jewish identity in his literary work, Albie Sachs was 'irritated' (Suttner 1997, 343) by the general omission of cultural representation of Jewish involvement in democratic politics, and particularly in a permanent photographic exhibition of South African Jewish life at the University of Cape Town. As a result, in 1998 he co-curated an exhibition called 'Looking Back: Jews in the Struggle for Democracy and Human Rights in South Africa,' which amplified the significance of Jewish identity in the lives and work of anti-apartheid activists.[53] As such, it indicated a publicly visible post-apartheid engagement with Jewishness. It restored memory to some existing silences about Jewish identity that were constructed within Jewish left discourse itself, including by Sachs in his *Jail Diary*. So too did the interviews with South African Jewish activists in *Cutting Through the Mountain* (Suttner 1997). 'Fifteen years ago I would have said that [Jewish assimilation is] fine, because internationalism is what we want, and one of the roots of our problem is that people are separated into ethnic groups,' said Taffy Adler, for instance (1997, 18). 'I still think ethnicity is a major problem, but I now recognise the value of different cultural systems, and I have come to believe that diversity is an important element in human existence, as long as it doesn't degenerate into the kind of horrible ethnic violence that we see all around the world,' he said (18). In this context, Gordimer's 'My Father Leaves Home' assumes additional significance. Her belated attempt to fill in gaps in her knowledge about the derided parts of her father's life is characterized by this post-apartheid comfort with acknowledging and rendering visible aspects of Jewish identity that previously had been suppressed.

Of all the pieces in this anthology, the actor, writer, and editor Matthew Krouse's (b. 1961) story 'The Mythological Structure of Time' most strongly indicates the fundamental change that has occurred in the landscape of post-apartheid South African Jewish consciousness and memory. Strongly influenced by Barney Simon's 'Our War,' parts of the story occur in the synagogue during the holiday of Purim when the biblical story of Esther is read. Like Millin, who modeled her self-perception on Esther, Krouse's protagonist identifies with Esther. 'On Purim we also dress up. They say it's the only time of the year when a Jewish man may wear a woman's dress. But this I've never seen. I've seen hundreds of girls dressed up as Queen Esther, but never a man dressed as her. I'd like to make up as Queen Esther though, but in a real crown, with jewelled earings, and not just a paper crown painted a shoddy gold,' writes Krouse. Identification with the figure of Esther, however, has radically different implications and consequences. Krouse uses Esther to integrate representation of gay and Jewish aspects of his identity. Krouse edited The Invisible Ghetto (1993), the first South African (and indeed African) anthology of gay and lesbian writing. He did so during a period that witnessed the shaping of the constitution that includes provisions for freedom of sexual orientation, as well as a bill of rights that outlaws all forms of racism. In that context, he described the imperative for gay and lesbian self-expression to emerge from invisibility (xi) as part of 'the development of human self-realization . . . crucial [to] overcoming the imbalances created by apartheid' (xv).

In desiring to dress up as Esther in 'The Mythological Structure of Time,' Krouse simultaneously renders visible the autobiographical protagonist's gay and Jewish identities. He implicitly abandons the fear-driven pursuit of invisibility and thereby acceptance within white supremacist society which Millin and the leaders of establishment Jewish community anxiously sought. While he is fully cognizant of the fears, they do not fuel his writing.[54] Instead, consistent with the contemporary pursuit of a new South African society free from the perceptions of the apartheid past, Krouse seeks fundamentally new ways to liberate from fear. Using humor, he turns

his mocking gaze to anti-Semitic perceptions and subverts their
Jewish internalization: 'It's Purim of course. Haman, as we know,
was a previous Hitler. He also hated us, and it's obvious why. It's
because we behave like a herd of cattle, and we look like moneylending, baby blood drinkers. We can't seem to change. History
never worked the stinky-herring-look out of our genes.' Krouse
satirizes anti-Semitic perceptions of Jews as ritual baby killers,
Shylock, animals to be sent to the slaughter. In keeping with the
anti- and post-apartheid projects of creating a nonracist, nonsexist,
nonhomophobic society, he also attempts to reconcile traditionally
separated lifestyles and communities. Like Sachs, he interprets his
position in post-apartheid South African society through positive
reference to his Jewishness. Krouse is fully conscious of the 'irreconcilable irony' involved in his celebration of his love for a Muslim
man through reference to Jewish rituals and beliefs, which traditionally reject interreligious and homoerotic contact. His love is
doubly taboo. As it is forbidden to eat meat and milk together, so
are forbidden both the love of two men and the love of a Jew and a
Muslim. Unlike his grandmother's cutlery, the lovers cannot be
cleansed into familial acceptance by a day's burial in the garden.
Krouse, however, denies that they have little in common (both, for
instance, are children of immigrants). Most significantly, they
share their love. In contrast with the mother in 'God Help Us,'
Krouse's concern is neither to protect the dietary laws nor his privileged position in a racist social hierarchy. Bringing Jewish identity
and history to bear on other aspects of South African experience,
'The Mythological Structure of Time' marks the literary point at
which affirmation of Jewish culture and identity converges with
participation in and engagement with the broader life of the South
African nation. 'The Mythological Structure of Time' signposts a
fundamental rupture from the literary tradition that had, at its
center, anxiety about Jewish racial status in a white supremacist
environment.

Ronald Segal attributed the origins of The Black Diaspora: Five Centuries of the Black Experience Outside Africa (1995) to his Jewish South
African childhood and upbringing. He related black and Jewish
histories in their respective diasporas:

This is a book whose beginning reaches back into my childhood. I was born into a Diaspora myself, the Jewish Diaspora, in a country, South Africa, where Jews occupied both a privileged and a perilous position. . . . My late mother used to say that she was in love with the Jewish people. In writing this book, I fell in love with the Black Diaspora. She would not, in her demanding devotion, have appreciated the object of mine, but she would have understood the ways and the reasons by which I reached it. (xi–xv)

At a time when South Africa is reestablishing itself in the region of southern Africa and on the African continent, bringing Jewish and African history to bear on each other provides a welcome indication of the possibility of conceptualizing an Afro-Jewish experience and historiography and of integration not only in the life of the South African nation but in a Pan-African context as well.

Notes

1. See De Kok and Press, *Spring Is Rebellious*.

2. See Gilman, *Jew's Body*, 169–93.

3. Zuma became South Africa's second democratically elected deputy president, under President Thabo Mbeki.

4. Figures supplied by the Jewish Board of Deputies.

5. Krut, 'The Making of a South African Jewish Community,' 150.

6. Sherman, *From a Land Far Off*, 75.

7. Sherman, *From a Land Far Off*, 72.

8. Sherman, *From a Land Far Off*, 72.

9. Ellen Hellman, 'Dr Wulf Sachs: A Tribute,' in *Zionist Record*, 1 July 1949.

10. He did so sufficiently successfully to deceive as insightful a reader as Jacqueline Rose. In her introduction to the recent reprint of *Black Hamlet*, she considers the relation between Sachs's and Chavafambira's language. Rose incorrectly argues that Sachs 'was wholly proficient' in English, the language of the European colonizer, which was 'the first and perhaps most crucial boundary' between the two men. Wulf Sachs, 'Introduction,' 45.

11. See Coetzee, *White Writing*, 150 n.7.

12. The father Gordimer acknowledged as her own in 'My Father Leaves

Home' had a literary precursor in Saiyetovitz in her story 'The Defeated.' Though 'a gentle man,' when Saiyetovitz 'was trading with the natives, strange blasts of power seemed to blow up in his soul.' 'Moving in jerks of rage' and 'roughly bullying the boy into a decision,' if Saiyetovitz 'treated the natives honestly,' he did so 'with bad grace': 'He forced them to feel their ignorance, their inadequacy, and their submission to the white man's world of money' (1953, 181–82).

13. See Leveson, *People of the Book*, 177.

14. Sparks, *Mind of South Africa*, 161–62. See also Bunting, *Rise of the South African Reich*.

15. Meyer, *Nog nie ver genoeg nie*, 12.

16. Feldberg, *South African Jewry—1965*, 303.

17. See Millin, *War Diary*, Vol. 1: *World Blackout*, 1944; Vol. 2: *The Reeling Earth*, 1945; Vol. 3: *The Pit of the Abyss*, 1946; Vol. 4: *The Sound of the Trumpet*, 1947; Vol. 5: *Fire out of Heaven*, 1947; Vol. 6: *The Seven Thunders*, 1948.

18. See also Millin, ed., *White Africans Are Also People*, 20: 'The South Africans saw South-West [Africa] as a land from which the Germans might spring upon South Africa. . . . Six years before the Kaiser's war, ex-President Steyn of the Orange Free State said: ". . . What else is German-West but a jumping-off place to attack us from the north while their ships destroy our ports?" For the Boers knew what the British refused to know.'

19. Justice Millin, judgment in case *Verwoerd v. The Star*, July 13, 1943, quoted in Mzimela, *Nazism and Apartheid*, 103.

20. His brother J. D. Vorster, later a leading figure of the Dutch Reformed Church, regarded Adolf Hitler as his authority: 'Hitler's *Mein Kampf* shows the way to greatness—the path of South Africa. Hitler gave the Germans a calling. He gave them a fanaticism which causes them to stand back for no one. We must follow his example because only by such a holy fanaticism can the Afrikaner nation achieve its calling' (Mzimela, *Nazism and Apartheid*, 112).

21. Simon, *Jo'burg Sis!*

22. Unpublished interview by Matthew Krouse, Johannesburg, 1995. A similar interview with Joseph Sherman is published in Suttner, *Cutting Through the Mountain*, 117–41.

23. Until 1951 Jews, however, were still prohibited from joining the NP in the then Transvaal Province. Sounding something akin to classic Groucho Marx, Strijdom justified this by saying that 'decent Jews would not want to join a Christian Party [like the *Herenigde* National Party] and such Jews as

had so little decency as to want to join it—they did not want as members' (Shimoni, *Jews and Zionism*, 211).

24. Most of the contributions to a special edition of *Jewish Affairs*, mouthpiece of the SAJBD, dedicated to 'Jews and Apartheid,' apologetically stressed the fear of anti-Semitism as a justification for the SAJBD's unwillingness to speak out against apartheid (*Jewish Affairs* 52, no. 1 [1997]).

25. On one occasion, he inscribed and signed a copy in his capacity as general secretary to 'His Worship the Mayor of Johannesburg, Aleck Jaffe Esq. With the best wishes of the South African Jewish Board of Deputies. 25 March 1965.' Author's private collection.

26. Saks, 'Jews on Commando,' 23.

27. Schwarz, 'Jewish Modes of Opposition,' 29.

28. Schwarz, 'Jewish Modes of Opposition,' 29.

29. Shain and Frankental, 'Accommodation, Activism and Apathy,' 55.

30. Johan van Vuuren, former chief executive and chairman of Armscor. Quoted in Melman, 'Exposed,' 17.

31. Melman, 'Exposed,' 17.

32. Perhaps the most consistent promoter of such affinities was the journalist Henry Katzew. For example, he wrote that 'two small nations are fighting for survival in our days: the 1½ million Jews of Israel surrounded by 40 million Arabs; and the Afrikaner nation of South Africa in a continent of awakening black men.' See *Solution for South Africa* (no page).

33. See Braude, 'From the Brotherhood of Man to the World to Come,' 259–87.

34. Bernhard, 'The Row Rumbles On,' and *Jewish Affairs*, Autumn 1997, 71–73.

35. See, for example, Suttner, *Cutting Through the Mountain*, 615.

36. Shain and Frankental, 'Accommodation, Activism and Apathy,' 56.

37. Auerbach, 'Do We Apologise?' 34.

38. Shain and Frankental, 'Accommodation, Activism and Apathy,' 55.

39. Segal edited *Africa South*, a journal to which seminal liberation movement intellectual and political figures, including assassinated anti-apartheid activist Ruth First, ANC stalwart Walter Sisulu, and current Speaker of Parliament Frene Ginwala, contributed on issues of the day.

40. *Sunday Independent*, 21 April 1996.

41. The TRC is based on the final clause of the Interim Constitution of 1993

and passed in Parliament as the Promotion of National Unity and Reconciliation Act, no. 34 of 1995.

42. Promotion of National Unity and Reconciliation Act, 3.1.a.

43. AZAPO, para 58. For a discussion of this aspect of the TRC, see Braude and Spitz, 'Memory and the Spectre of International Justice,' 275–77.

44. Promotion of National Unity and Reconciliation Act, 20(2). For a discussion of this aspect of the TRC, see Braude and Spitz, 'Memory and the Spectre of International Justice,' 273.

45. Giliomee said that 'the main sponsors of the resolution and the idea of a convention [on the Suppression of the Crime of Apartheid] were the Union of Soviet Socialist Republics (USSR) and Ghana. The Convention came into force in 1976 after 20 countries had ratified it. Almost all of these 20 countries were either dominated or heavily under the influence of the Soviets ... Almost without exception the "democracy" and "human rights" which existed at that stage in these countries are now recognised as a cruel farce. How seriously must we take people who take seriously the judgements of those countries on human rights abuses in South Africa?' Giliomee, 1996: 8–9.

46. 13–14 September 1998, South African Jewish Board of Deputies, Johannesburg.

47. South African Jewish historian Gideon Shimoni agreed with him. 'Any attempt to suggest a prognosis for South African Jewry in the new South African polity and society must inquire into the prospects of ethnic identity and expression in general and within the minority groupings and above all within the white segment to which the Jews belong. The future of the Jews in this sense is very much linked with the future of the Afrikaners, as has always been the case in the past,' he said (1999, 47).

48. Workshop Proceedings, 'The Truth Commission—A Jewish Issue? Jewish Perspectives on Justice and Forgiveness in South Africa,' Gesher Workshop, 19 May 1996, Johannesburg.

49. Auerbach, 'South African Jewry,' 3.

50. Auerbach, 'South African Jewry,' 2.

51. Garber, *Vested Interests*, 17.

52. Unpublished interview with Uys, Johannesburg, 1994.

53. The Kaplan Centre for Jewish Studies, University of Cape Town, 2 April–5 June 1998.

54. The voice of Stephen Cohen, gay, Jewish South African artist, is also

audible. At the 1996 Gay and Lesbian Pride Parade in Johannesburg, Cohen brandished a banner that provocatively proclaimed: 'Give us your children—what we can't fuck we eat.' Cohen satirizes homophobic perceptions of gays as cannibals and child molesters. Like Krouse, he has explored the relation between sexuality and nationalism under apartheid alongside his exploration of issues of Jewish identity. Strongly informed by recognition of the historical links between Afrikaans and German nationalism and of their similar impact on the life of the nation, including the constructions of ethnic and sexual identities, his representations of aspects of the apartheid police state in the 1980s were littered with visual references to Nazism. Through these, Cohen engaged critically with apartheid constructions of national and sexual identity. More recently, Cohen's work has dealt explicitly with Jewishness, including a piece of his performance art in the streets of Johannesburg entitled 'Jews' that dealt with the hunted and persecuted in history.

Bibliography

Abrahams, Lionel. 1986. *The Celibacy of Felix Greenspan*. Johannesburg: A. D. Donker
——. 1988. *A Reader*, Johannesburg: A. D. Donker.
——. 1996. *The Democratic Chorus and Individual Choice*. Johannesburg: South African Institute of Race Relations.
Adler, Taffy. 1979. 'Lithuania's Diaspora: The Johannesburg Jewish Workers' Club, 1928–1948.' *Journal of Southern African Studies* 6, no. 1:70–92.
Asmal, Kader, Louise Asmal, and Ronald Suresh Roberts. 1996. *Reconciliation Through Truth: A Reckoning of Apartheid's Criminal Governance*. Cape Town: David Philips.
Auerbach, Franz. 1996. 'South African Jewry and the Truth Commission.' Unpublished.
——. 1997. 'Do We Apologise? South African Jewish Community Responses to Apartheid.' *Jewish Affairs* 52, no. 1:31–35.
Azanian Peoples Organisation (AZAPO) and Others v. President of the Republic of South Africa and Others 1996 (4) SA 671 (South African Constitutional Court).
Barney, Simon. 1974. *Jo'burg Sis!* Johannesburg: Bateleur Press.
Bernard, Norman. 1997. 'Conscientising the Jewish Community: An Orthodox Rabbi Looks Back.' *Jewish Affairs* 52, no. 1:71–73.
Bernhard, Norman. 'The Row Rumbles On' (letter to the editor). *Mail and Guardian*, 11–17 April.

Bernstein, Edgar. 1962. *My Judaism, My Jews*, Johannesburg: Exclusive Books.

Braude, Claudia. 1999. 'From the Brotherhood of Man to the World to Come: Rabbinic Writing Under Apartheid.' In *Jewries at the Frontier: Accommodation, Identity, Conflict*, edited by Sander L. Gilman and Milton Shain. Urbana: University of Illinois Press.

Braude, Claudia, and Derek Spitz. 1997. 'Memory and the Spectre of International Justice: A Comment on AZAPO.' *South African Journal on Human Rights*, 13, no. 2:269–82.

Bunting, Brian. 1964. *The Rise of the South African Reich*. London: Penguin Africa Library.

Coetzee, J. M. 1988. *White Writing: On the Culture of Letters in South Africa*. Sandton: Century Hutchinson.

De Klerk, F. W. 1996. 'National Party Submission to the Truth and Reconciliation Commission.' Cape Town.

De Kok, Ingrid, and Karen Press. 1990. *Spring Is Rebellious: Arguments About Cultural Freedom by Albie Sachs and Respondents*. Cape Town: Buchu Books.

Feldberg, Leon. 1965. *South African Jewry—1965*. Johannesburg: Fieldhill.

Friedman, Graeme, and Roy Blumenthal. 1998. *A Writer in Stone: South African Writers Celebrate the 70th Birthday of Lionel Abrahams*. Cape Town: David Philip.

Furlong, Patrick. 1991. *Between Crown and Swastika: The Impact of the Radical Right on the Afrikaner Nationalist Movement in the Fascist Era*. Johannesburg: Witwatersrand University Press.

Garber, Marjorie. 1992. *Vested Interests: Cross-Dressing and Cultural Anxiety*. New York: Harper Collins.

Giliomee, Hermann. 1996. 'Liberal and Populist Democracy in South Africa: Challenges, New Threats to Liberalism.' Johannesburg: South African Institute of Race Relations.

———. 1999. 'The Cultural Survival of Afrikaners and Afrikaans-Speakers in a Democratic South Africa.' *Jewish Affairs* 54, no. 1:24–35.

Gilman, Sander. 1991. *The Jew's Body*. New York: Routledge.

Gordimer, Nadine. 1949. *Face to Face*, Johannesburg: Silver Leaf Books.

———. 1953. *The Soft Voice of the Serpent and Other Stories*. London: Gollancz.

———. 1960. *Friday's Footprint*. London: Gollancz.

———. 1990. *My Son's Story*. London: Penguin Books.

———. 1991. *Jump and Other Stories*. New York: Farrar, Straus and Giroux.

———. 1992. 'Writing and Being.' *Staffrider* 10, no. 2:5–10.

Herber, Avril. 1979. *Conversations*. Johannesburg: Bateleur Press.

Jacobson, Dan. 1998. *Heshel's Kingdom*. London: Hamish Hamilton.

Katzew, Henry. N.d. *Solution for South Africa: A Jewish View*. Cape Town: Nasionale Boekhandel.

Kentridge, Morris. 1934. 'South African Jewry in 1934.' *Almanac*, September, 10.

———. 1959. *I Recall.* Johannesburg: Free Press.

Krouse, Matthew, ed. 1993. *The Invisible Ghetto: Lesbian and Gay Writing from South Africa*, Johannesburg: COSAW Publishing.

Krut, Riva. 1987. 'The Making of a South African Jewish Community in Johannesburg, 1886–1914.' In Belinda Bozzoli, ed., *Class, Community and Conflict: South African Perspectives*. Johannesburg: Ravan Press, 135–59.

Leveson, Marcia. 1996. *The People of the Book.* Johannesburg: Witwatersrand University Press.

Melman, Yossi. 'Exposed: SA's Clandestine Nuclear Dealings with Israel.' *Sunday Independent*, 4 May 1997, 15–17.

Meyer, P. J. 1984. *Nog nie ver genoeg nie: 'n persoonlike rekenskap van vyftig jaar georganiseerde Afrikanerskap.* Johannesburg: Perskor.

Millin, Sarah Gertrude. 1926. *The South Africans.* London: Constable.

———. 1928. *The Coming of the Lord.* London: Constable.

———. 1941a. *The Night Is Long.* London: Faber and Faber.

———. 1941b. *South Africa.* London: Collins.

———. 1944. *World Blackout.* London: Faber and Faber.

———. 1945. *The Reeling Earth.* London: Faber and Faber.

———. 1946. *The Pit of the Abyss.* London: Faber and Faber.

———. 1947a. *The Sound of the Trumpet.* London: Faber and Faber.

———. 1947b. *Fire out of Heaven.* London: Faber and Faber.

———. 1948. *The Seven Thunders.* London: Faber and Faber.

———. 1962. *The Wizard Bird.* N.p.: Central News Agency.

———. 1968. 'Time Is No Longer.' Unpublished article. S. G. Millin Papers, A539/M8. Manuscript Collection, University of the Witwatersrand Library.

———. 1986. *God's Stepchildren.* Johannesburg: A. D. Donker.

———. N.d. 'The Jewess Esther: A Play in Fifteen Scenes Adapted from the Story in the Bible.' Unpublished article. S. G. Millin Papers, A539/M5. Manuscript Collection, University of the Witwatersrand Library.

———, ed. 1966. *White Africans Are Also People.* Cape Town: Howard Timmins.

Mzimela, Sipo. 1980. *Nazism and Apartheid: The Role of the Christian Churches in Nazi Germany and Apartheid South Africa.* New York: New York University Press.

Podbrey, Pauline. 1993. *White Girl in Search of the Party.* Pietermaritzburg: Hadeda Books.

Promotion of National Unity and Reconciliation Act, No. 34 of 1995. *Government Gazette* 16579, Vol. 361, July 1995, 4–48.

Rubin, Martin. 1977. *Sarah Gertrude Millin: A South African Life.* Johannesburg: A. D. Donker.

Sachs, Albie. 1990a. *Protecting Human Rights in a New South Africa*. Cape Town: Oxford University Press.

———. 1990b. *The Jail Diary of Albie Sachs*. London: Paladin.

———. 1991. *The Soft Vengeance of a Freedom Fighter*. London: Paladin.

———. 1992. *Advancing Human Rights in South Africa*. Cape Town: Oxford University Press.

———. 1993a. 'Being the Same and Being Different.' *Jewish Quarterly* 40, no. 1:13–16.

———. 1993b. 'Reparation—Political and Psychological Considerations.' *Psycho-Analytic Psychotherapy in South Africa* 2:18–27.

Sachs, Bernard. 1949. *Multitude of Dreams*. Johannesburg: Kayor.

———. 1959. *South African Personalities and Places*. Johannesburg: Kayor.

Sachs, Wulf. 1996. *Black Hamlet*. Johannesburg: Witwatersrand University Press.

Saks, David. 1999. 'Jews on Commando.' *Jewish Affairs* 54, no. 3:23–30.

Saron, Gustav, and Louis Hotz. 1955. *The Jews in South Africa: A History*. Cape Town: Oxford University Press.

Schwarz, Harry. 1997, Autumn. 'Jewish Modes of Opposition.' *Jewish Affairs*, 29.

Segal, Ronald. 1963. *Into Exile*. London: McGraw-Hill.

———. 1995. *The Black Diaspora: Five Centuries of the Black Experience Outside Africa*. New York: Farrar, Straus and Giroux.

Serote, Mongane Wally. 1972. *Yakhal'inkomo*. Johannesburg: Renoster Books.

Shain, Milton. 1994. *The Roots of Antisemitism in South Africa*. Johannesburg: Witwatersrand University Press.

Shain, Milton, and Sally Frankental. 1997. 'Accommodation, Activism and Apathy: Reflections on Jewish Political Behaviour During the Apartheid Era.' *Jewish Affairs*, 52, no. 1:53–57.

Sherman, Joseph. 1987. *From a Land Far Off: A Selection of South African Yiddish Stories*. 1987. Cape Town: Jewish Publications.

Shimoni, Gideon. 1980. *Jews and Zionism: The South African Experience, 1910–1967*. Cape Town: Oxford University Press.

———. 1999. 'South African Jewry in the Context of World Jewry.' *Jewish Affairs*, 54, no. 1:45–47.

Sifrin, Geoff, Steven Friedman, and Daniel Beller. 1997. 'Can Reconciliation Take Root in Post-Apartheid South African Society? A Jewish View on the Process.' *Jewish Affairs*, 52, no. 1:63–68.

Sparks, Allister. 1990. *The Mind of South Africa: The Story of the Rise and Fall of Apartheid*. New York: Ballantine.

Suttner, Immanuel. 1997. *Cutting Through the Mountain: Interviews with South African Jewish Activists*. London: Penguin Books.

Ungar, André. 1959. 'The Abdication of a Community.' *Africa South*, 3, no. 2:29–38.

Uys, Pieter-Dirk. 1994. *A Part Hate a Part Love: The Legend of Evita Bezuidenhout*. Groenkloof: Hond.

Wade, Michael. 1993. 'A Sport of Nature: Identity and Repression of the Jewish Subject.' In B. King, ed. *The Later Fiction of Nadine Gordimer*. London: Macmillan.

Zwi, Rose. 1980. *Another Year in Africa*. Johannesburg: Bateleur Press.

——. 1998. *Last Walk in Naryshkin Park*. Johannesburg: Witwatersrand University Press.

Rose Zwi

EXCERPT FROM Another Year in Africa

I

Berka Feldman spat out the nails from between his lips, cleared the table of leather, tacks, and thread, and left the shoe on the last, to be repaired the following morning. It was only ten to five. He seldom left the workshop before six, but today he felt restive. After an oppressively hot morning the sky had suddenly darkened and distant thunder had rolled like wagon wheels over rocky ground. Ripped by forked lightning the clouds emptied themselves over the suburb then drifted away, leaving a brilliant sunset and steaming streets.

From the doorway he watched the water gurgle down the gutters towards the Dip. He drew a deep breath. His lungs caught sharply on the smell of damp concrete and a sudden yearning for the wet-straw smell of the veld washed over him. He longed to be on his wagon again, enclosed in the silence and emptiness of the veld, with only his voorloper to lead the oxen. In summer he had watched the grass bend and sway like Jews at prayer while he hummed the half-forgotten songs and psalms of his childhood. In winter he listened to the susurrus of the wind through the dry grass, rising to a mournful swell as it swept over the veld. Towards evening a thin spiral of smoke might appear on the horizon. He savoured his solitude, certain that it would end. Soon he would walk into a mud-walled farmhouse filled with the smell of coffee and griddle cakes baking on an open fire. Hanging from the rafters of the reed-and-thatch roof would be cobs of dried mealies, twisted rolls of tobacco, and strips of biltong. From the earthen floor into which peach pips had been beaten would rise the faint sweet smell of cowdung . . .

How free, how lonely that life had been.

He took off his leather apron, washed his hands in the cracked basin at the back of the shop and rinsed out his mouth. The taste of nails persisted. Only a drink would remove that metallic taste, but if he came home on a·Friday evening smelling of beer, Yenta would have another weapon in her armoury of abuse. He put his cap over his thick grey hair and walked out of the shop, squinting up at the sun which hung low over Main Street.

From where he stood he could see the eastern part of the suburb; from the top of Main Street he would see the rest. The city lay to the east, its tall grey towers rosy in the dying light, a coppery blaze piercing the eye as the sun reflected off glass and steel.

To think that forty-five years ago it had been little more than a miners' village with row upon row of tin shanties, rough men, horses, ox wagons. Berka shrugged his shoulders at the miracle of its growth.

His shop was a mile and a half from town, but the Dip brought the buildings nearer and they towered like a fortified city over a village at its gates. Although he might yearn, occasionally, for his carefree days as an itinerant cobbler, he had lived in the shadow of the city for so long that he gladly accepted the boundaries of his world: The sun rose to the east of Main Street, and set over the hill, to the west of it.

Berka recalled early his arrival in South Africa, early in 1892.

'It's a bad time to have come,' his uncle reproached him. The pogrom should have coincided with a boom in South Africa. 'There's no gold in the streets nor, it seems, in the mines,' he continued crossly as he led Berka into a small room at the back of the Concession Store. 'You'll have to work hard. I pay five pounds a month with free board and lodging. If you want to get rich, save.'

For several years Berka sold blankets and trinkets to black miners. On week-ends he helped in the Kaffir Eating House attached to the store. The smell of burned entrails and cooked meat clung to his clothes and cleaved to his nostrils. His cousins sniffed fastidiously when he came to his uncle's house for an occasional meal.

In his sparsely furnished room he studied English from a tattered grammar book. The bar was his elocution class. From the English miners he acquired a Midlands accent which, coupled with impeccable Yiddish inflexions, made his teachers roar with good-natured laughter. He read voraciously. This improved his English, widened his knowledge, and assuaged the loneliness of his years as a kaffer-itnik. He worked for long enough to buy the tools of the trade he had learned in the old country, then started on his life of wandering.

His uncle never forgave him his ingratitude.

'If you'd remained with me instead of running off into the veld like a wild chatas,' he said to Berka, 'you'd have been a rich man. Today you don't even own the house you live in.'

'Property is theft,' Berka had replied. 'I want nothing that I haven't earned with my own labour.'

They never spoke to one another again.

Berka stood at the corner of Main Street and Lovers' Lane. Wherever he looked he saw Uncle Feldman's possessions. He had become a man of property over the years. But Uncle Feldman was not a happy man: he had little joy from his sons. They had not gone beyond Standard Seven in school and proved equally inept in business. He would be lucky if they said a decent kaddish for him when he died—at a hundred and twenty years, please God. Berka chuckled. He could think of no greater punishment for his sons.

Uncle Feldman had moved out of Mayfontein twenty years ago but he retained his Concession Store, the source of all his wealth. He hired a manager and although he was almost eighty, he still went to the business. At irregular hours, Berka thought grimly, so that he could catch the manager stealing. Uncle Feldman was certain that everyone stole from him.

Berka spat into the gutter.

Uncle Feldman was one of the few people towards whom Berka could not extend tolerance, an attribute which he valued above most others. Yenta, who had never really understood him, claimed that his tolerance stopped at his own front door.

He began walking up Main Street, aware that his tall bulky figure was as much an institution in Mayfontein as the headgear of the mine, the white dumps on its outskirts or the bar. As he walked to and from work every day he was hailed from all sides. His heart swelled with emotion: He was the friend of Jew and Gentile, the arbiter in disputes, the consoler in sorrow. In short, he was loved.

'Feldman!' came a deep voice from the smithy across the road. 'Why do you stand there in the middle of the street, smiting yourself on the chest, smiling, spitting, shaking your fist?'

Leib Schwartzman emerged from the smithy. He was a stocky man whose powerful shoulders gleamed with sweat under his grease-stained vest.

'Are you sick that you're shutting shop so early, or has your uncle written you into his will?' he asked with a grin.

'Neither. I calculated that if I worked an hour less today, I'd become a millionaire that much later. How's business?'

'Bad, bad.' Leib wiped his forehead with the back of his hand. 'Cars, trams, bicycles. Where have all the horses gone?'

'To the Free State, to become rabbis like that ass Benjamin,' Berka said.

'Don't blaspheme against the servants of the Lord. What will happen when you have to account to Him one day?'

'If God is just, as you claim he is, he'll distinguish between those with kosher stomachs and unkosher souls. I may not get to heaven but neither will my reverend brother-in-law Benjamin. The only trouble is that I'll probably meet him in the Other Place.'

Leib laughed. He had studied Law in Kovno but influenced by the workers' movement he had given up Torah for a trade. The future of society, after all, lay in the hands of the proletariat. But he had retained his love for Jewish tradition and went to shul, to synagogue, regularly. Opiate of the masses, he'd exclaim angrily when Berka defined religion for him. What's a worse opiate? Going to shul or going to the bar? Meet my learned friend Bernard, he would mock. He's so thirsty for Justice that he's been called to the Bar.

'When I saw you packing up early I thought perhaps you wanted to get to shul in time,' Leib smiled.

'Don't joke,' Berka said gloomily. 'I'll probably land up doing that to please Ruth. It's not easy being an honorary grandfather. Ruth's afraid I'll land up in Hell because she once heard me say that there was no God. She wants me to look for Him in shul.'

'Strange child,' Leib said rubbing a grease spot off his arm. 'Last week your sister-in-law sent Ruth to borrow a pot from us. "Mrs. Blackman," says Ruth to the wife because she's speaking English now so the name's Blackman not Schwartzman, "mine grenny vants to lend your big bleck pot." Why doesn't she speak Yiddish to my Chaya? They're both a pair of English scholars, Ruth and Chaya.'

'Because she doesn't know Chaya well and to strangers she speaks only English.' Berka looked angry, upset. 'I must be getting along. I'll stop off at the bar to chat with our local proletarians.'

Leib put his hand on Berka's shoulder.

'Don't be angry with me, Berka, I know how fond you are of the child. But to whom can one speak? To her father the dreamer? Or her mother who's always wrapped up in Vicks and cottonwool?'

'Ruth's not strange, Leib. She's got too much imagination and too few friends. The kids tease her because she doesn't speak English properly. She'll learn. She begins school on Monday where she'll mix with other children. Have a good sabbath. See you at the poker game on Sunday night.'

The sun had almost disappeared behind the Main Street hill and Berka stepped up his pace. He wanted to see it set behind the mine dumps. There were few sights he loved more.

Poor Ruthie. She'd have to learn to live in the present. A child of six burdened with a consciousness of tragedy and persecution, with memories that weren't even hers. He himself was guilty of telling the story of his family's massacre in her presence. He had broken down that time and shouted:

'There is no God!'

Berka coughed to clear the heaviness on his chest. He hummed tunelessly for a while then remembered the song about the drunkard:

When they write my epitaph
It'll read 'Here lies a drunk,'
And I'll answer with a laugh,
'There's no brandy here, I'm sunk!'

He must sing that for Yenta. She said that real Jews didn't booze. Yet here, immortalised in a Yiddish folk song, was the lament of a Jewish drunkard. Let her explain that one away. Berka walked on, humming the jaunty tune.

There were few people in Main Street. The Jewish housewives were at home preparing the sabbath meal and the miners' wives shopped on Saturday morning. Haggard, often toothless, their hair perpetually in curlers, they trudged across the veld in their slippers from the mine's Married Quarters to do their weekly shopping.

There was little enough in their purses after their men had stopped off at the bar and at the bucket shop on Friday evenings. Their children, thin and snot-nosed, ran wild through the suburb.

Harsh men, these miners, yet who could judge them? Here he was, walking in the clear rain-washed air while they were thousands of feet below surface, drilling into stubborn rock, breathing in poisonous fumes, stumbling through the tunnels that honeycombed the earth beneath his feet. Underground was Hell. Dark tunnels of damp rock, slippery passages, unbearable heat, pressure bursts, rock falls. Could these conditions produce gentle compassionate men? And what was it all for anyway? They wrested a few grains of gold from tons of rock, then buried it again in underground vaults.

He had watched the men come off shift, their faces pale with dust and fatigue, tin hats in one hand, carbide lamps in the other, blinking in the unaccustomed light of day. They washed down the mine dust with drink and beat up their wives, their children, and the hapless mine kaffirs. To them, the blacks were barely human.

Every year Berka watched the black recruits arriving at Mayfontein Railway Station clad in loin cloths and blankets. They were tall sturdy men, selected for their strength and good health. For two shillings a day, a pot of mealie meal, and kaffir beer, they travelled hundreds of miles from their kraals and their families to live in crowded mine compounds and to do the hardest work underground. When their nine months' contract ended, they might be a few pounds richer, wear trousers and a shirt, and carry away with them, under their gay blankets, a lung disease.

And the white miners organised unions to protect themselves from the blacks' cheap labour, but left them to be slaves to the mine bosses.

'Berka! You look as though you're carrying the world on your shoulders,' a gentle voice said at his side. 'And all the way uphill too.'

'Reb Hershl! Just the man I need to see.' Berka stopped at the bakery door and sniffed. 'Ah, you perfume the suburb. There's such comfort in the smell of fresh bread. Little wonder I've got such a big nose. All my emotions are filtered through it.' He put his arm around Hershl's shoulders and walked into the bakery with him.

He had time. There would be another sunset tomorrow evening. Such a pessimist he wasn't. A few words with Hershl would remove the metallic taste from his mouth and the ash from his soul.

Hershl took off his floury apron and hung it on a nail behind the counter. The bakery was small. The front portion had been divided off from the wall ovens at the back by a thin wooden partition. There was a glass-fronted counter which displayed iced cakes, buns, and several kinds of bread: rye with aniseed, special sabbath kitkes, and sandwich loaves. Through the opening in the partition came a surge of hot air as the iron doors of the wall ovens swung open to receive another load of bread. A loud crash of metal trays and bread tins drowned the first part of Hershl's sentence:

'. . . the last lot of loaves for the night,' he said as the noise died down. 'Dirk will lock up. Since I took him on I can go to the synagogue on Friday evenings.'

'How's business?' Berka asked.

'Excellent, improving all the time. It paid to take on a trained baker. Faigel works up front now and only does the confectionery for special occasions. I bought a horse and cart this week. The deliveries were getting too big for my bicycle.'

'Leib will be pleased to hear there's another horse in town,' Berka said. 'He thought they'd all gone to the Free State.'

'Free State?' Hershl looked puzzled. He did not always under-stand Berka's jokes. 'Did I tell you I'd made an offer for Sharp's delicatessen? It's much bigger than my shop and I can build in extra ovens. Now that I've got contracts with a few Concession stores I shall need it. I saw Uncle Feldman the other day,' Hershl added. 'For two reasons. To get an order for the bakery and to ask for a donation for the Refugees' Fund.'

'Let me guess,' Berka said drily. 'The order you got at cut prices. And if you did get a donation, you had to sweat blood first.'

'You know the man. He denied he was stingy. All rumours, he said. People thought he was mean because he didn't advertise his charitable deeds as others did. He gave anonymously.'

'So anonymously that he doesn't even sign his cheques,' Berka retorted. 'Let's talk of cheerful things.'

'Cheerful things?' Hershl's face dropped. 'There's nothing cheer-ful in 1937. Look at Germany: Jews thrown out of jobs, property confiscated, schools closed, people shut up in ghettos. That's cheerful? And suddenly the world's too overcrowded to take in a few Jewish refugees.'

'They let some Jews into South Africa from Germany.'

'And are drafting the Aliens Act to keep the others out. They hate the Jews as much as the Nazis do.'

'But what's happening in Germany couldn't happen here,' Berka persisted.

'You've been saying that for years, Berka. This isn't the same South Africa you knew in the old days. All those stories you tell of Boer hospitality and respect for the people of the Book. When they're in the Book they're all right, but when the farmer's crops fail and he comes to borrow from the Jewish storekeeper at interest, it's a different matter. When the Jew was a smous, a pedlar, they tolerated him. When he holds the purse strings or he's in competition, they fear him. And where there's fear, there'll be persecution.'

'Nonsense. There may be hotheads among them but has there ever been a pogrom here?'

'What do you think the Greyshirts are planning, a Purim party?'

'So, where's it better?'

'Where's it better he asks,' Hershl appealed to the ceiling. 'Berka, we need a home of our own, without Aliens Acts and without anyone's kind permission to exist.'

'Spare me the Zionism. Bought any good stands in the sea lately?'

Hershl laughed, not without embarrassment. I shall die in Jerusalem, he predicted when he argued about Zionism with Berka. That I can believe, Berka would reply. To live there is another matter. Emissaries from Palestine had an easy time with Hershl. Two years earlier an imposing man with a dark flowing beard and side curls had sold Hershl a stand in Palestine. A few months later he discovered it was situated a mile off the coast of Jaffa, in the sea.

'Nu, in Lithuania I was a Hebrew teacher,' Hershl said. 'Here I am a baker. In Palestine I'll become a fisherman. Remember how furious Faigel was? She doesn't understand how I feel about Palestine. Buying trees, making an annual contribution to Zionist funds, sending other people, that she doesn't mind. But the idea of settling there is beyond her comprehension.'

'And mine. It's too remote and strange to me. How's the family?'

'Fine. Daniel starts school on Monday.'

'So does Ruthie. It's a pity they don't play together. It'd help if Ruth had friends her own age.'

'Daniel's also shy. Children of immigrant parents have a hard time. Torn between different ways of life. If we lived in Palestine . . .'

'There he goes again,' Berka said walking towards the door. 'I live in the present and you live in an impossible dream of the future. It's better, I suppose, than living in the past like our Dovidke. Come here, Hershl. Look at him standing there at his window, dreaming of the old country no doubt, where the fields were greener and the fruit sweeter.'

'He often stands like that,' Hershl said looking up at Dovid Erlich at his workshop window over the road, gazing sightlessly into the distance. 'He's got problems. Not much work coming in, mostly alterations. And Sheinka is a nagging wife.'

'Is there another kind?' Berka asked.

'Poor Ruthie. She's caught in the middle. They can't be easy parents to live with. I wonder what went wrong? Sheinka was a lovely woman when they came out from Lithuania eight years ago. A little melancholic perhaps, but charming. She's grown bitter over the last few years.'

Berka was looking up at Dovid. From his first floor workshop, he thought enviously, he can see over the ridge of the hill where the sun will soon set. And he's not even aware of what he's seeing. Berka turned to leave the bakery.

'Have a good sabbath, Hershl. Come over and kibbitz on Sunday night. Leib and I have arranged a game of bloff. Low stakes.'

He shook Hershl's floury hand warmly. He loved the man; he renewed Berka's faith in humanity.

Main Street was shining after the rain. A tram car clambered heavily up the hill, packed with people returning from work. Their faces looked soft and warm in the golden light. Berka loved them all. Even that thief Steinberg who gave short weight in his butchery; and Chidrawi, the swarthy Syrian who was arranging a pyramid of yellow peaches in his window; and Levin the outfitter who stood in his doorway, a tape measure around his neck. And all those children outside the fish and chips shop watching wistfully as Ronnie Davis sprinkled vinegar over someone else's chips. He even felt a fleeting affection for the miser Pinn who owned the second-hand shop. His wife stood in the doorway, fluffing her hair this way and that, before embarking on what must be a two-hour journey home. She stopped off all along Main Street, garnering the news of the day, which she then embellished and disseminated among the housewives of First Avenue. She often knew better than they what was happening in the house next door. Some people were entirely unlovable.

Berka looked into the dark interior of Nathan's Drapery Store where his daughter Raizel worked. She was probably cashing up now. She had worked for the Nathans for four years, since she matriculated. At first she was a counter hand, measuring out elastic, hair ribbons, and dress material. Today she practically ran the business. Mrs. Nathan spent most of her time in the city, drinking tea at the Corner Lounge, or walking about from shop to shop. Getting ideas for the trade, she called it. Mr. Nathan was almost blind. My eyes, he called Raizel. My heart, Berka murmured as he passed the shop.

The barbershop next to Nathan's was crowded with miners. Not, God forbid, having haircuts, but placing bets for the dog races.

Friday Night is Wanderers Night,
Night for Greyhound Racing.

read a poster on the wall. Next to it hung a framed picture of water-waved ladies. And Wednesday night was Wembley Night, yet another night for dog racing.

Berka walked resolutely past the hotel bar. The Siren-sounds of clinking glasses and loud laughter would not tempt him tonight.

From the bar onwards Main Street ran a flat course for half a mile towards the large bluegum plantation which flanked the suburb on the west. The plantation stretched from the end of Main Street southwards towards the mine dumps. Below the dumps was a small dam into which water was pumped from underground. If Berka had seen snow-capped mountains, pine forests and an inland lake as he turned the corner from Main Street into First Avenue, he would not have been happier. He remembered when the first saplings had been planted. He had watched the mine dump grow as the coco-pans crawled up its sandy slopes depositing yet another load of finely crushed rock onto the chalky hill. And next to it the yellow slimes dam also grew slowly, hardening towards its final shape as a truncated pyramid.

He never tired of this constant yet ever-changing scene. On rainy days the dump stained deep yellow, the trees washed a lighter green, and the leaden skies reflected dully in the cyanic dam. Under the clear winter skies the dam sparkled like a jewel, and the whiteness of the dump was blinding. He loved it most at sunset, however, when the dump became a mountain of gold dust and the dam liquid amber.

They could keep their gold bars in their vaults. He was satisfied with the refuse. From the top of First Avenue he surveyed his kingdom. King of the Rubbish Heaps, he thought with a smile. Beyond the veld which separated Mayfontein from the mine, the wheels of the headgear turned ceaselessly and the stentorian voice of the crushers echoed throughout the suburb, day and night, week after week, year after year, until it seemed to be the very breath of the suburb. He breathed in unison with it.

At this time of the day the rows of the red-bricked semi-detached houses glowed like live coals and the whole suburb caught fire. Only the plane trees cast a cooling shadow across the hot sandy roads. Yanka the fruit vendor came into view, driving his horses hard in his effort to reach home before the sabbath. Billowing clouds of red dust rose in his wake. Like the cumulus clouds which hung over the dump, like the dust raised by Boers on commando.

'This is my world,' Berka sighed as he walked down First Avenue towards his house, 'and I'm glad of it.'

2

'I should've had that drink!' Berka looked regretfully up First Avenue then back again to the veranda where Yenta, her ample bosom resting on its polished ledge, was waiting for him. Her hair was combed and she was wearing her best brown dress. That could mean one of two things: that she wanted a favour from him in which case she would have overlooked his beery breath, or that she had unpleasant news, in which case he would need a drink.

'Benjamin's in for the week-end,' she greeted him apologetically. 'He's come to see a doctor. Please be patient with him, Berrala. He's a sick man.'

Berrala. A man had as many names as his wife had moods. He was Berka when she talked about him to others; Berra when she was annoyed with him which was most of the time; Bernard when he had been to the bar with his non-Jewish friends; and Berrala when she wanted something from him. In her fantasies she undoubtedly saw him sitting in a plush office with 'Bernard K. Feldman' gilded on the door. If he did not have a middle name, she'd provide one.

'That's not all.' She put a restraining hand on his sleeve as he brushed past impatiently. 'Ruthie's in the lounge with that scabby dog of hers, Zutzke.'

Berka stopped. His gruffness could not hide his concern.

'What now?' he asked.

'This afternoon,' Yenta said replacing her bosom on the ledge, assured of his attention, 'when Gittel went out to feed the chickens, she noticed a piece of roof missing from the chicken run. And the chicken she'd been fattening for Purim had flown.'

'So?'

'So poor Gittel chased all over First Avenue looking for the silly chicken. She finally found it on Reb Hershl's kitchen table, pecking at the farfel which Faigel had put out to dry.'

'So now we've completed the saga of the chicken. What about Ruth?'

'Wait. Sheinka at the same time noticed that Ruth and Zutzke were missing. She went to the veld where Ruth had run away last time and saw her, followed by the dog, climbing up the mine dump. She was dragging that piece of corrugated iron behind her, like a sled. When she saw Sheinka, she fled into the plantation as though a horde of Cossacks were after her. Pregnant as she is, Sheinka dragged herself across the wet veld and found Ruth lying under the trees, crying her heart out. She wouldn't say why. You know a mother's heart: Sheinka feared she'd been raped by those wild mine kaffirs . . .'

'Stop talking like a stupid yiddine. So what happened then?'

'So what happened then he asks. Nothing.' Yenta hated interruptions. She liked to tell a story in her own time, with suitable digressions. But she remembered that Benjamin was in from the Free State and controlled her temper. 'So what happened? Ruth ranted like a meshugene about pogroms, blood, and snow. The piece of iron, she said, was her sled and she was running away from the Cossacks. Then she ran away from Sheinka. She's been in the lounge for the last hour, waiting for you.'

Yenta looked grave. Berka hated the gravity, the muted tones in which they spoke about Ruth. As though the child were an idiot, a cripple.

He walked into the dark airless passage from which all the rooms in the house led off. It had pockets of smells which evoked the week's meals: pickled brisket, sauerkraut, cauliflower, gefilte fish, not to mention the all-pervading smell of pickling cucumbers and fermenting wine. He screwed up his nose and lit his pipe. In the far corner of the lounge Ruth lay sprawled out in a large armchair, her ginger head against Zutke's spotted one. They were both asleep.

Berka sat down on a chair near the door. He really needed a drink but he'd wait for Raizel. When she came home she would pour him a schnapps and amuse him with tales about Nathan's. A perceptive girl, his Raizel. Perhaps he should have let her become a teacher. In the five years that Dovid had gone to night school he had not learned as much English as in the last year when Raizel had begun to teach him. But Berka had been afraid; so many teachers remain old maids.

With boys it was different. They needed a trade, a profession. Yenta had wanted their son Joel to be a doctor. When he had apprenticed himself to a pharmacist, Yenta consoled herself: They understand more than doctors, these chemists, she said. When I've got a pain, a cold, anything, I go to Brown the chemist, he gives me a mixture and in a few days I'm as strong as a horse again. What's so marvellous about doctors? In the old country the sick died of their diseases and the doctor died of starvation. Please God when Joel finishes, I'll give him with what to start his own little chemist shop.

Towards this end Yenta had been pickling cucumbers and fermenting wine in the cellar for years. Her products were snapped up by the neighbours and by Sharp's Delicatessen as soon as they matured. How's Joel's little chemist shop coming along, Berka would ask with heavy sarcasm. His earnings had kept them in relative comfort during all the years of their married life but he did not have a penny in the bank. Laugh, laugh, Yenta would reply. One day you'll see.

Joel's boss was complimentary about him. So charming with the clients, he told Berka. Clients yet; he, Berka, had customers. And so charming. For that he got an education? He wished Joel would shed a little more charm at home. Since he was asked out to his rich clients' homes he had grown so high and mighty. Bring your friends here one Friday night, Yenta had offered in her innocence. You must reciprocate. I'll make noodle soup, tzimmes, a stuffed duck.

Berka had watched Joel take in her untidy hair, her ill-fitting false teeth which clattered loosely as she spoke, her nails which were blackened from the coal stove and from her wine making. He followed Joel's eyes down to Berka's slippers which she always wore. I can't ma, he told her turning away. We're not geared for visitors. Bring them, bring them, I can manage. Last Pesach I had twenty people here for the seder. I can . . . She had broken off abruptly, rubbed her nose vigorously, and ended lamely: Oh, I understand. Well, perhaps we do need new curtains. And the sofa is a little worn . . .

That was education for you.

Their house did look shabby. The lace curtains were yellow with dust, the floral linoleum needed a good scrubbing and the heavy rust-coloured settee and armchairs threw up clouds of dust when one sat down. Phthisis one could get. But Yenta would not spring-clean until Passover. This vestigial behaviour stemmed from the old country where the housewives waited for the long cold winter to pass and for the snows to melt before they took down their curtains, polished the windows and scrubbed the floors. The fact that Passover occurred in autumn in South Africa, not in the spring, did not deflect Yenta from her girlhood rituals.

It was hard to keep the mine dust out of the house. In the dry winter months the wind whipped up the loose sand from the dumps, covering everything and everyone with a fine layer of dust. Yet Sheinka and Gittel, Yenta's sister, managed to keep their house clean. Like a chemist shop—Yenta herself said. But it was to Yenta's house that the visitors flocked, not to Gittel's. They dropped in for a chat, for a game of klabberjas; they sat on the veranda in summer and around the kitchen stove in winter. There was always enough to eat for those who were tardy in leaving at mealtimes. Everyone responded to Yenta's warmth and kindness, and ignored the smells, the dust, and the general untidiness of the house. They visited Gittel and Sheinka only by invitation.

But she could keep the place cleaner, Berka brooded. The only pretty thing in the lounge was a vase of marigolds which Raizel had put on the little glass table. When he suggested to Yenta that she take in a native servant she said: I don't want blacks in the house; they stink.

Her cucumbers and her wine didn't stink. Berka struck a match. Ruth stirred. She's emotionally exhausted, Berka thought as she moaned quietly and fell asleep again. Since her tonsilectomy she suffered badly from nightmares. They're choking me, they're choking me! she'd cry leaping out of bed. They said they'd take out my tonsils with a teaspoon, she told Berka reproachfully when she came out of hospital. A big light shone on me. They put a black smelly thing over my nose and I couldn't breathe. Afterwards I knew I wasn't dead because my throat was so sore. They didn't take them out with a spoon. And they didn't give me ice cream and jelly afterwards like mamma said.

Like an orphan they treated her. To have left a sensitive seven-year-old all alone in the hospital; Berka still couldn't get over it. Yenta had taken Ruth into hospital by tram and Raizel had brought her home next day in a taxi. Dovid was working, Sheinka was pregnant, and Gittel couldn't speak English.

Berka's pipe went out again. He did not risk lighting another match. He put the pipe into the ashtray and looked at the pictures on the wall. Yenta's sepia-tinted mother and father hung above the settee in matching oval frames. Their features had been blurred by time and enlargement and they could have been anybody's mother and father. The mother, a dark round-faced woman, wore a wig. The father's face was covered with a long beard, a thick moustache, and a forelock which was combed low over his forehead. Only his large brown eyes—like Raizel's—were visible above an aquiline nose. He wore a yarmulka.

The other walls were covered with haughty uncles and smug aunts under whose noses Berka longed to draw big black moustaches. Yenta was proud of her family. They certainly had had the time and money to make frequent visits to the photographer.

Berka marvelled at the speed with which his feelings of universal love and tolerance dissipated when he stepped into his house. He smiled, however, when he looked at the picture of Raizel and Joel as children. Even Joel looked lovable.

There were photographs of picnics in Lithuanian woods, of the village choir, of the river. There was also a street scene in Ragaza, a broad sandy road with little wooden houses under shingled roofs; a horse and cart in the distance and an occasional tree growing in a garden. Berka had often seen Ruth standing in front of this picture, staring at it, almost fearfully.

On the wall behind him was a wedding photo of Dovid and Sheinka. She looked dark and lovely and he proud and studious. A pair of gold-rimmed glasses rested lightly on his nose. Berka smiled. Dovid's eyesight was as good as his own. The gold-rimmed glasses and the book under the arm were the emblems of the Lithuanian intellectual. They carried the best literature under their arms.

There were no pictures of Berka's family. These had been destroyed together with everything else. To look at the walls one would think he had been born from a stone.

To his right were his and Yenta's wedding pictures. They were separate and had not been taken at their wedding but Berka insisted on calling them his wedding pictures. One was a picture of Yenta and her sister Gittel. Gittel's round pretty face was in the full light. Her hair was draped back into a soft chignon and she smiled with the assurance of a pretty woman. Yenta's face receded into the dark background. Her beaked nose was skilfully touched up by the photographer and her intelligent scornful smile acknowledged that she was a foil for her older sister's good looks. Only her large brown eyes—again like Raizel's—brightened up her long dark face.

This was the picture with which Benjamin had wooed Berka on her behalf. The other one is prettier, he agreed, but she's eight years older and she's married. Yenta may not be the most beautiful woman in the world but what a character she's got, what a character! And what a character she turned out to have. Berka should have been warned by that all-knowing smile.

Next to it hung the second half of the wedding picture, the one of Berka which Benjamin had sent to Yenta. He stood in front of a mining magnate's house and his features were sacrificed to background. He leaned possessively against an ornate iron gate, his thumb lightly hooked into the chain of a watch—kindly lent by the photographer. His hair was parted in the centre and his moustache, which he later trimmed down to Yenta's specifications, stretched from ear to ear, like his smile.

'I thought the house belonged to you,' Yenta would throw up at him in later matrimonial disputes.

'And I thought you had character,' he countered. 'Looks I could see you didn't have.'

'So, who asked you to bring me out from Ragaza?'

'Your brother. And I was tired of wandering about. They all said I needed a good Jewish wife, a home. Some home you made me. A bed of nails.'

'If not for me you wouldn't have had nails either.'

'I should have married Maria du Toit. Her father promised me the farm when he died.'

'You deserve a goya. You're a peasant. Who else but a poor orphan like me, living with her married sister, would have come out to a strange country to marry an even stranger man?'

'On your holy brother's recommendation. For once he showed good judgement, on your behalf. And tell me: Who brought out your sister and her children to South Africa when her husband died? Benjamin or me?'

'Who said you didn't? Will you throw that up at me for the rest of my life?'

Berka sighed. He never won an argument with Yenta. She was convinced that he disliked Benjamin because he had been instrumental in their marriage. She could not conceive of the fact that Benjamin was a repulsive human being in his own right.

Berka heard a light shuffle of feet behind him. Yenta stood in the passage with a large cup of coffee in her hand, motioning him towards the veranda. Benjamin was probably staying all week. He got up quietly and followed her. She waited until he had settled himself in the cane chair before she handed him the strong sweet coffee. Then she leaned against the veranda ledge again, looking expectantly up the street.

Raizel was due home, her sabbath dinner was ready, and when Benjamin returned from synagogue they would eat. Not that the sabbath dinner differed much from weekday meals. Berka had discouraged her years ago from making a fuss of the sabbath. A white table cloth and her mother's silver candlesticks were the only concessions to tradition which Berka, after many battles, had allowed her.

The sun had already set behind the plantation and the air was fresh and cool. The smell of warm damp earth and bruised marigolds mingled with that of sabbath cooking which floated down the street. On every block from the top of Main Street to the end of First Avenue, lived at least two Jewish families. On their own block there was their landlady Mrs. Zaidman and her spinster daughter; the Schwartzmans and Dovid's family. Over the road lived the Pinns and Reb Hershl's family. They were surrounded by friends. Except, of course, for their new neighbours, the Burgers.

Berka sipped his coffee loudly then listened. Old man Burger sat just behind the wall which separated their verandas. He was also drinking coffee, noisily. He had moved into the other half of the semi-detached house a few months ago. A balding bull-necked man with a red angry face, he had barely returned Berka's greetings since he moved in. His wife and six children—goodness only knew where they all slept in their two-bedroomed house—were no friendlier. Only their eldest son Jan whom he often met in the bar, greeted him politely.

Perhaps Hershl was right. He would have to revise his ideas of Boer friendliness and hospitality.

The Burgers were urbanised Afrikaners but the dedication with which the old man tended his garden made Berka suspect that he had once been a farmer. All the other houses had crushed stone from the mines covering their tiny patch of garden. Burger dug and manured the soil, planted sweet-smelling flowers, bushes, and creepers, and spent all his free time either in the garden or hammering in the cellar which he had converted into a workshop.

Aaron Blecher and his family had been very different neighbours. Trust his wife to drag him off to a 'better' suburb, to provide a good address for their marriageable daughters. When they left, Berka lost an invaluable klabberjas hand and Yenta a close friend. The low backyard wall which divided their houses had hummed with a constant traffic of loaned cups of oil, flour, and sugar. Now Yenta was greeted by the implacable pale face of Mrs. Burger. In spite of this Yenta still wanted to buy the house they had lived in for the past twenty years.

'Mrs. Zaidman was here again today,' she said as she took away Berka's empty cup. 'She only wants a hundred pounds down, the rest to be paid in monthly instalments. She says . . .'

'She's selling cheap because she needs hard cash for her krasa-vitza's dowry,' Berka said irritably.

'Molly's not ugly and she's not unmarriageable. She's only twenty-seven.'

'Not counting Mondays and Thursdays.'

'She wouldn't even sell it, but since her husband died . . .'

'Forget it, Yenta. I'm not going into real estate.'

Yenta sighed. Why did she persist? She and Berka had discovered long ago just how far they could push one another. In fact, they understood one another so well that there seemed little point in talking at all. The turbulent days of their marriage when Mrs. Pinn on her veranda could report word for word of an argument taking place in their own kitchen, were over. If they argued now it was simply a matter of form, to acknowledge that the other existed.

'I had the strangest dream last night,' Yenta changed the subject. She rarely had ordinary dreams. 'I dreamed I ordered two baskets of black grapes from Yanka to make wine. His horse ate half of one basket. I was so angry that I went to the Syrian and he delivered two baskets to the house. As I sat down to press them into the wine barrel, I discovered that there were cucumbers in the baskets, not grapes.'

'And so?' Berka asked, waiting for the inevitable interpretation of signs and portents which always had a bearing on dog racing.

'The double for tonight will be two and two,' she said. 'I've already placed a bet.'

'Foolish woman. One of the baskets was half empty. The double for tonight will be two and one and a half. Or, if you add the Syrian's baskets to Yanka's and subtract . . .'

'Another Joseph!' she said with infinite contempt. 'Go tell it to Pharaoh.'

She watched Mrs. Pinn's progress down the street. Yenta had seen her turning into First Avenue when she went into the kitchen to make coffee for Berka. So far she had only covered three quarters of the street, describing a zig-zag course as she crossed from one house to another. To beat a hasty retreat into the house as Mrs. Pinn approached meant you had something to hide. To receive her with equanimity was a sure sign of a clear conscience. Unlike the Angel of Death she passed over all the non-Jewish houses, stopping only at her co-religionists'. The goyim's gossip, it seemed, was not worth collecting.

Tonight her stops were shorter than usual. Mrs. Pinn observed the sabbath and she wanted to be home in time to light the candles.

'Have you seen mine Raizel?' Yenta asked when she finally arrived at her veranda. She always spoke English to Mrs. Pinn although the latter, who was born in South Africa, had learned to speak Yiddish after the first lot of immigrants arrived from Lithuania. In a suburb of immigrants Yiddish was an occupational imperative.

'Oh yes,' Mrs. Pinn answered in her gritty voice. She felt slighted by Berka's curt nod. 'She was walking slowly along Main Street with Mr. Erlich. They seemed in no great hurry to get home.'

She watched Berka for a reaction. When she got none, she gave Yenta her news: They said the Syrian had rejected Yanka's offer for his fruit shop. He wanted an extra hundred pounds' goodwill. They said that Reb Hershl had made a secret offer for Sharp's Delicatessen. As an old friend she was tipping off Yenta to approach Reb Hershl about selling him her cucumbers. The rebbetzin, they said, had already offered him wine for the Passover. They also said that Schumacher, the German refugee who had opened an ice-cream shop next to the police station, was only half-Jewish and that his wife was a full-blooded German, a terrible anti-semite. She for one would not buy his ice-cream. Who knew what they put into it?

'They say,' Berka mumbled angrily, walking into the house. 'They say. Who the hell is They?'

'They say,' Mrs. Pinn continued, disconcerted by Berka's abrupt withdrawal but refusing to be silenced, 'that Yaakov Koren has stopped sending money to his wife and child and that they're living on charity from the shtetl. He's sending her a divorce instead and he's going to marry the widow Kagan before Rosh Hashana.'

When Berka came into the lounge he found Ruth sitting upright in the chair, a dazed sleepy expression on her face. Zutzke was stretching himself luxuriously at her feet. She smiled happily as Berka picked her up and she put her thin arms around his neck. The smell of bluegums and acidic dump sand clung to her curly ginger hair. He hugged her warmly then sat on the armchair, holding her in his lap.

'Ruthie's had a hard day. Tell me about it,' he said softly in Yiddish.

She leaned contentedly against his chest, saying nothing.

'Tell Zeide Berka what you did today, Ruthie.'

'I, I don't know if I dreamed it or if it really happened,' she said with a frown.

'Tell me the dream then. Bobbe Yenta always tells me her dreams. Maybe if I know what you dreamed we'll be able to work out the double for tonight's dog racing.'

Ruth smiled. Everybody knew about Yenta's dreams.

'It was like last time,' she began, hiding her head on Berka's shoulder. 'I dreamed, I think I dreamed, that I heard horses and I knew that I must run away. In the snow it's hard without a sled, so I took the iron from Bobbe Gittel's chicken run. And I ran to the dumps, to the snow mountain. With the lake and the forest, like Daddy told me.'

She dug her face into his shoulder again and was quiet for a while.

'And it happened again, like last time. It didn't look like Mayfontein. It looked like that picture on the wall, that one,' she pointed without looking at the street scene of Ragaza. 'All the houses were on fire and those men with the big swords came on horses and, and . . .' She burst into tears.

'Finish, my child. Then it will be over and out.'

'And they killed everybody who was running out of the houses. And the snow in the street was red,' she blurted out, 'and I ran into the forest.'

Berka sat, silent with guilt, holding her tightly against his chest.

'And I didn't know if I dreamed it or thought it or if it really happened,' Ruth said. 'And Mamma shouted and hit me and said I was a liar.'

'Shah, shah. It did happen, my poor child, but not to you. To someone else and a very long time ago. It is all over now and it will never happen again, so you mustn't worry. It will never never happen again.'

He sat very still until he felt all the tension leave her thin body. Then he heard a loud voice on the veranda. Within seconds Sheinka had rushed into the lounge, preceded by a strong smell of Vicks.

'I knew she'd be here, the little liar! Steals the iron off the roof to play dangerous games on the dumps, then tells silly stories about pogroms. She's either crazy and doesn't know what she's talking about or she's an out and out liar. Come home immediately!'

Ruth clung to Berka.

'Quietly, quietly,' Berka told Sheinka sternly. 'I've just managed to calm her.'

'It's you and Dovid who fill her head with nonsense!' Sheinka cried. 'Stories, stories, stories! No wonder the child's an idiot. She doesn't know what or where she is half the time.'

'Sit down, Sheinkala, and don't excite yourself. Remember your health,' Berka said quietly.

At the mention of her health Sheinka collapsed into a chair with one hand over her heart and the other over her stomach.

'The baby will be born dead, I know it!' she wailed. 'How can any living thing survive such upsets? And it will be her fault.'

Ruth tensed up against Berka and looked at him in mute appeal. He tightened his hold on her.

'Yenta, bring Sheinkala a cup of that delicious hot coffee,' he said.

'No. I'm going home. Come,' she said to Ruth as she wriggled out of the chair.

Ruth turned around slowly to face her mother and said haltingly, in English.

'I don't want to go home mit you.'

Sheinka fell back into the chair. Her face crumbled as she cried: 'In English! Did you hear? She spoke to me in English! What am I, a stranger? Gott in Himmel! What sin have I committed to deserve such a strange child?'

Nadine Gordimer

My Father Leaves Home

The houses turn aside, lengthwise from the village street, to be private. But they're painted with flowery and fruity scrolls and garlands. Blossoming vines are strung like washing along the narrow porches' diminishing perspective. Tomatoes and daisies climb together behind picket fences. Crowded in a slot of garden are pens and cages for chickens and ducks, and there's a pig. But not in the house he came from; there wouldn't have been a pig.

The post office is made of slatted wood with a carved valance under the roof—a post-office sign is recognizable anywhere, in any language, although it's one from a time before airmail: not a stylized bird but a curved post-horn with cord and tassels. It's from here that the letters would have gone, arranging the passage. There's a bench outside and an old woman sits there shelling peas. She's wearing a black scarf tied over her head and an apron, she has the lipless closed mouth of someone who has lost teeth. How old? The age of a woman without oestrogen pills, hair tint charts, sunscreen, and anti-wrinkle creams. She packed for him. The clothes of a cold country, he had no other. She sewed up rents and darned socks; and what else? A cap, a coat; a boy of thirteen might not have owned a hand-me-down suit, yet. Or one might have been obtained specially for him, for the voyage, for the future.

Horse-drawn carts clomp and rattle along the streets. Wagons sway to the gait of fringe-hooved teams on the roads between towns, delaying cars and buses back into another century. He was hoisted to one of these carts with his bag, wearing the suit; certainly the cap. Boots newly mended by the member of the family whose trade this was. There must have been a shoemaker among them; that was the other choice open to him: he could have learnt shoe-making but had decided for watch-making. They must have equipped him with the loupe for his eye and the miniature screw-drivers and screws, the hairsprings, the fish-scale watch glasses; these would be in his bag as well. And some religious necessities. The shawl, the things to wind round his arm and brow. She wouldn't have forgotten those; he was thirteen, they had kept him home and fed him, at least until their religion said he was a man.

At the station the gypsies are singing in the bar. It's night. The train sweats a fog of steam in the autumn cold and he could be standing there somewhere, beside his bag, waiting to board. She might have come with him as far as this, but more likely not. When he clambered up to the cart, that was the end, for her. She never saw him again. The man with the beard, the family head, was there. He was the one who had saved for the train ticket and ship's passage. There are no farewells; there's no room for sorrow in the drunken joy of the gypsies filling the bar, the shack glows with their heat, a hearth in the dark of the night. The bearded man is going with his son to the sea, where the old life ends. He will find him a place in the lower levels of the ship, he will hand over the tickets and bits of paper that will tell the future who the boy was.

We had bought smoked paprika sausage and slivovitz for the trip—the party was too big to fit into one car, so it was more fun to take a train. Among the padded shotgun sleeves and embossed leather gun cases we sang and passed the bottle round, finding one another's remarks uproarious. The Frenchman had a nest of thimble-sized silver cups and he sliced the sausage towards his thumb, using a horn-handled knife from the hotel gift shop in the capital. The Englishman tried to read a copy of Cobbett's *Rural Rides* but it lay on his lap while the white liquor opened up in him unhappiness in his marriage, confided to a woman he had not met before. Restless with pleasure, people went in and out of the compartment, letting in a turned-up volume of motion and buffets of fresh air; outside, seen with a forehead resting against the corridor window, nothing but trees, trees, the twist of a river with a rotting boat, the fading Eastern European summer, distant from the sun.

Back inside to catch up with the party: someone was being applauded for producing a bottle of wine, someone else was taking teasing instruction on how to photograph with a newfangled camera. At the stations of towns nobody looked at—the same industrial intestines of factory yards and junk tips passed through by railway lines anywhere in the world we came from—local people boarded and sat on suitcases in the corridors. One man peered in persistently and the mood was to make room for him somehow in the compartment. Nobody could speak the language and he couldn't speak ours, but the wine and sausage brought instant surprised communication, we talked to him whether he could follow the words or not, and he shrugged and smiled with the delighted and anguished responses of one struck dumb by strangers. He asserted his position only by waving away the slivovitz—that was what foreigners naturally would feel obliged to drink. And when we forgot about him while arguing over a curious map the State hunting organization had given us, not ethno- or geographic but showing the distribution of water- and wildfowl in the area we were approaching, I caught him looking over us, one by one, trying to read the lives we came from, uncertain, from unfamiliar signs, whether to envy, to regard with cynicism, or to be amused. He fell asleep. And I studied him.

There was no one from the hunting lodge come to meet us at the village station ringed on the map. It was night. Autumn cold. We stood about and stamped our feet in the adventure of it. There was no station-master. A telephone booth, but whom could we call upon? All inclusive; you will be escorted by a guide and interpreter everywhere—so we had not thought to take the telephone number of the lodge. There was a wooden shack in the darkness, blurry with thick yellow light and noise. A bar! The men of the party went over to join the one male club that has reciprocal membership everywhere; the women were uncertain whether they would be acceptable—the customs of each country have to be observed, in some you can bare your breasts, in others you are indecent if wearing trousers. The Englishman came back and forth to report. Men were having a wild time in the shack, they must be celebrating something, they were some kind of brotherhood, black-haired and unshaven, drunk. We sat on our baggage in the mist of steam left by the train, a dim caul of visibility lit by the glow of the bar, and our world fell away sheer from the edge of the platform. Nothing. At an unknown stage of a journey to an unknown place, suddenly unimaginable.

An old car splashed into the station yard. The lodge manager fell
out on his feet like a racing driver. He wore a green felt hat with
badges and feathers fastened round the band. He spoke our language, yes. It's not good there, he said when the men of the party
came out of the bar. You watch your pocket. Gypsies. They don't
work, only steal, and make children so the government gives them
money every time.

The moon on its back.
     One of the first things he will have noticed when he arrived was
that the moon in the Southern Hemisphere lies the wrong way
round. The sun still rises in the east and sets in the west but the one
other certainty to be counted on, that the same sky that covers the
village covers the whole earth, is gone. What greater confirmation
of how far away; as you look up, on the first night.
     He might have learnt a few words on the ship. Perhaps someone
who had preceded him by a year or so met him. He was put on a
train that travelled for two days through vineyards and mountains
and then the desert; but long before the ship landed already he
must have been too hot in the suit, coming south. On the high
plateau he arrived at the gold mines to be entrusted to a relative.
The relative had been too proud to have explained by post that he
was too poor to take him in but the wife made this clear. He took
the watch-making tools he had been provided with and went to the
mines. And then? He waylaid white miners and replaced balance
wheels and broken watch-faces while-you-wait, he went to the
compounds where black miners had proudly acquired watches as
the manacles of their new slavery: to shift work. In this, their own
country, they were migrants from their homes, like him. They had
only a few words of the language, like him. While he picked up
English he also picked up the terse jargon of English and their
languages the miners were taught so that work orders could be
understood. Fanagalo: 'Do this, do it like this.' A vocabulary of
command. So straight away he knew that if he was poor and alien at
least he was white, he spoke his broken phrases from the rank of
the commanders to the commanded: the first indication of who he
was, now. And the black miners' watches were mostly cheap ones

not worth mending. They could buy a new one for the price he would have to ask for repairs; he bought a small supply of Zobo pocket watches and hawked them at the compounds. So it was because of the blacks he became a business man; another indication.

And then?

Zobos were fat metal circles with a stout ring at the top and a loud tick tramping out time. He had a corrugated-tin-roofed shop with his watch-maker's bench in a corner and watches, clocks, and engagement and wedding rings for sale. The white miners were the ones whose custom it was to mark betrothals with adornments bought on the instalment plan. They promised to pay so-much-a-month; on the last Friday, when they had their wages, they came in from the hotel bar smelling of brandy. He taught himself to keep books and carried bad debts into the Depression of the Thirties.

He was married, with children, by then. Perhaps they had offered to send a girl out for him, a home girl with whom he could make love in his own language, who would cook according to the dietary rules. It was the custom for those from the villages; he surely could have afforded the fare. But if they knew he had left the tin shack behind the shop where he had slept when first he became a business man, surely they couldn't imagine him living in the local hotel where the white miners drank and he ate meat cooked by blacks. He took singing lessons and was inducted at the Masonic Lodge. Above the roll-top desk in the office behind his new shop, with its sign WATCHMAKER JEWELLER & SILVERSMITH, was an oval gilt-framed studio photograph of him in the apron of his Masonic rank. He made another move; he successfully courted a young woman whose mother tongue was English. From the village above which the moon turned the other way there came as a wedding gift only a strip of grey linen covered with silk embroidery in flowers and scrolls. The old woman who sat on the bench must have done the needlework long before, kept it for the anticipated occasion, because by the time of the distant marriage she was blind (so someone wrote). Injured in a pogrom—was that a supposition, an exaggeration of woes back there, that those who had left all behind used to dramatize an escape? More likely cataracts, in that village, and no surgeon available. The granddaughters discovered the piece

of embroidery stuck away behind lavender-scented towels and pil-
lowcases in their mother's linen cupboard and used it as a carpet
for their dolls' house.

The English wife played the piano and the children sang round
her but he didn't sing. Apparently the lessons were given up; sometimes she laughed with friends over how he had been told he was a
light baritone and at Masonic concerts sang ballads with words
by Tennyson. As if he knew who Tennyson was! By the time the
younger daughter became curious about the photograph looking
down behind its bulge of convex glass in the office, he had stopped
going to Masonic meetings. Once he had driven into the garage
wall when coming home from such an occasion; the damage was
referred to in moments of tension, again and again. But perhaps he
gave up that rank because when he got into bed beside his wife in
the dark after those Masonic gatherings she turned away, with her
potent disgust, from the smell of whisky on him. If the phylacteries
and skull-cap were kept somewhere the children never saw them.
He went fasting to the synagogue on the Day of Atonement and
each year, on the anniversaries of the deaths of the old people in
that village whom the wife and children had never seen, went again
to light a candle. Feeble flame: who were they? In the quarrels
between husband and wife, she saw them as ignorant and dirty; she
must have read something somewhere that served as a taunt: you
slept like animals round a stove, stinking of garlic, you bathed once
a week. The children knew how low it was to be unwashed. And
whipped into anger, he knew the lowest category of all in her country, this country.

You speak to me as if I was a kaffir.

The silence of cold countries at the approach of winter. On an
island of mud, still standing where a village track parts like two
locks of wet hair, a war memorial is crowned with the emblem of a
lost occupying empire that has been succeeded by others, and still
others. Under one or the other they lived, mending shoes and
watches. Eating garlic and sleeping round the stove. In the graveyard stones lean against one another and sink at levels from one
occupation and revolution to the next, the Zobos tick them off, the

old woman shelling peas on the bench and the bearded man at the
dockside are in mounds that are all cenotaphs because the script
that records their names is a language he forgot and his daughters
never knew. A burst of children out of school alights like pigeons
round the monument. How is it possible that they cannot be understood as they stare, giggle, and—the bold ones—question. As with
the man in the train: from the tone, the expression on the faces, the
curiosity, meaning is clear.

Who are you?

Where do you come from?

A map of Africa drawn with a stick in the mud.

Africa! The children punch each other and jig in recognition.
They close in. One of them tugs at the gilt ring glinting in the ear of
a little girl dark and hairy-curly as a poodle. They point: gold.

Those others knew about gold, long ago; for the poor and despised there is always the idea of gold somewhere else. That's why
they packed him off when he was thirteen and according to their
beliefs, a man.

At four in the afternoon the old moon bleeds radiance into the grey
sky. In the wood a thick plumage of fallen oak leaves is laid reveren-
tially as the feathers of the dead pheasants swinging from the
beaters' belts. The beaters are coming across the great fields of
maize in the first light of the moon. The guns probe its halo. Where
I wait, apart, out of the way, hidden, I hear the rustle of fear among
creatures. Their feathers swish against stalks and leaves. The cluck-
ing to gather in the young; the spurting squawks of terror as the
men with their thrashing sticks drive the prey racing on, rushing
this way and that, no way where there are not men and sticks, men
and guns. They have wings but dare not fly and reveal themselves,
there was nowhere to run to from the village to the fields as they
came on and on, the kick of a cossack's mount ready to strike
creeping heads, the thrust of a bayonet lifting a man by the heart
like a piece of meat on a fork. Death advancing and nowhere to go.
Blindness coming by fire or shot and no way out to see, shelling
peas by feel. Cracks of detonation and wild agony of flutter all
around me, I crouch away from the sound and sight, only a spectator, only a spectator, please, but the cossacks' hooves rode those

pleading wretches down. A bird thus dead, striking my shoulder before it hits the soft bed of leaves beside me.

Six leaves from my father's country.

When I began to know him, in his shop, as someone distinct from a lap I sat on, he shouted at the black man on the other side of the counter who swept the floor and ran errands, and he threw the man's weekly pay grudgingly at him. I saw there was someone my father had made afraid of him. A child understands fear, and the hurt and hate it brings.

I gathered the leaves for their pretty autumn stains, not out of any sentiment. This village where we've rented the State hunting lodge is not my father's village. I don't know where, in his country, it was, only the name of the port at which he left it behind. I didn't ask him about his village. He never told me; or I didn't listen. I have the leaves in my hand. I did not know that I would find, here in the wood, the beaters advancing, advancing across the world.

Dan Jacobson

The Zulu and the Zeide

Old man Grossman was worse than a nuisance. He was a source of constant anxiety and irritation; he was a menace to himself and to the passing motorists into whose path he would step, to the children in the streets whose games he would break up, sending them flying, to the householders who at night would approach him with clubs in their hands, fearing him a burglar; he was a butt and a jest to the African servants who would tease him on street corners.

It was impossible to keep him in the house. He would take any opportunity to slip out—a door left open meant that he was on the streets, a window unlatched was a challenge to his agility, a walk in the park was as much a game of hide-and-seek as a walk. The old man's health was good, physically; he was quite spry, and he could walk far, and he could jump and duck if he had to. And all his physical activity was put to only one purpose: to running away. It was a passion for freedom that the old man might have been said to have, could anyone have seen what joy there could have been for him in wandering aimlessly about the streets, in sitting footsore on pavements, in entering other people's homes, in stumbling behind advertisement hoardings across undeveloped building plots, in toiling up the stairs of fifteen-storey blocks of flats in which he had no business, in being brought home by large young policemen who winked at Harry Grossman, the old man's son, as they gently hauled his father out of their flying-squad cars.

'He's always been like this,' Harry would say, when people asked him about his father. And when they smiled and said: 'Always?' Harry would say, 'Always. I know what I'm talking about. He's my father, and I know what he's like. He gave my mother enough grey hairs before her time. All he knew was to run away.'

Harry's reward would come when the visitors would say: 'Well, at least you're being as dutiful to him as anyone can be.'

It was a reward that Harry always refused. 'Dutiful? What can you do? There's nothing else you can do.' Harry Grossman knew that there was nothing else he could do. Dutifulness had been his habit of life: it had had to be, having the sort of father he had, and the strain of duty had made him abrupt and begrudging: he even carried his thick, powerful shoulders curved inwards, to keep what he had to himself. He was a thick-set, bunch-faced man, with large bones, and short, jabbing gestures; he was in the prime of life, and he would point at the father from whom he had inherited his strength, and on whom the largeness of bone showed now only as so much extra leanness that the clothing had to cover, and say: 'You see him? Do you know what he once did? My poor mother saved enough money to send him from the old country to South Africa; she bought clothes for him, and a ticket, and she sent him to her brother, who was already here. He was going to make enough money to bring me out, and my mother and my brother, all of us. But on the boat from Bremen to London he met some other Jews who were going to South America, and they said to him: "Why are you going to South Africa? It's a wild country, the savages will eat you. Come to South America and you'll make a fortune." So in London he exchanges his ticket. And we don't hear from him for six months. Six months later he gets a friend to write to my mother asking her please to send him enough money to pay for his ticket back to the old country—he's dying in the Argentine, the Spaniards are killing him, he says, and he must come home. So my mother borrows from her brother to bring him back again. Instead of a fortune he brought her a new debt, and that was all.'

But Harry was dutiful, how dutiful his friends had reason to see again when they would urge him to try sending the old man to a home for the aged. 'No,' Harry would reply, his features moving heavily and reluctantly to a frown, a pout, as he showed how little the suggestion appealed to him. 'I don't like the idea. Maybe one day when he needs medical attention all the time I'll feel differently about it, but not now, not now. He wouldn't like it, he'd be unhappy. We'll look after him as long as we can. It's a job. It's something you've got to do.'

More eagerly Harry would go back to a recital of the old man's past. 'He couldn't even pay for his own passage out. I had to pay the loan back. We came out together—my mother wouldn't let him go by himself again, and I had to pay off her brother who advanced the money for us. I was a boy—what was I?—sixteen, seventeen, but I paid for his passage, and my own, and my mother's and then my brother's. It took me a long time, let me tell you. And then my troubles with him weren't over.' Harry even reproached his father for his myopia; he could clearly enough remember his chagrin when shortly after their arrival in South Africa, after it had become clear that Harry would be able to make his way in the world and be a support to the whole family, the old man—who at that time had not really been so old—had suddenly, almost dramatically, grown so short-sighted that he had been almost blind without the glasses that Harry had had to buy for him. And Harry could remember too how he had then made a practice of losing the glasses or breaking them with the greatest frequency, until it had been made clear to him that he was no longer expected to do any work. 'He doesn't do that any more. When he wants to run away now he sees to it that he's wearing his glasses. That's how he's always been. Sometimes he recognizes me, at other times, when he doesn't want to, he just doesn't know who I am.'

What Harry said about his father sometimes failing to recognize him was true. Sometimes the old man would call out to his son, when he would see him at the end of a passage, 'Who are you?' Or he would come upon Harry in a room and demand of him, 'What do you want in my house?'

'Your house?' Harry would say, when he felt like teasing the old man. 'Your house?'

'Out of my house!' the old man would shout back.

'Your house? Do you call this your house?' Harry would reply, smiling at the old man's fury.

Harry was the only one in the house who talked to the old man, and then he did not so much talk to him, as talk of him to others. Harry's wife was a dim and silent women, crowded out by her husband and the large-boned sons like himself that she had borne him, and she would gladly have seen the old man in an old-age home. But her husband had said no, so she put up with the old man, though for herself she could see no possible better end for him than a period of residence in a home for aged Jews which she had once visited, and which had impressed her most favourably with its glass and yellow brick, the noiseless rubber tiles in its corridors, its secluded grassed grounds, and the uniforms worn by the attendants to the establishment. But she put up with the old man; she did not talk to him. The grandchildren had nothing to do with their grandfather—they were busy at school, playing rugby and cricket, they could hardly speak Yiddish, and they were embarrassed by him in front of their friends; and when the grandfather did take any notice of them it was only to call them Boers and *goyim* and *shkotzim* in sudden quavering rages which did not disturb them at all.

The house itself—a big single-storeyed place of brick, with a corrugated-iron roof above and a wide stoep all round—Harry Grossman had bought years before, and in the continual rebuilding the suburb was undergoing it was beginning to look old-fashioned. But it was solid and prosperous, and withindoors curiously masculine in appearance, like the house of a widower. The furniture was of the heaviest African woods, dark, and built to last, the passages were lined with bare linoleum, and the few pictures on the walls, big brown and grey mezzotints in heavy frames, had not been looked at for years. The servants were both men, large ignored Zulus who did their work and kept up the brown gleam of the furniture.

It was from this house that old man Grossman tried to escape. He fled through the doors and the windows and out into the wide sunlit streets of the town in Africa, where the blocks of flats were encroaching upon the single-storeyed houses behind their gardens. And in these streets he wandered.

It was Johannes, one of the Zulu servants, who suggested a way of dealing with old man Grossman. He brought to the house one afternoon Paulus, whom he described as his 'brother.' Harry Grossman knew enough to know that 'brother' in this context could mean anything from the son of one's mother to a friend from a neighbouring kraal, but by the speech that Johannes made on Paulus's behalf he might indeed have been the latter's brother. Johannes had to speak for Paulus, for Paulus knew no English. Paulus was a 'raw boy,' as raw as a boy could possibly come. He was a muscular, moustached and bearded African, with pendulous ear-lobes showing the slits in which the tribal plugs had once hung; and on his feet he wore sandals, the soles of which were cut from old motor-car tyres, the thongs from red inner tubing. He wore neither hat nor socks, but he did have a pair of khaki shorts which were too small for him, and a shirt without any buttons: buttons would in any case have been of no use for the shirt could never have closed over his chest. He swelled magnificently out of his cloth-ing, and above there was a head carried well back, so that his beard, which had been trained to grow in two sharp points from his chin, bristled ferociously forward under his melancholy and almost mandarin-like moustache. When he smiled, as he did once or twice during Johannes's speech, he showed his white, even teeth, but for the most part he stood looking rather shyly to the side of Harry Grossman's head, with his hands behind his back and his bare knees bent a little forward, as if to show how little he was as-serting himself, no matter what his 'brother' might have been say-ing about him.

His expression did not change when Harry said that it seemed hopeless, that Paulus was too raw, and Johannes explained what the baas had just said. He nodded agreement when Johannes explained to him that the baas said that it was a pity that he knew no English. But whenever Harry looked at him, he smiled, not ingratiatingly, but simply smiling above his beard, as though saying: 'Try me.' Then he looked grave again as Johannes expatiated on his virtues. Johannes pleaded for his 'brother.' He said that the baas knew that he, Johannes, was a good boy. Would he, then, recommend to the baas a boy who was not a good boy too? The baas could see for himself, Johannes said, that Paulus was not one of these town boys, these street loafers: he was a good boy, come straight from the kraal. He was not a thief or a drinker. He was strong, he was a hard worker, he was clean, and he could be as gentle as a woman. If he, Johannes, were not telling the truth about all these things, then he deserved to be chased away. If Paulus failed in any single respect, then he, Johannes, would voluntarily leave the service of the baas, because he had said untrue things to the baas. But if the baas believed him, and gave Paulus his chance, then he, Johannes, would teach Paulus all the things of the house and the garden, so that

Paulus would be useful to the baas in ways other than the particular task for which he was asking the baas to hire him. And, rather daringly, Johannes said that it did not matter so much if Paulus knew no English, because the old baas, the oubaas, knew no English either.

It was as something in the nature of a joke—almost a joke against his father—that Harry Grossman gave Paulus his chance. For Paulus was given his chance. He was given a room in the servants' quarters in the back yard, into which he brought a tin trunk painted red and black, a roll of blankets, and a guitar with a picture of a cowboy on the back. He was given a house-boy's outfit of blue denim blouse and shorts, with red piping round the edges, into which he fitted, with his beard and his physique, like a king in exile in some pantomime. He was given his food three times a day, after the white people had eaten, a bar of soap every week, cast-off clothing at odd intervals, and the sum of one pound five shillings per week, five shillings of which he took, the rest being left at his request, with the baas, as savings. He had a free afternoon once a week, and he was allowed to entertain not more than two friends at any one time in his room. And in all the particulars that Johannes had enumerated, Johannes was proved reliable. Paulus was not one of these town boys, these street loafers. He did not steal or drink, he was clean and he was honest and hard-working. And he could be as gentle as a woman.

It took Paulus some time to settle down to his job; he had to conquer not only his own shyness and strangeness in the new house filled with strange people—let alone the city, which, since taking occupation of his room, he had hardly dared to enter—but also the hostility of old man Grossman, who took immediate fright at Paulus and redoubled his efforts to get away from the house upon Paulus's entry into it. As it happened, the first result of this persistence on the part of the old man was that Paulus was able to get the measure of the job, for he came to it with a willingness of spirit that the old man could not vanquish, but could only teach. Paulus had been given no instructions, he had merely been told to see that the old man did not get himself into trouble, and after a few days of bewilderment Paulus found his way. He simply went along with the old man.

At first he did so cautiously, following the old man at a distance, for he knew the other had no trust in him. But later he was able to follow the old man openly; still later he was able to walk side by side with him, and the old man did not try to escape from him. When old man Grossman went out, Paulus went too, and there was no longer any need for the doors and windows to be watched, or the police to be telephoned. The young bearded Zulu and the old bearded Jew from Lithuania walked together in the streets of the town that was strange to them both; together they looked over the fences of the large gardens and into the shining foyers of the blocks of flats; together they stood on the pavements of the main arterial roads and watched the cars and trucks rush between the tall buildings; together they walked in the small, sandy parks, and when the old man was tired Paulus saw to it that he sat on a bench and rested. They could not sit on the bench together, for only whites were allowed to sit on the benches, but Paulus would squat on the ground at the old man's feet and wait until he judged the old man had rested long enough, before moving on again. Together they stared into the windows of the suburban shops, and though neither of them could read the signs outside the shops, the advertisements on billboards, the traffic signs at the side of the road, Paulus learned to wait for the traffic lights to change from red to green before crossing a street, and together they stared at the Coca-Cola girls and the advertisements for beer and the cinema posters. On a piece of cardboard which Paulus carried in the pocket of his blouse Harry had had one of his sons print the old man's name and address, and whenever Paulus was uncertain of the way home, he would approach an African or a friendly-looking white man and show him the card, and try his best to follow the instructions, or at least the gesticulations which were all of the answers of the white men that meant anything to him. But there were enough Africans to be found, usually, who were more sophisticated than himself, and though they teased him for his 'rawness' and for holding the sort of job he had, they helped him too. And neither Paulus nor old man Grossman were aware that when they crossed a street hand-in-hand, as they sometimes did when the traffic was particularly heavy, there were white men who averted their eyes from the sight of this degradation, which could come upon a white man when he was old and senile and dependent.

Paulus knew only Zulu, the old man knew only Yiddish, so there was no language in which they could talk to one another. But they talked all the same: they both explained, commented, and complained to each other of the things they saw around them, and often they agreed with one another, smiling and nodding their heads and explaining again with their hands what each happened to be talking about. They both seemed to believe that they were talking about the same things, and often they undoubtedly were, when they lifted their heads sharply to see an aeroplane cross the blue sky between two buildings, or when they reached the top of a steep road and turned to look back the way they had come, and saw below them the clean impervious towers of the city thrust nakedly against the sky in brand-new piles of concrete and glass and facebrick. Then down they would go again, among the houses and the gardens where the beneficent climate encouraged both palms and oak trees to grow indiscriminately among each other—as they did in the garden of the house to which, in the evenings, Paulus and old man Grossman would eventually return.

In and about the house Paulus soon became as indispensable to the old man as he was on their expeditions out of it. Paulus dressed him and bathed him and trimmed his beard, and when the old man woke distressed in the middle of the night it would be for Paulus that he would call—'Der schwarzer,' he would shout (for he never learned Paulus's name), 'vo's der schwarzer?'[1]—and Paulus would change his sheets and pyjamas and put him back to bed again. 'Baas Zeide,' Paulus called the old man, picking up the Yiddish word for grandfather from the children of the house.

And that was something that Harry Grossman told everyone of. For Harry persisted in regarding the arrangement as a kind of joke, and the more the arrangement succeeded the more determinedly did he try to spread the joke, so that it should be a joke not only against his father but a joke against Paulus too. It had been a joke that his father should be looked after by a raw Zulu: it was going to be a joke that the Zulu was successful at it. 'Baas Zeide! That's what der schwarzer calls him—have you ever heard the like of it? And you should see the two of them, walking about in the streets hand-in-

1. Where's the black man?

hand like two schoolgirls. Two clever ones, *der schwarzer* and my father going for a promenade, and between them I tell you you wouldn't be able to find out what day of the week or what time of day it is.'

And when people said, 'Still that Paulus seems a very good boy,' Harry would reply:

'Why shouldn't he be? With all his knowledge, are there so many better jobs that he'd be able to find? He keeps the old man happy— very good, very nice, but don't forget that that's what he's paid to do. What does he know any better to do, a simple kaffir from the kraal? He knows he's got a good job, and he'd be a fool if he threw it away. Do you think,' Harry would say, and this too would insistently be part of the joke, 'if I had nothing else to do with my time I wouldn't be able to make the old man happy?' Harry would look about his sitting-room, where the floorboards bore the weight of his furniture, or when they sat on the stoep he would measure with his glance the spacious garden aloof from the street beyond the hedge. 'I've got other things to do. And I had other things to do, plenty of them, all my life, and not only for myself.' What these things were that he had had to do all his life would send him back to his joke. 'No, I think the old man has just found his level in *der schwarzer*—and I don't think *der schwarzer* could cope with anything else.'

Harry teased the old man to his face too, about his 'black friend,' and he would ask his father what he would do if Paulus went away; once he jokingly threatened to send the Zulu away. But the old man didn't believe the threat, for Paulus was in the house when the threat was made, and the old man simply left his son and went straight to Paulus's room, and sat there with Paulus for security. Harry did not follow him: he would never have gone into any of his servants' rooms, least of all that of Paulus. For though he made a joke of him to others, to Paulus himself Harry always spoke gruffly, unjokingly, with no patience. On that day he had merely shouted after the old man, 'Another time he won't be there.'

Yet it was strange to see how Harry Grossman would always be drawn to the room in which he knew his father and Paulus to be. Night after night he came into the old man's bedroom when Paulus was dressing or undressing the old man; almost as often Harry stood in the steamy, untidy bathroom when the old man was being bathed. At these times he hardly spoke, he offered no explanation of his presence: he stood dourly and silently in the room, in his customary powerful and begrudging stance, with one hand clasping the wrist of the other and both supporting his waist, and he watched Paulus at work. The backs of Paulus's hands were smooth and black and hairless, they were paler on the palms and at the finger-nails, and they worked deftly about the body of the old man, who was submissive under the ministrations of the other. At first Paulus had sometimes smiled at Harry while he worked, with his straightforward, even smile in which there was no invitation to a complicity in patronage, but rather an encouragement to Harry to draw forward. But after the first few evenings of this work that Harry had watched, Paulus no longer smiled at his master. And while he worked Paulus could not restrain himself, even under Harry's stare from talking in a soft, continuous flow of Zulu, to encourage the old man and to exhort him to be helpful and to express his pleasure in how well the work was going. When Paulus would at last wipe the gleaming soap-flakes from his dark hands he would sometimes, when the old man was tired, stoop low and with a laugh pick up the old man and carry him easily down the passage to his bedroom. Harry would follow; he would stand in the passage and watch the burdened, bare-footed Zulu until the door of his father's room closed behind them both.

Only once did Harry wait on such an evening for Paulus to re-appear from his father's room. Paulus had already come out, had passed him in the narrow passage, and had already subduedly said: 'Good night, baas,' before Harry called suddenly:

'Hey! Wait!'

'Baas,' Paulus said, turning his head. Then he came quickly to Harry. 'Baas,' he said again, puzzled and anxious to know why his baas, who so rarely spoke to him, should suddenly have called him like this, at the end of the day, when his work was over.

Harry waited again before speaking, waited long enough for Paulus to say: 'Baas?' once more, and to move a little closer, and to lift his head for a moment before letting it drop respectfully down.

'The oubaas was tired tonight,' Harry said. 'Where did you take him? What did you do with him?'

'Baas?' Paulus said quickly. Harry's tone was so brusque that the smile Paulus gave asked for no more than a moment's remission of the other's anger.

But Harry went on loudly: 'You heard what I said. What did you do with him that he looked so tired?'

'Baas—I—' Paulus was flustered, and his hands beat in the air for a moment, but with care, so that he would not touch his baas. 'Please baas.' He brought both hands to his mouth, closing it forcibly. He flung his hands away. 'Johannes,' he said with relief, and he had already taken the first step down the passage to call his interpreter.

'No!' Harry called. 'You mean you don't understand what I say? I know you don't,' Harry shouted, though in fact he had forgotten until Paulus had reminded him. The sight of Paulus's startled, puzzled, and guilty face before him filled him with a lust to see this man, this nurse with the face and the figure of a warrior, look more startled, puzzled, and guilty yet; and Harry knew that it could so easily be done, it could be done simply by talking to him in the language he could not understand. 'You're a fool,' Harry said. 'You're like a child. You understand nothing, and it's just as well for you that you need nothing. You'll always be where you are, running to do what the white baas tells you to do. Look how you stand! Do you think I understood English when I came here?' Harry said, and then with contempt, using one of the few Zulu words he knew: 'Hamba! Go! Do you think I want to see you?'

'Au baas!' Paulus exclaimed in distress. He could not remonstrate; he could only open his hands in a gesture to show that he knew neither the words Harry used, nor in what he had been remiss that Harry should have spoken in such angry tones to him. But Harry gestured him away, and had the satisfaction of seeing Paulus shuffle off like a schoolboy.

Harry was the only person who knew that he and his father had quarrelled shortly before the accident that ended the old man's life took place; this was something that Harry was to keep secret for the rest of his life.

Late in the afternoon they quarrelled, after Harry had come back from the shop out of which he made his living. Harry came back to find his father wandering about the house, shouting for *der schwarzer*, and his wife complaining that she had already told the old man at least five times that *der schwarzer* was not in the house: it was Paulus's afternoon off.

Harry went to his father, and when his father came eagerly to him, he told the old man, '*Der schwarzer*'s not here.' So the old man, with Harry following, turned away and continued going from room to room, peering in through the doors. '*Der schwarzer*'s not here,' Harry said. 'What do you want him for?'

Still the old man ignored him. He went down the passage towards the bedrooms. 'What do you want him for?' Harry called after him.

The old man went into every bedroom, still shouting for *der schwarzer*. Only when he was in his own bare bedroom did he look at Harry. 'Where's *der schwarzer*?' he asked.

'I've told you ten times I don't know where he is. What do you want him for?'

'I want *der schwarzer*.'

'I know you want him. But he isn't here.'

'I want *der schwarzer*.'

'Do you think I haven't heard you? He isn't here.'

'Bring him to me,' the old man said.

'I can't bring him to you. I don't know where he is.'

Then Harry steadied himself against his own anger. He said quietly: 'Tell me what you want. I'll do it for you. I'm here, I can do what *der schwarzer* can do for you.'

'Where's *der schwarzer*?'

'I've told you he isn't here,' Harry shouted, the angrier for his previous moment's patience. 'Why don't you tell me what you want? What's the matter with me—can't you tell me what you want?'

'I want *der schwarzer*.'

'Please,' Harry said. He threw out his arms, towards his father, but the gesture was abrupt, almost as though he were thrusting his father away from him. 'Why can't you ask it of me? You can ask me—haven't I done enough for you already? Do you want to go for a walk?—I'll take you for a walk. What do you want? Do you want—do you want—?' Harry could not think what his father might want. 'I'll do it,' he said. 'You don't need *der schwarzer*.'

Then Harry saw that his father was weeping. The old man was standing up and weeping, with his eyes hidden behind the thick glasses that he had to wear: his glasses and his beard made his face a mask of age, as though time had left him nothing but the frame of his body on which the clothing could hang, and this mask of his face above. But Harry knew when the old man was weeping—he had seen him crying too often before, when they had found him at the end of a street after he had wandered away, or even, years earlier, when he had lost another of the miserable jobs that seemed to be the only one he could find in a country in which his son had, later, been able to run a good business, drive a large car, own a big house.

'Father,' Harry asked, 'what have I done? Do you think I've sent *der schwarzer* away?' Harry saw his father turn away, between the narrow bed and the narrow wardrobe. 'He's coming—' Harry said, but he could not look at his father's back, he could not look at his father's hollowed neck, on which the hairs that Paulus had clipped glistened above the pale brown discolorations of age—Harry could not look at the neck turned stiffly away from him while he had to try to promise the return of the Zulu. Harry dropped his hands and walked out of the room.

No one knew how the old man managed to get out of the house and through the front gate without having been seen. But he did manage it, and in the road he was struck down. Only a man on a bicycle struck him down, but it was enough, and he died a few days later in the hospital.

Harry's wife wept, even the grandsons wept; Paulus wept. Harry himself was stony, and his bunched, protuberant features were immovable; they seemed locked upon the bones of his face. A few days after the funeral he called Paulus and Johannes into the kitchen and said to Johannes: 'Tell him he must go. His work is finished.'

Johannes translated for Paulus, and then, after Paulus had spoken, he turned to Harry. 'He says, yes baas.' Paulus kept his eyes on the ground; he did not look up even when Harry looked directly at him, and Harry knew that this was not out of fear or shyness, but out of courtesy for his master's grief—which was what they could not but be talking of, when they talked of his work.

'Here's his pay.' Harry thrust a few notes towards Paulus, who took them in his cupped hands, and retreated.

Harry waited for them to go, but Paulus stayed in the room, and consulted with Johannes in a low voice. Johannes turned to his master. 'He says, baas, that the baas still has his savings.'

Harry had forgotten about Paulus's savings. He told Johannes that he had forgotten, and that he did not have enough money at the moment, but would bring the money the next day. Johannes translated and Paulus nodded gratefully. Both he and Johannes were subdued by the death there had been in the house.

And Harry's dealings with Paulus were over. He took what was to have been his last look at Paulus, but this look stirred him again against the Zulu. As harshly as he told Paulus that he had to go, so now, implacably, seeing Paulus in the mockery and simplicity of his houseboy's clothing, to feed his anger to the very end, Harry said. 'Ask him what he's been saving for. What's he going to do with the fortune he's made?'

Johannes spoke to Paulus and came back with a reply. 'He says, baas, that he is saving to bring his wife and children from Zululand to Johannesburg. He is saving, baas,' Johannes said, for Harry had not seemed to understand, 'to bring his family to this town also.'

The two Zulus were bewildered to know why it should have been at that moment that Harry Grossman's clenched, fist-like features should suddenly seem to have fallen from one another, nor why he should have stared with such guilt and despair at Paulus, while he cried, 'What else could I have done? I did my best,' before the first tears came.

Sarah Gertrude Millin

Esther's Daughter

I

One thing that used to annoy our cook Alita very much was the fact
that Esther, the cook next door, being coloured, could ride in a
tram, while she, Alita, being black, could not.

'In Bloemfontein,' she said, 'they don't make this nonsense. In
Bloemfontein it is not as here, in Johannesburg. The first thing is
they don't let the Indians or the Chinamen live there at all. And the
second thing is that there a Bastaard is a black person and not a
white person, and we don't any of us ride in the tram. Black or
brown or yellow, it is all the same. And so it should be.'

But, of course, Alita never let Esther know that she had heart-
burnings over the social distinctions which exist in Johannesburg
between black and brown. Indeed, she even went so far as to tell her
that she would much rather walk the two miles to town than be
grudgingly accommodated, as is Esther, on top of a tram.

'I am my master's and my missis' Kaffir,' she said to her, 'but not
everybody's Kaffir!'

Whether Esther really believed, as she self-consciously stepped
on the tram, and rode past poor, trudging Alita, that Alita did not
envy her her privilege, I should not like to say.

But, in any case, Alita has had her revenge.

2

It was not only the matter of tram-riding that troubled Alita in her
relationship with Esther. It was that Esther generally put on airs
with Alita.

Quite soon after Esther arrived next door, Alita went to see her.
She pressed her white apron very carefully, and she put on her
Sunday head-cloth, and she brought as an offering a pumpkin of

her own growing and some mint, which we are unsuccessfully trying to eradicate from the flower-beds.

Esther accepted the pumpkin and the mint, and Alita stayed for about half an hour gallantly making formal conversation about the Church and the rain and things like that. I say 'gallantly' because, from what I could gather, Esther did not give Alita much encouragement. 'I think, missis,' Alita explained wistfully, 'I think Esther is going to keep herself high with me.'

That was not treatment to which Alita is accustomed. Even the white nurse-girls stop their perambulators while Alita leans over to comment on the beauty of their charges, and the bigger children who walk with the nurses have learnt to expect that Alita will give them the sweets she buys with the money she makes by the sale of bones and bottles. They even come, the nurses and children, to play in our back garden.

Esther apparently did not realise that Alita was a privileged person in our street.

'Perhaps she feels strange,' I comforted Alita. 'Perhaps she will behave differently when she comes to see you.'

'Will she come to see me?' said Alita.

We both awaited with anxiety the return call of Esther.

3

But the weeks passed and Esther did not come. She sent the houseboy sometimes to borrow household things, she spoke a chance word or two over the garden wall, but she never herself walked into our kitchen to have a little friendly chat with Alita.

In a way, I did not exactly blame Esther. It was not as if, like the nursemaids, she was so safe about her colour that there could be no question of equality between her and Alita. After all, even white people are like that. They are less friendly with oncoming potential associates than they are with their unquestionable inferiors.

And then Esther was, in other ways too, in a difficult position. She really had to hold on most desperately to what was hers. The trouble with Esther was that she had once had a white husband, and that her child had inherited his white skin. What would Esther's daughter say if she saw her mother hob-nobbing with Alita?

Alita pointed Elizabeth out to me one day as she was walking past our house to see her mother.

'Missis! Quick! Make as if you are not looking. It is the daughter of Esther. It is Elizabeth.'

'That white girl!'

Alita nodded. She had created the sensation she wanted to create. I really was surprised. For I have seen colour manifesting itself in many ways, but I have not seen anything stranger than that a thoroughly brown woman like Esther should have a child as fair as Elizabeth.

'The nursemaid that comes here with the twins,' Alita went on, 'tells me that this Elizabeth has got a young man, and he works on one of the mines. His name is Mr. Periguano.'

I noted how Alita gave to the man his courtesy title, but not to the girl who was the daughter of Esther.

'He must be an Italian,' I commented, and it ran quickly through my mind that if Elizabeth should, by an unlucky chance, have very dark children, it could always be pointed out that they were of Italian descent. I was relieved to think that Elizabeth was going to marry an Italian.

But Alita denied Elizabeth's young man the grandeur that was Rome.

'He is not an Italian, missis. They say he is English, or perhaps Irish, and that his hair is red.'

'Periguano is not an English or Irish name, Alita,' I said.

Alita yielded politely.

'Misses knows, of course. But still that is what he is called. I have heard it with my own ears. Mr. Periguano.'

'You have not seen him yourself?' I asked.

Alita shook her head.

'He does not visit Esther,' she said very pleasantly.

4

And why was that, I wondered. Why did not Mr. Periguano visit his future mother-in-law? . . .

Esther was always going about these days with sewing in her hand. So Alita told me. 'She is making things for her daughter like the white people have. In two months' time they are going to marry. It will be a grand wedding, I hear, with flower-girls and what-not, and Esther is putting all her money in the post-office for the wedding-dress. Missis, I would like very much to see the wedding.'

'Well, you can go if you want to,' I told her.

'I would not give Esther the pleasure,' said Alita, 'to stand like a dog outside the church making 'Aie-ie' when her daughter walks in to get married.'

Nevertheless, in the end, she did go. 'I will stand behind the crowd,' she said. 'As long as Esther does not see me, that is all that matters.'

She returned after a while, and I asked her how it had been.

There was, I thought, a curiously charged expression on Alita's face, as if she were primed to the very edge with excitement. Although she spoke equably, it was only, I could see, from the surface.

'Well, and so the people came, missis, and there were three motor-cars. In one was Mr. Periguano with a friend, and it is true he has red hair. And in another was Elizabeth with a man, and the flower-girls. And in another were folk I don't know. Then some came in carriages, and some came walking. And everyone was really white, missis.'

'And did the bride look beautiful?'

Alita made a sound signifying the very absolute in appreciation. 'Missis should have seen her. The veil and the lace and the dress all full of beads. I can swear that dress must have cost Esther more than a little money. Perhaps five pounds. No, what do I say? Five pounds? Six or seven pounds even!'

I expressed my overwhelmed astonishment.

'And Esther?' I asked. 'What was she wearing? Had she a nice dress, too?'

Alita did not reply. It was the dramatic pause. I had leapt to the very heart of Alita's story.

'Esther?' she said, tasting privately her thrilling climax.

'Yes. How did she look?'

'Esther?' Alita repeated in a quiet, demure voice. 'No, she was not looking very wonderful. She came just as missis can see her every day.'

I certainly was surprised.

'But why was that? Was it because all her money was spent on Elizabeth's clothes?'

Alita shook her hand.

'No, missis.'

She spread out her arms, and delivered herself of her news. 'No, it was not for that. It was because it did not matter how Esther looked. Esther, my missis, was not in the motor-cars. She was not in the carriages. She was not in the church. Esther. . . . Esther was standing at the back of the crowd where Alita was standing. And when Elizabeth drives past, she puts out her head, and she makes a little noise in her throat, and then she quickly hides herself that Elizabeth shall not see her. And I too—that she may not be shamed more—I look too as if I don't see Esther. And that, missis, is how Esther went to her child's wedding.'

It was not necessary that Alita should speak further. We both understood what had happened between Esther and Elizabeth. Elizabeth had married white, and was done with her mother. Quite probably Mr. Periguano had never even seen his mother-in-law, and knew nothing of Elizabeth's African blood.

'Are you not sorry for Esther, Alita?' I asked, after a few moments.

'Yes, I am sorry,' said Alita. 'I hoped evil would happen to Esther because she kept herself proud with me. I said, in my heart, "Let the Old Man On High show Esther what it is to feel as she makes Alita feel." But now I wish He had not listened to me.'

5

In the newspaper next morning I saw the announcement of a marriage between Joseph Baragwanath and Elizabeth Twentyman. For a second it conveyed nothing to me. Then I realised that Joseph Baragwanath must be Alita's Mr. Periguano; and I thought to myself how, if Elizabeth's children were not white, she would not, after all, be able to excuse their colour by an Italian ancestry.

Barney Simon

Our War

About Us and Our War

Well, this is about our war. Whenever I complained about it, the noise and the dirt and the stinking and the dying, Mama used to say, 'Listen, Leiba, be grateful for what you've got. That you're not in London or Moscow or New York or somewhere. Be grateful you're here where things always happen easier.' When I got upset about Lily Fine losing her leg, she said, 'So, but she's still got her head.' And when our house went up in the second bombardment (which was famous for the first usage outside of Asia and the Middle East of .22238 Ziggmutt Mortars) and we built a shelter and it rained all those October days, the way she behaved you would've thought that it was the Christmas holidays and we were on holiday at the Imperial Hotel in Muizenberg. But if you think I was a moaner, you should've heard Rochella. She cried if there were lumps in the mealie-meal porridge or hair on the soap. She wouldn't wear a dress if it was dirty and if there was skin on the milk (when there was any) she'd rather go thirsty. When the mortars got going and there were blasts and quakes and screams, she complained that she couldn't go to sleep. But, to be fair, that was toward the beginning.

One Sunday, which turned out to be the day of the eighteen-hour blast (the fourth time in the whole world an entire ground-to-ground operation was carried out by the crews of Donizetti rocket units), the Mizroch family, Zaidah Mizroch, Mrs. Mizroch, his daughter-in-law, and little Mitzi and Mike all went to collect what firewood they could from Gilooly's Farm, and when they hadn't come back by Friday, we moved into their house which was a little small for us, but still.

About Mama

Mama worked at the Bertha Solomon Social Centre, which was used as a hospital and house for old people since our war began. She did shift work, sometimes at night, sometimes during the day. She cleaned and scrubbed and nursed and sometimes she even helped in the surgery. She didn't like us to come there, but once I did. There were old people all over. On the veranda, on beds, on mattresses, on the floor, all calling her Malka, which is her first name, and asking her to sing. She didn't have a good voice—you know, she never got the tune nicely, but everybody used to ask her to sing because she knew nice songs with nice words. Then they asked her to tell them a joke. It wasn't so good but when she told it she was laughing so much she made us all laugh too.

Old Mr. Lapinsky said that she had hands of solid gold. Everybody called for her to turn them over or rub them or massage them where they were sore. Especially Mr. Lapinsky whose eyes were all white, and when he died, he left her his watch. At first we thought it was real gold, but when we took it to Maishke, he said it wasn't gold, just golden. She had friends who worked there too, like Mrs. Pinchuk, Mrs. Maganoff, and Bessie Finestein. They weren't friends like she had in the old days like Pearl Reichman, but they were nice all the same.

At home our best times were when she made us potato sweets, and night, when we used to push our mattresses together and lie there in the dark. If you got there first, you lay next to her. First nobody talked and we just breathed. And then she told us about how she was a little girl in a little village in Lithuania and how she was scared of ice-skates, but she used to 'glitzzzz' on her shoes across the ice and how she used to find strawberries in the forests that smelt as sweet as flowers and covered her whole hand and how they used to sleep on the stove (that was always Mendel's favourite) in winter and how when she came here her best friend was the beauty queen and whistler Pearl Reichman and how they used to copy the movie stars' make-up with luscious lips and gipsy eyes, and how when she first came she thought the traffic cop stopped the traffic for her to cross the street and what a nice man she thought he was to do that (that was Rochella's favourite) and how once when somebody asked her to make a bet, she said she could

make her own bed thank you (that was mine). Laykella had her own
bed-time because she (slept in a little hammock and) went to bed
early. Her favourite story was about the Reb and the Rebbitsen. But
that's too long to tell now.

How We Lost Hindella

Three days after we moved into the Mizroch house, we lost Hindella. There was some street fighting, no mortar or artillery, just
rifle and a grenade or two. God knows what was happening in
Pandora Street. It sounded like hell. Anyway, we were all lying flat
on the lounge floor because we were all going out when it started
and it didn't sound bad enough for the cellar when Hindella, God
knows why, got up, peeped out of the window, and plop was down
with us again flat on her back with a bright red spot between her
eyes.

After that, even before the funeral, Mama couldn't stand the
Mizroch house any more, so she sent me out to Auntie Ada in
Greenside where we heard it was pretty quiet to ask if we could
move in with her and also to tell her about Hindella and her funeral,
but when I got there, her house was full of other people who said
they didn't know where Auntie Ada was and we couldn't come. So
we just stayed on at the Mizroch house and Mama and Rochella
spoke and cried in their sleep every night. Mendel and me mind you
went on sleeping like logs and Baby Layka of course just went on
snoring like an angel.

Hindella's Funeral

We buried Hindella in the cemetery that had been made on the
soccer-field in Rhodes Park. On the way there, Rochella asked me
to pinch her or something if she started to giggle because she
always does. It was a hot day with a very blue sky. Mrs Maganoff,
Mrs Katzen, and Mrs Pinchuk, who worked with Mama at the
Bertha Solomon Social Centre, were there, and Mama and me and
Rochella and Tiny Yiddel from Belgravia Shul (he's the one Chesterfield's Circus wanted but he wouldn't take the job and kept his old
one opening the shul in the morning and locking it at night and

setting out the prayer books) and Rabbi Spitz with his yellow-and-black beard. He was there to say the prayers, but before he did, Yiddel and me dug the grave, and when the service began, we were covered with orange dust. Rabbi Spitz first sang a song and then we put Hindella's coffin into the hole and then we all began to say prayers and old Mrs Pinchuk started crying and Mama lent her her hanky and she started crying too and the wind came up and blew the dust into our faces and when Mama stepped back from Mrs Pinchuk, some ground gave way underneath her and she nearly fell into Hindella's grave. Then Rabbi Spitz took off his torn coat and gave it to Yiddel, and he had on a nice shiny one underneath and Yiddel gave him his prayer-shawl and he put it on and then he took off his black hat and handed it to Yiddel and he had a little yarmulka on the back of his head and then Yiddel handed him his prayer-book and he was ready, with Yiddel holding everything behind him. I tiptoed over to Yiddel and asked him if I could help him, and he said he was fine, but did I hear about the saltanossas he made. When he starts talking about saltanossas it's the end of you, so I tiptoed back to Rochella, and Rabbi Spitz began to talk about the ten plagues of Egypt and how the worst of all was the plague that caused the plagues—the hatred between men, the hatred that rises when we forget about God. Mama was dusting herself off and she asked him to stop talking and just help bury Hindella and Rabbi Spitz said why was he asked to come then and Mama said she never asked him to come, Mrs Pinchuk did, and so Rabbi Spitz took his hat from the top of Yiddel and put it back on his head over the yarmulka, and then he put his prayer-book where the hat had been on Yiddel and he took off his prayer-shawl and began to fold it and Mrs Pinchuk said he should be ashamed to leave the grave of a Jewish child and Mama said, 'Look at us, look where my child is— and he talks about Moses and the ten commandments!' 'The Ten Plagues!' Rabbi Spitz shouted.

'What's the difference?' Mama screamed. 'Don't talk to me about God. His is the place they should bomb and his churches and his shuls—let him know what it's all about.'

Little Yiddel was standing on the tips of his toes holding onto the prayer-book and the prayer-shawl and helping Rabbi Spitz struggle into his coat. I could feel Rochella shaking next to me, so I pinched her arm. Mama got onto her knees next to the grave and she picked up a pile of sand in her arms and threw it onto the coffin—'There!' she shouted in Yiddish, 'Nuh!' and she picked up more, and threw and threw shouting, 'Nuh! Nuh! Nuh!' The dust was flying all over, covering her face and her body and all of us. Mrs Pinchuk and Mrs Maganoff and Mrs Katzen also ran to the grave and started throwing sand too, all together, and Rabbi Spitz, still fighting with his coat, started to run away across the field, with little Yiddel following on his little legs, still all orange, carrying the prayer-book and the prayer-shawl.

Mama, Mrs Katzen, Mrs Pinchuk, and Mrs Maganoff went on throwing, tearing at the ground when the dug-up sand was finished, until there was a mound on top of Hindella's grave. Everybody was cursing and crying, turning the dust to mud on their faces, and beside me I felt Rochella still shaking.

'Stop laughing!' I shouted, and everybody stopped in the dust and stared at us and Rochella began to cry.

About Pearl Reichman

Pearl Reichman was Mama's best friend from long ago. She used to live down the street when we lived in Troyville. Sometimes she used to go to the movies with us, to the musicals. She had black hair and a shiny mouth which she always painted red. She was famous as a whistler. People said she should be in Hollywood and when Tyrone Power came to visit South Africa she was one of the girls they took his photograph with at the airport. The publicity men put her third from the left, but when Tyrone Power had to kiss someone on the cheek for a photo, he chose Pearl, and she had to pretend to faint and when she did it was marvellous and then she had to pretend to whistle and she *really* whistled, her speciality, a canary whistling 'Swanee' and Tyrone Power got a real surprise and asked her to do it again so she did a whole performance there in the airport and her picture was in every paper, him kissing her on the cheek and her whistling and everybody thought now she must go to Hollywood because there'd never been a whistling movie star—singers yes, like Jeannette Macdonald, Kathryn Grayson, Jane Powell, Illona Massey, Rise Stevens, Carmen Miranda or organ players like Ethel

Smith playing 'Tico Tico' and there were rumours that Pearl was leaving any day so people began to get her to whistle at Bar Mitzvahs and weddings and birthday parties and over the radio once and once when my mother and me were in town with her somebody stopped her in the street and asked her to whistle what she whistled for Tyrone Power so she whistled her speciality, 'Swanee' like a canary, and everyone stood around us and when she finished we all clapped and a woman and a little girl and a boy, all separately asked her for her autograph. Anyway then one summer she went on a tour of all the holiday places like Port Elizabeth, East London, Durban, and Mossel Bay and she married a Mr Salzman in Durban who had a shop near the dock which sold everything from a thimble to an elephant (which was his motto, the elephant being a brooch actually) then once when we were in Durban on holiday we saw her at a concert at the Jewish Club and after the concert we went back behind the curtain to see her and everything. But I don't remember much about her there except that her arms were very white and she had a gold filling in her side tooth and a rose in her hair because I had bad sunburn and that was what was really worrying me. Then when the war began and there was a big bombardment of the Natal coast, Mr Saltzman's shop went up and him too and Pearl came back to her family, old Mrs Reichman, the only one left. She called herself Pearl Reichman again and used to walk around in her nightie because she said it was an evening dress. Even Rochella could understand but couldn't explain to her that a nightie isn't an evening dress. Anyhow, the nightie was how we first knew she was going funny and then it just got worse and Pearl got thinner and thinner and then old Mrs Reichman died of natural causes not just our war, and the Reichman house got mortar-blasted and Pearl lived on the veranda swing seat and all the time she went up and down the street looking for food and whistling and sometimes it was beautiful and sometimes it got on your nerves. Then one day we found her in her backyard, dead. It was after the rain and she was lying on her back with her eyes open and her mouth open and her nightie was wet and you could see everything. That's what happened to Pearl Reichman. When Mama came home and I told her how we found Pearl Reichman, she cried and I asked her why.

She never cried when Jossel Hurwitz died or Cousin Lily was blown up and lots of other people and she said I didn't know Pearl when she was beautiful and dreaming all the time and Tyrone Power kissed her and she wore her ruby red evening dress at weddings and Bar Mitzvahs. God, Mama said, what dreams she had—sequins and gold handbags and Hollywood and look how she died—dreaming of bread!

The Reb and the Rebbitsen: Laykella's Favourite Story Told by Mama

Every morning Laykella was the first one up. She used to climb out of her hammock and then into my mother's bed and then into mine and each of us had to tell her a story and she would tell us one back.

The Reb and the Rebbitsen

Once upon a time (Mama used to say) there was a Rabbi and his wife, the Rebbitsen. They had lots, l-o-o-o-ts of little children. The biggest one was called Leibella, the next was called Laykella and there were many more, whose names are too many to tell, but the last one, the very, very last one was called Mottel. He was tiny. Tinier than Yiddel of Belgravia Shul, tinier than Laykella. Maybe he was as tiny as the Englishman Tom Thumb (Laykella always used to say that), maybe he was the tiniest boy in the world. Well, one day the Rabbi put on his yarmulka and his black top hat, and the Rebbitsen put on her shaitel (her wig) and her pink flower-hat and they went to shul where everybody said how nice they looked. But before they went, the Reb and the Rebbitsen said, 'Children we're leaving you alone at home. Whatever you do, don't open the doors for anyone. No matter what they say, what they play, don't open the door.' And the children all said, 'No matter what they say, what they play, we won't open the door!'

Well, there they were, laughing and happy and playing games and singing songs when a big white bear came to the door. 'Kinder-lach, konderlach, lost mir arein,' the bear said, 'children, children, let me in—I'll give you honey and sugar.'

'Nein! Nein!' The children called, 'Wir haben alein! We have our own!'

'Kinderlach, konderlach,' the bear began again, 'lost mir arein—
ich et dir gebben putter mit breit! Butter and bread!'

'Nein, nein, wir haben alein!'

So the bear gave a graiser forts—a big fart—which blew down
the door and he ran in and swallowed all the little children. All
except little Mottel who hid in a bottle. And when the Reb and the
Rebbitsen came home, he in his tall black top hat and she in her
pink flower-hat, they found the door broken down and all their
children gone. All except Mottel who was banging on his bottle.
Well, they helped Mottel out of the bottle and he told them what
had happened. How the bear with one graiser forts had broken
down the door and then swallowed up all their children. The Rebbitsen was very clever. If you've swallowed so many children what
do you do? You take a drink of water and you lie down in a cool
place. So she took off her pink flower-hat to disguise herself and
she took her scissors and her needle and her cotton and she went
down to the river. And there under a big shady tree was the bear
with a graiser boich—a big stomach—fast asleep. So she tiptoed up
to him and cut open his stomach with her scissors and she took all
her children out and then she got some smooth warm stones from
the river-bank and she packed them where her children had been
and sewed the bear's stomach so neatly together that he never
noticed a stitch. And soon the children were all home again, laughing and happy and playing games and singing songs, and when the
bear woke up he stretched and yawned and went to look for honey.

How We Lost Laykella

One morning, on the 16th of April, we all slept late, mostly because
Laykella hadn't woken us. I went in to see Mama at about nine
o'clock. She was sleeping with her arm over her eyes. Laykella was
still curled up in her little hammock. I tiptoed up in case she was
pretending and I could give her a fright. I swung the hammock up
and down but she didn't move inside it. I twanged the strings but
she didn't pretend to snore or bark or poop or anything. I tickled
where her backside was and waited. Then I slowly pulled the sides
apart and peeped inside. Her face was very white, the skin around
her mouth was very blue and her eyes were half-open. Her lips were

moving. I shouted and Mama jumped up and grabbed Laykella from me and put her on the bed and pumped her legs up and down and kissed her feet and her face. She pulled a dress on and rolled Laykella up in a blanket and picked her up and ran into the street, her feet bare, her hair all over her face. I ran behind. There was a doctor's house on the corner of Phoenix Street and Roberts Avenue. The door was locked and the windows closed. I ran around to the back. It was burnt out. Only one room was left and it was black with soot. There was a dinner-wagon with plates still inside against one wall. I opened the door from the inside and Mama thought it was the doctor and she started to cry when she saw that it was me. We ran ten blocks to the sanatorium shouting for help and for a doctor all the way and Laykella flapping in our arms and people running away when they saw what she looked like.

First we came to the side of the sanatorium. There was a line curled around and around the stairs, the garden, and the pavement. Sick people and wounded people were sitting around crying and calling and there was a stink like rotten mangoes. Nobody took any notice of us there. A man in a dirty white coat told us to stand in the line. He wouldn't listen when I told him about Laykella, so we went to the front where nobody was supposed to go and I banged on the doors, then Mama gave me Laykella and she banged even harder and then a woman in a brown overall and a white nurse's hat opened it and said what did we want and Mama showed her Laykella and the nurse said yes, it was typhoid but she couldn't do anything we should try the General Hospital. Behind her I could see people lying on benches in the passage and on the floor and there was the same smell of mangoes. Mama said please to just show Laykella to a doctor and the nurse said what doctor and slammed the door. Then suddenly Mama wrapped up Laykella tight and put her down on the top stair and pulled me up and we ran across the street and as we were about to hide behind a wall, the door opened and the woman came out screaming at us—'What are you doing?' she shouted. 'Leave me alone!' and she burst into tears and slammed the door shut again. We went back to Laykella on the stair and Laykella was dead. We couldn't give her a proper family funeral like Hindella because she had to be buried in a special typhoid place on the other side of Cyrildene.

Yiddel Saltanossas and Mama

On Thursday, the 26th of July, I was out in Pandora Street with Rochella looking for wood. Pandora Street had gone down in the big four-day bombardment around about the time Hindella was shot. They used the new A40A bazookas for the first time, but if you looked hard enough among the rubble you could find some floor-boards and cellar beams. It was very cold and we were wrapped up with everything we could find, like blacks and sacks and old socks on our hands, so it was hard to even move. Rochella kept complaining, and then she found some marbles and some pieces of a jigsaw puzzle with flowers on it and she started to play with them so I left her, as long as she was quiet.

Anyway, I was climbing all over, pulling and pushing around deep in the cellar, when I heard her calling again. I looked up, and there against the sky was tiny little Yiddel of Belgravia Shul. He's the one Chesterfield's Circus wanted (but he wouldn't take the job and kept his old one opening the shul in the morning and locking it at night and setting out the prayer-books).

'Mrs Pinchuk wants you,' he said.

'What for?' I asked.

'I don't know,' he said, 'but she said you must come now.'

'Okay,' I said, 'I will.'

'No,' he said, 'you must come now.'

'Okay,' I said, 'you go and I'll come.'

'It's all right,' he said, 'I'll walk with you.'

I couldn't think of anything more to say, so that was that. I was stuck with him and his saltanossas, there was no way out. All he talks about is the saltanossas his late mother used to make and how he got those eggs that time when a somebody, a stranger, came to the shul and gave him two and he got some flour and milk which isn't as good as cream (which is *really* what you're supposed to bake saltanossas in) but still good enough when *he* does them, and he made his own saltanossa lokshen, and how yellow they were because he used *real* eggs, not like the white lokshen he used to buy. 'Egg lokshen they used to call them,' he said sarcastically, 'but what does that mean? Egg lokshen have to have *eggs* in them, otherwise don't call them egg lokshen!' And then he described how Mrs Pinchuk gave him a little white cheese and how *thin* his lokshen

were because he rolled them so hard and he had to use a vinegar
bottle because somebody had stolen his late mother's rolling pin
(for firewood most probably) and then when he put it all in the oven
and he baked them, how the milk bubbled and how beautiful and
brown they were on top, and the *smell*—with his eyes closed, he was
in his late mother's kitchen, waiting with his plate. Everybody, he
said, the whole street, smelt his saltanossas and Mrs Pinchuk,
when she smelt them, said to herself (she told him after), 'Es
gezunterheit, Yiddel, eat in good health,' and he did! He always
laughed at the same point and grepsed on purpose. That's a story
you can hear once or twice, but if you hear it too much it can get on
your nerves. And then when we were passing the shul he started to
look for the key that hung from a pin on his coat but he couldn't
find it so we stood there while he pulled his pockets inside out and
stuck his fingers through the holes until he saw the door was open
and he remembered he had given the rabbi the key. Then while he
was pushing his pockets back in, he started to tell me how he only
wore tennis shoes on Yom Kippur before our war, but now they
were all he had and he showed me how they were glued together,
and rags and cardboard. Then he asked me if I knew where there
were some eggs, and if that is what we were *really* looking for up
there in Pandora Street. He was sure he heard a chicken when he
was coming up the road. I said it must have been Rochella playing
with the marbles and he said why should she sound like a chicken
when she's playing with marbles and that he noticed feathers
among the bricks, and I tried to get him onto the subject of birds in
general and how even the sparrows had gone in our war, but he
shot back to eggs and saltanossas again, and then just when he got
to the part about the milk and how it was bubbling, we got to
Pinchuk's house and old Mrs Pinchuk was waiting outside and
Yiddel said, 'Here he is,' and Mrs Pinchuk squeezed me and took
me into a room and there was a body on the floor covered with
sacks and she bent down and lifted some sack from the head and it
was my mother's face. Somebody had just washed it. It was very
clean and the hair was wet. Mrs Pinchuk said somebody had started
shooting at the corner of Marshall and Browning Streets and my
mother got shot. Mrs Pinchuk asked me if I wanted to kiss my
mother and I said no. My mother's feet were showing at the other

end of the sacks. They were dirty. Mrs Pinchuk asked me if I wanted
to bring Rochella and Mendel to see her and I said no, so she
walked with me down the street to Headquarters where she said we
must see the Captain. She had her hand at the back of my neck and
some people were staring at me.

The Captain

The Captain was eating stew. There was a little left. I could see some
potato, beans, and meat and something red. He stopped when Mrs
Pinchuk said who I was and he showed me my mother's papers that
they found on her when she was shot and he said she was forty-two.

'That's right,' Mrs Pinchuk said.

'She misses category 627VX/A by seven months and four days,'
said the Captain, 'luck of the game. If she'd been born that much
later or killed that much earlier, she would've been IN. Yesterday
there was a case—mother of two—who made it by one single day.'

'I think I know who it was,' said Mrs Pinchuk. 'Is it a Mrs Katzoff
by any chance? Two girls—Maisie and Lynette.'

'How many children?' the Captain asked me, but I was watching
the stew.

'How many?' he asked Mrs Pinchuk.

'Five,' she said. He wrote down five.

'Sorry,' she said, 'is it in ink? Two dead.'

'So that's . . . ,' he calculated, 'two living . . .' He scratched a two
over the five.

'Sorry,' Mrs Pinchuk said, 'I think it's three.'

'Five—two—,' the Captain said. 'You're right—three.' He
blacked out the five with the two over it and wrote a three beside.

'Names?'

'Leiba—that's him—Rochella and Mendel.'

'Ages?'

'Twelve, seven,' Mrs Pinchuk said, 'and . . . and how old's
Mendel?'

'Five,' I said.

The Captain looked at me. 'Do you want some stew?' he asked.

'Yes,' I said. I took the socks off my hands and rolled them
together into a ball. Outside, a siren was going, but none of us took

any notice. I could hear people running. He gave me his plate and spoon and they watched me finish what was there. I ate fast, staring down at the plate and listening to every chew and swallow in my head and every scrape of the spoon on the plate.

'Your relationship?' he asked Mrs Pinchuk.

'We worked together at the Bertha Solomon Social Centre.'

I licked the plate.

'Did you deal with Mrs Maganoff?' Mrs Pinchuk asked, 'I was with her too. That sniper got her in Flossie Street.'

'. . . C-e-n-t-r-e . . .' the Captain was still writing. I put the plate back on his desk.

'Now,' said the Captain, 'we've got to add a little, multiply a little and divide by three.' He scribbled on a piece of paper. I noticed a streak of gravy still left on the stew plate, so I picked it up and licked it away. The Captain was adding next to a doodle of a girl's face.

'One times one is one and one is two. Twenty-eight pounds thirteen and sixpence. Let me check. Three children. Forty-two years old. Category 627vx/B. Right. You see, if she'd made A, it would've been thirty-eight pounds.'

'You can't do anything more?' Mrs Pinchuk asked. 'They're lovely children.'

'How do you want it?' the Captain asked. 'In cash?'

'I suppose so,' Mrs Pinchuk said, 'what do you say, Leiba?' I didn't say anything.

'Do you want me to keep it for you?' Mrs Pinchuk asked.

'No,' I said.

'So then how do you want it?'

'I don't know.'

'I'll give it to you in notes and silver,' the Captain said. He took money out of a metal box and counted it into a paper-bag. Ten— twenty—thirty—a five—one—two—three—in notes—Good— now— two (silver clinked)—four—six—eight—ten—onetwo— three—thirteen shillings—and—six—pence! Do you want to check?'

I didn't say anything and Mrs Pinchuk said, 'Don't worry, we trust you.' He gave me the paper-bag.

Mrs Pinchuk was on her way back to the Bertha Solomon Social Centre, and it was on the way home, so I walked with her. She put her hand on the back of my neck again and I was carrying the paper-bag. At the gate to the Bertha Solomon Social Centre she asked me if I wanted to come in with her. I said no. There were some old people on the veranda and I thought I saw Mr Lapinsky among them and I was about to say hello when I remembered that he was dead, but I waved anyway and the other old man waved back. Then Mrs Pinchuk squeezed me and kissed me and told me to look after the money and the children and she went in and I started to walk home.

I walked first to Pandora Street, but Rochella wasn't there any-more, just little Yiddel looking for eggs where we had been. There was nobody at the house either. I didn't want to go inside. I called Rochella's name and Mendel's, walking up and down the street. The all-clear had sounded half an hour before, but nobody in the street had returned. I seemed to be the last person left on earth. I went back to our house, but couldn't stay there. I called their names from the door. Rifle fire began again in the distance. It was an evening sound, like trains shunting or children calling long ago. I went up Highlands Road, now just saying Rochella and Mendel's names. I turned down a side-street, stopping to kick around among the bricks and ashes of a ruined house. Suddenly I heard a bird. Only a bit of a sound, but real and clear. I stood still for a long time, hardly breathing, waiting for it to come again. The rifle fire was getting heavier, somewhere deep in Hillbrow. I moved to where the bird sound had come from and came to a big curly-iron gate still standing between two burnt black pillars. I walked around them into a broken garden, the trees twisted and scattered, the house a pile of rubble glistening with glass. Beyond, I suddenly saw more trees, green and straight, forgotten by our war. I climbed over the house to reach them and when I got there I didn't know properly what to do. I just touched them a bit, the fir needles and the bark. I began to cry and I tried to remember my mother. I tried to remem-ber her living but it was hard. Whenever I concentrated on her I saw her dead, and when I didn't concentrate I saw only the trees. I called again for Rochella and Mendel and then I remembered the bird. I stood still to hear it again, but there was no sound or sight of one.

I went back to the street. It was full of people now and when I got to the house, Rochella and Mendel were waiting for me at the door.

When I told them about Mama, Rochella started to cry and Mendel wasn't listening properly. And when I told them about the money, they asked to look into the paper-bag and I let them. Then Rochella said she wanted a cardigan like Leila Schlossburg's and Mendel went outside again to play.

The next day I bought:

   5 lbs mealie-meal porridge,
   3 lbs sugar,
   3 chops (I don't know what kind),
   2 loaves of bread,
   1 tin Golden Syrup,
   2 tins Captain Albert's Sardines,
   3 marshmallow fishes,
   4 carrots,
   1 package salt.

Oh yes, and the cardigan for Rochella. A white one. That really got on my nerves. But she wouldn't stop crying for it.

Nehemiah Levinsky

In the Shadow of Nuremberg

The sun was setting behind the large black mountain, as though lowered on long golden strands. These strands shimmered in the sunlight, weaving a multi-coloured carpet below, so that from one side the mountain was bathed in gold, while the other began to darken with shadows.

The hotel nestled at the foot of the mountain, and looked like an outsize phylactery on a gigantic head. Screwing up his eyes as he gazed up at it, Hanns stood on the verandah taking in the sunset, the surrounding landscape, and the loneliness which breathed heavily from the mountain.

Hanns was a travelling salesman. He drove from town to town and as soon as he spotted a store of sizeable proportions, he would stop the car, haul out his samples and order book, and step inside with a broad greeting. The wide selection of his goods, and the reputation of the firms he represented, were sufficient to ensure that he could always meet his customers' needs, so that he seldom came away without an order. A German Jew, he spoke English with a distinct German accent, but felt quite at ease chatting to those who did business with him.

From the hotel bar Hanns could hear the drunken laughter of his fellow travellers who, like himself, were staying overnight—here, in this God-forsaken place, where the only form of entertainment was drink. Hanns had been partial to a tot now and then, but had recently resolved to stop drinking altogether. Right now he was waiting for a telephone call from his wife, Helen, whom he had only this week, for the first time, left alone to go on the road.

Helen was his second wife. He and Dorothy, his first wife—a tall, slim, Afrikaner blonde, had parted mainly because of his heavy drinking. His earnings were simply insufficient for their expensive habits: her mania for clothes, and his addiction to drink. This led to quarrels which ultimately ended in divorce.

Dorothy was very like the other, the one whose name he still carried in his heart, for she had been part of his life, part of the golden dream—a dream turned nightmare . . . But her name—Marlene—inevitably recalled Germany to him, his former 'home' which he wanted to forget, to expunge from his memory.

But then he met Dorothy, and his peace was shattered. When he first saw her, his heart leaped for joy: Marlene!—the same lovely face, the same golden tresses . . . all but the gentle Madonna smile he so loved in Marlene. Also, on closer acquaintance he saw that she lacked Marlene's simplicity, tenderness, and compassion. But Marlene belonged to the past, and in Dorothy he saw his present and his future. He fell deeply in love with her.

They were soon married. They leased a flat, bought furniture, and when all was ready, they began to throw lavish parties. Their circle of friends grew, they entertained, were invited in return, and their life became an endless succession of partying and entertainment. Hanns, who had to be on the road to attend to his customers, couldn't always keep up with Dorothy. As for Dorothy herself, alone in the flat, time hung heavily on her hands. She had no wish to do office work, and would stay in bed till noon. Then she'd get up, dress, paint her face, and go out to tea with her friends. There she'd stay till nightfall, come home, change her dress, and await her visitors. She started going out with other men, a fact which could not long be kept secret from Hanns.

Now, as he stood in the twilight looking at the mountain, visions of his past life began to assail him, passing like a panorama before him. He saw them clearly—drifting clouds, golden, light and airy, but also heavy, dark and lowering, like the shadows on the mountain. Here's the day he parted from Marlene . . . They had driven far out into the country, and come to a village, stopped for tea, then walked to a nearby forest. There, along the silent pathways, arm in arm, their fingers interlocking, they strolled. He told her of his deep love for her but also of his dreadful misgivings. Hitler's Nuremberg Laws had made him a pariah, had outlawed him from German society. They must part. Marlene wouldn't hear of this.

Hitler's madness would pass, she said, the German people could not be duped; they'd soon see his threats for what they were—mere soap bubbles—and get rid of him. Hanns shook his head sadly. Desperately they sought a way out. Marlene suggested they leave Germany and marry in their new country. But Hanns, the more practical, knew that without money they could not live abroad where his profession—law—would be useless. At last they reached a decision: Hanns would go to America or South Africa, where she would eventually join him and they would marry.

'This could take years,' he said, with a sigh. 'Could you really wait for me that long?'

'I'll wait!' she said, as she looked at him, love in her eyes, and with a kiss they sealed their bond.

They left the forest in the late afternoon, walking as on a cloud, intoxicated with love and daydreaming of their future. So engrossed were they with each other that they failed to notice a group of Brownshirts come marching in formation from a side street. The young Nazis, their manoeuvres over, were on their way to their barracks. They might have passed them unnoticed had not one of them, an old schoolmate of Hanns's, recognized him and shouted:

'There goes an Ike—a Jew—with an Aryan girl'

The peace of the quiet village was suddenly shattered. Hanns was set upon by the hoodlums. Blows rained on him from every side. As though from afar he heard Marlene's screams:

'Leave him alone! He's my fiancé, my husband . . .'

He saw a Nazi gripping her head between his legs, while another was pulling her golden tresses and cutting away at them. For months afterwards, during the year he had spent in prison and concentration camp, Marlene's last screams still echoed in his ears.

He was released. Began to look for Marlene. Was told she was ill in hospital. He longed to see her, talk to her, but was advised against it. It could only make things worse for her. Even a letter was out of the question—it might fall into the wrong hands. Nor could he risk drawing attention to himself. He felt like a whipped cur who had to creep into a corner to hide in his own homeland. Now all he wanted was to get out of Germany, and as quickly as possible. He was just waiting for his papers so he could leave for South Africa.

From his new home he wrote to Marlene. He sat writing far into the night, and when he finally sealed the envelope, he felt that his very soul was enclosed in it. He waited long, but there was no answer. Desperate, he wrote to a friend. The reply came. Hanns opened the letter. A newspaper cutting within a black border fell out—Marlene was dead . . .

Now, as he looked at the black mountain, the death notice again flashed before his eyes. He shuddered at the necromantic vision.

A voice broke into his thoughts.

'*Baas*, your telephone call to Johannesburg,' a black youth shouted in his ear.

He roused himself as though from a dream, murmured 'Marlene . . .' and ran to the phone.

'Oh! it's you, Helen! Helen, my darling,' and his voice trembled with excitement.

'I've been to the doctor,' she said.

'The doctor? What do you mean? Are you ill?' and again he had a vision of death.

'No,' he heard her say, followed by a soft laugh—'oh you big, silly, darling Hanns. Can't you guess? A baby.'

Helen was born a Christian. Though her religious upbringing had not been rigid, she, like most of her friends in the neighbourhood, went to church and attended Sunday school. Her contact with Jews had been minimal—the odd purchase at a Jewish store or visit to an office.

They had met at a dance. At first she thought Hanns was a German. Later, when they had learnt to know each other better, he told her that he was a Jew, and gradually began to confide in her and tell her of his past life. She listened and her heart went out to him. But he had one fault she could not condone—his heavy drinking.

'You know, Hanns, I've heard that Jews aren't usually heavy drinkers. How come you are? You know what?' she quipped, 'I don't believe you're a Jew!' Then added: 'As for me, I can't see myself ever marrying an alcoholic.'

Hanns bristled. 'Helen, if you really love me, you must take me as I am—with all my faults.'

'You're right,' she said, 'but addiction to liquor is not a fault—it's a sickness, and sickness can be cured.'

Finally his love for Helen triumphed—he kicked the habit entirely. It was a gradual and painful process, but by the time they married he had stopped drinking for good. A new life began for him. Helen came with him to the city, she met his friends. She had no taste for parties, and preferred to work rather than stay home alone. Hanns, knowing that he must spend weeks on end in the country, agreed.

It was Sunday morning. Hanns and Helen were at home, playing with their baby daughter. Suddenly Helen turned to Hanns and said that she would like their little girl to have a Jewish name. Hanns, surprised but pleased, suggested 'Dina,' which had been his mother's name. Then Helen told him:

'Hanns, I want to become Jewish. I want my children to grow up as Jews.'

Hanns looked at her and gave a wistful smile. 'My dear Helen, according to Hitler's Nuremberg Laws you are already Jewish, and so is Dina. So why bother with rituals and all that rigmarole?'

'True,' she replied, 'I don't care much for rituals and ceremonies, but if that's the only way to become a Jewess, I'll gladly go through with it.'

'Yes, dear Helen, I see. You honestly believe that a few rituals, a few prayers by a rabbi will make you into a true Jewish daughter. For my part, though, I feel that our marriage in court is both legal and binding in my eyes and in the eyes of those people, and I don't need a kosher stamp to prove it. But if you really want to belong to our people, then study our culture, our history of martyrdom, and you'll come to love us and feel like one of us.'

'I'll do as you say,' Helen answered meekly.

His work in the country finished, Hanns set off for home. He was in excellent spirits. He'd had a bumper week, orders galore, and now looked forward to a few days' relaxation with Helen and little Dina. He hummed a tune as he drove along the highway.

In the distance he saw a car parked alongside the road. Next to it stood a man with arm upraised. Hanns slowed down, stopped, and to his surprise saw that it was one of his fellow travellers, often referred to as 'Jack Souse.' Jack told him his car had broken down and that he needed a lift to the nearest garage to fetch a mechanic.

'Okay, come on, hop in!' said Hanns.

Jack got in and as he seated himself in the front passenger seat, Hanns caught a strong whiff of liquor from his breath.

On the way Jack became expansive.

'Hanns, you're a first-class chap, a thorough gentleman, and your wife is a perfect lady. You mustn't take any notice of what some nasty people are saying about her.'

Hanns burst out laughing. 'I'm divorced from Dorothy and don't care a damn what people say about her, so long as it's not about Helen.'

'True, I agree,' said Jack. 'Helen is a one-hundred-percent white lady. They must be mad to think she's a Coloured!'

'What? My wife a Coloured?' cried Hanns, and in his agitation lost control. The car swerved, left the road, and started bumping over the veld.

Back on the highway, Hanns sat silent. Jack too held his peace. Arriving at the garage, Jack jumped out and thanked him. Hanns nodded and drove off.

He stormed into the house, looking like thunder, threw his sample case into a corner, ignored Helen who came to meet him, and made straight for little Dina who lay peacefully asleep in her cot. He roughly turned her over and began to scrutinise her little hands.

Helen had followed him into the bedroom. Perhaps he'd had a few drinks, she thought, and had become jealous. She turned to him, irony in her voice, and said: 'What are you looking for? Are you trying to make sure she is your daughter?'

'They say you're a Coloured,' he stammered, and looked around him bewildered.

'A Coloured!' Helen gave a bitter laugh. 'You're mad, Hanns— you're infected with the Nuremberg madness!' And then, almost in tears, she began pleading with him: 'Aren't you ashamed of yourself? In your own child you look for racial flaws! You, of all people? Haven't you yourself suffered enough from this nonsense?'

Her words hit him like rocks. He stood there, his shoulders drooping, his head bowed. At last he cried out: 'Forgive me, Helen, please forgive me! I don't want to hear anything. Just tell me you forgive me. And I give you my word, it'll never happen again.'

He seized her by the hand, drew her close, and with burning lips began to kiss her—kiss and weep . . . kiss and weep . . .

Dov Fedler

EXCERPTS FROM Gagman

This One's Gonna Killya'

In the camp I was called a collaborator. I was told I was worse than
a kapo because I made jokes of my comrades' deaths. I was under
threat from all sides. If I made it through the camps—and there was
to be a liberation—the survivors would still want my blood.

Every day in that hellhole, Feldshon would swear his oath to me.
'When this is over we'll get you!' It sounded like a prayer.

'Promises, promises . . .' I would taunt him.

He would glare at me from behind those cracked and broken
glasses. I believe it is only his hatred of me that sustained him
through that terrible place. And yet he would never thank me for it.
One day, I knew I would have to take Feldshon seriously. But for
now it was the commandant I had to keep amused. Every night a
different act—new material. I would have done anything for a new
joke. I used to swop my meagre rations for jokes—any gag as long
as it was new. Jokes became more precious than bread. They became my staff of life.

How long can a man go without food? Feed me a line and I'll
show you.

That's the sort of gag that went down well with the commandant.
Only he appreciated what I went through to keep him entertained.
He knew that humour springs from the deepest wells of despair.
The more I suffered, the louder he laughed. I would bathe in the
radiance of his chuckles, I was raised to sublime ecstasies by his
chortles.

Forgive my melodramatic descriptions, but I do not exaggerate.

The merest hint of a smile from him was enough to transport
me. I would focus on just one detail of his face when I performed
for him—the left corner of his mouth. That is where his laughter
began. That was the source of my river of life. How I dreaded a

drought in that area. And of course, he knew exactly how carefully I watched that one spot. And so, he would twitch and snarl just so he could delight in my responsive terror. Nothing made him laugh quite as hard, as that demonstration of his absolute power. He loved to see me terrified. Naturally, I played that emotion harder than any other. I rehearsed it every moment on and off stage until it became second nature to me.

The secret, as some great comedian once noted (it may have been me), is Sincerity. If one can but fake that.

My greatest fear was the moment I knew must come. It is every comedian's greatest fear. It is the moment that the audience becomes familiar with one's patter, the moment it can tell where you are coming from and can anticipate the joke and loses interest. The moment that happens, you're dead.

In my case, the poignancy of that statement was sharper than for most. I could not afford to lose him, for even one brief second.

'If you must kill me, please make me into a lampshade—let my punishment be a light one.' I once quipped hysterically.

He loved lines like that. Of course, I joked about what my own fate would be. One has to draw from one's own life to wring out an authentic laugh. If somehow I could have got him to like me, I understood that there would never be any question of mercy in our relationship. No, the moment I ceased to be amusing, would be my last.

Fear can inspire great performances. One needs the adrenalin to go on stage. One needs that edge. The heart pounds furiously, the head buzzes. Blood and humour become a heady mix and the gags go off like firecrackers.

Everyone has bad nights. I had not had one yet. The law of averages dictated that one would have to come up sometime. It was due. It was overdue.

I could not, like Scheherezade, go on for a thousand one performances. That was too much. I knew that there was soon to be that fateful event—my final performance. 'By all means laugh, but please don't let the last laugh be on me.' That one, too, broke him up. That kind of line held his interest in the contest of my wit versus his attention, but gave him yet another weapon to wield. It allowed him to feign disinterest and that would paralyse me with fear.

I was like spit hanging from the corner of his mouth waiting for gravity to do its work. It just could not go on like this.

I don't remember when the possibility of escape first occurred to me, but as the cliche tells it 'Hope springs eternal, etc.' I fantasised about a life of freedom. I had reached the end of yet another cliche: 'All I feared was fear itself.' I stopped thinking about how long I would live. After all, how long could I keep it up? How long is a piece of string? How long the hangman's noose? All I could think of was snappy answers to these existential questions.

It was in this turbulent state of mental activity that I suddenly had insight into his dependence on me. I saw with absolute clarity that it was I who made him omnipotent. Nothing else responded so totally to his will. The merest flicker of emotion on his face reflected in me as bizarrely as the images in the mirrors of an amusement arcade. His anger was caricatured in my terror.

I learnt to anticipate his moods and I was as attentive as a new lover. I studied the language of his countenance, learning that a slight flaring of the nostrils was the herald of a bout of petulance. At the first sign of such a storm I would throw myself at his feet, inviting the vicious kick that would divert his whim to destroy me into something more temporal.

I would then lie at the point of his boot in which I would study my reflection as I would nurse my bruised kidneys with a hug of self-congratulation and scream in genuine agony at the mastery of the beating. These multi-faceted performances were, I think, my best. At no time have I been able to fake sincerity better.

When it came, the end was sudden. I simply ran dry. And knowing that this had to be my last performance, I threw caution to the winds. What did I have to lose? I ridiculed everything mercilessly. I mocked the Fuhrer and, finally, life itself.

He laughed as never before. I knew that this was the pinnacle of my career. I could never rise to this height again. I could never top this. All I knew was that I had to keep him laughing. I also understood that he was the best audience that I would ever have. I wanted that moment to continue forever. All I desired was to keep him laughing. It was then that I realised that he could not stop and that it was I who was controlling the situation. The revelation was dizzying. It almost stopped me. His face had turned a bright beet red.

The veins of his temples throbbed and strained with the pressure of unrestrained mirth.

He tried to stop me speaking. He proffered a pleading hand.

'Me? You're asking me—for mercy?' I postured in my most obsequious attitude. This of course merely made him laugh harder. 'ME???' I squeezed the word for every ounce of insignificance that accurately depicted me. He began to choke with mirth. He had passed the limit we recognise as laughter. His body had no means of coping with the fits. It must be the moment that only the matador knows just as he takes breath to deliver the coup de grace. I held the servile pose and bowing low to look him in the eye, for he had fallen to the floor and lay there as helpless as a babe. I all but whispered: 'Doesn't that just kill you?'

His eyes widened for a brief moment of true understanding, but he could no longer resist the joke. His face turned purple, his eyes bulged and then suddenly he was still. There was no exhilation, no last breath. Whatever it was remained locked inside him.

It was a long time before I moved.

I remained transfixed in counterpoint to his rigid form until new life surged back in a joy of understanding that I was suddenly free.

It was the only occasion I remember actually laughing. How odd! My joy sprang from some primeval well and bubbled over. There was nothing that I could not conquer. I would simply walk out of this place and I would do it with nothing else but sheer chutzpah.

I do not remember formulating any plan. I merely followed the instinct that had preserved me thus far. I would continue the performance. The show must go on. The curtain was going up on another act. As I feverishly stripped him of his uniform, I rehearsed his posture and attitudes entirely in my head, correcting any flaw of interpretation even before playing it. But I was already expert in playing impossible roles and for once was not struck by stage fright.

As I slipped on the boots, I felt myself become him. I strode backstage knowing that the silhouette that flitted across the boards was his. The effect in the fragment of mirror, that for so long had watched me make up, was bizarre. The essence of the image was the commandant, but in close up it looked like a cadaver. What would carry the performance would be the uniform, I grudgingly conceded. What a triumph it would be to carry it off without props, without make-up; to do it on a wing and a prayer. I wondered that one's ego could still be so active at such a crucial juncture. How amazing to even briefly consider risking life for art now. Ah, but then artists are such vain creatures. All manner of madness passes through one's mind that moment before the curtain goes up, one becomes blind to everything but the play.

And then . . . you're on!

I remember only vaguely striding out into the night, greeting the guard with a perfunctory 'guten abend.' He returned the greeting with the respect befitting my rank. My confidence soared. I strode across the courtyard to the guard office, shouting at an orderly, demanding a car.

A lady awaited me in the town—schnell!! I muttered and cursed the inefficiency of the lower ranks and all in all conducted myself as an officer and a gentleman.

As the car swiftly swept through the gates of the camp, my heart fluttered like a wild bird wresting itself from the nest. I may have actually fainted, for I remember nothing of the journey to the town.

When it lurched to a sudden stop, I came back to my senses. I left the car hurriedly, admonishing the driver for his tardy work and with a dismissive wave of my gloved hand, strode into the square with all the assurance of a man with a pressing appointment.

Into the Land of Wham!

How I survived and finally set foot in The New World is a tale too oppressive to call to mind. Those were dark times, both physically and metaphorically.

I lived as a shadow, hiding all day and venturing furtively into the dark of night for a morsel of food.

I have no desire to chronicle those times.

I had, of course, become a hunted man, wanted by both the Nazis and the survivors of the Holocaust. The murder of a German officer was one that the die-hards would not allow to go unpunished. Hard to believe but it was the survivors who seemed to hound me more. I had colluded with the enemy by making him laugh. That was unforgiveable.

And so I had fled from the grave of Europe in search of new life in the New World. I became one of those huddled masses yearning to breathe free.

But even as I walked the streets in this land of freedom, I knew that I had escaped nothing. The shadows of the past still haunted me. I would still have to play a role rather than be myself. I would have to pretend to be a free man. If I allowed myself to be perceived as a stranger in the land, my pursuers would soon ferret me out. They would soon pick out my face from among those teeming hordes who scoured the streets in search of new hope.

It is so easy to spot a refugee. The loss of his home weighs him down. His posture is one of defeat. He stoops as he walks as if expecting the oppressor's lash across his back. My pursuers would soon find me were I to adopt that attitude. I knew I would have to be otherwise. Instead of stooping, I would strut. Yes, that was it—I must strut. I must be perceived as a bold man, a man of substance.

And so, I lifted my eyes above the huddled masses and sought out another role model.

Immediately, I was caught by the perpendicular line of his spine—
Hominus Erectus. He walked with the assurance of a man with a
pressing appointment. Where had I heard that line before? I followed like a shadow at first, studying the supple, lumbering rhythm
of his walk. I judged the clenching of his fists that demonstrated his
contained strength. I felt myself grow taller as I mimicked the way
he walked along the avenue with an independent air. By the time we
reached our destination, I was whistling that old tune along with
him.

He entered a building of some grandness. A uniformed attendant
stood at the door. He swept past the doorman with the self assurance of a landlord.

By now I was so in tune with his rhythm that I followed his
example, without pausing to consider my shabby condition and
treated the doorman as I had the guards at the gate of the camp.

I entered a gallery full of fantasy and glitter. The hall was filled
with people dressed in outrageous costume. Some wore masks and
others wore capes. Some seemed larger than life and not quite real.

Elsewhere a group of men dressed in ordinary street clothes
gathered in a corner deep in discussion. I thought I recognised
some of them, but could not quite remember from where. I felt
compelled to join them. I wanted so much to become part of this
gathering.

Instinctively I knew that I had stumbled on an opportunity to
create a new identity for myself. I lingered in the background and
listened. One who was leading the conversation was saying: 'I believe that change is still possible.'

He turned and looked directly at me and asked 'What do you
think, Gagman?'

Lionel Abrahams

Cut Glass

On each of the two days Felix sustained a small cut, the first on his forefinger, the second on his thumb. The last signs of them were healed in a week. Perhaps it was simply adult life—no less than it was child's life—to oscillate across the sharp divide between reality and reality and receive the occasional injury.

The episodes were minor. They occurred while his parents were abroad, and he, at his own choice, was staying alone at home, making, in a sense, his first naked confrontation with the city. Some friend's jocular reference, as they had driven along the easterly stretch of Jeppe Street, had identified a greasy looking black-and-brick three-storeyed block as a brothel, and Felix had eventually, one evening, essayed the bus journey and the seven blocks' walk to confront what the place had to offer. He had been lucky at first, for the girl who presented herself in response to his inarticulate signals and took him up to her room was pleasant-natured and patient. In some unvoiced way she accommodated their personalness in the mechanical situation. When he returned—he found himself wishing he could do so daily—he regularly asked for her, and took to bringing her little gifts, to turn what passed between them into something better than a transaction.

He found that the business went on at the brothel during the afternoons as well as the evenings, and the daylight jaunt was usually more convenient to him. But one afternoon his regular mate was not to be found, so, with hardly a tic of compunction, he took the service of another girl. She turned out stiff and remote, unfriendly in the nervous self-addressed exclamations she gave out at his caresses. In future, perhaps, he thought, he would forego the gratification—even after the journey—if the right girl were not there.

Then the series of his visits was interrupted for a few weeks because of a more fulfilling and intimate adventure. When that was over and he resorted to Jeppe Street again he found that 'his' girl no longer took a room there, and the others he spoke to could not tell him where to find her. So he abandoned his resolution, and went with the first girl who made herself available to him. His visits, after that, were irregular, and his rewards uneven. Once he found a thin redhaired girl, apparently new to the building, who clinched her deep admission of him with a vigorous pressure of thighs, belly, and loins which he found sharply delicious. Either she was a mistress of technique, or the voluptuary completeness came from the accidental fitting of their bodies. He would have liked her service again, but had not asked for her name. He glimpsed her once more several visits later, but she was sitting on a step, her mouth bleeding, yelling obscenities at someone invisible, apparently drunk.

Usually his encounters amounted to drab, awkward commerce. The place itself yielded nothing to colour or soften it. Some of the rooms were occupied by pensioners and indigent families: often there were children at play about the lobby, passages, and staircase, and they seemed simply knowing about the business of the building. He wondered dully about the harm to them that he might be contributing to. But that was momentary. He tried to lace the whole serial of his custom there with a tincture of luridness by the thought of his promiscuous ranging from woman to woman.

The day he nicked his finger eluded even this colouring. It marked the low point in the series and the beginning of its end (to which he resigned himself a bare month later, after the day he found the place unusually quiet and clean and his way blocked by an elderly woman with a look of authority who met his request for Marion with a contemptuous, threatening, dismissive jerk of her head). That was all there was to it, really. He could not hide from himself the fact that this visit was only squalid. He arrived at the building in a little turmoil of dark feeling, that was really no more than readiness for a routine placation, at an earlier hour than ever before—the afternoon was still callow after the lunch break. One woman only lounged in the doorway and he could see no others in the lobby beyond her. She was rather older, grosser, shabbier than most of the girls he usually saw there, and although she immediately assented to his mumbled proposition, she seemed some-how disconcerted, vaguely unready.

He was usually taken to one of the rooms on the first floor, but this time he had to climb higher, and it was on the second staircase that he passed a grimy window with a missing pane. He put his hand where the emptied steel frame offered him a more convenient leverage for his climb than closed window and blank wall, and it was there that a chip of glass, still embedded in the old putty and almost hidden in sooty dust, scratched a shred of skin from his forefinger. Only the dirt made him give the injury a second thought. He'd apply a disinfectant as soon as he got home.

He was always sticky with perspiration in that building after the walk from the bus stop, and on this hot day he was having to climb yet another flight above the second floor. At the top was an open door to the outside. They emerged on the tarmac of the roof area with a block of servants' rooms in the centre. There were several Africans about. One or two of them regarded him and spluttered with giggles of surprise and derision. The prostitute ignored these, exchanged a word with one of the others, produced a key and opened the padlock on the door to one of the rooms.

If this was her home there were signs that a man—her hus-band?—shared it with her. A jacket of his was draped on a hanger behind the door. Flustered, hot, confused in his feelings about the setting, Felix took what the woman, somehow wearily, gave him of her body. While upon her he noticed a rankness from her declivities which overwhelmed the smells of the room and of his sweating skin. It was a stink that clung first for hours to his own body, then for weeks in his imagination. This particular conjunction with an-other person seemed what such an event, he had thought, could never be: less meaningful than masturbation.

He had an invitation to lunch next day with his aunt. Auntie Sarah was the white-haired widow of Dad's brainy brother, Lewis, the daughter of a rabbi and the mother of two serious, brainy, academic children. Her life was replete with calamities, tragedies even, but she mother-of-pearled them with the stoicism of her silence about them, and the sheeny enamel of unflawed respectability in the order of her existence. Respectability had been the essential spirit of her home since his earliest memories of it, when his boisterously intellectual uncle—now sixteen years dead—and earnest cousins had been with her, still accumulating their tributes of social, scholarly, and connoisseuring glory. It was a stuffy, fussy, superficial attribute—but there was something incongruously strong in the way she had sustained it long after exile and death had robbed her of those three who had been the contributors of its substance. She had been left 'comfortably off,' and no doubt that had eased her way, but it did not empty the force of what, so unforcedly (with her petite physique and nervous tentative manners) she represented.

His conversations in her house long ago had always been with one of the other three. Between himself and her what passed was not substantial discussion but a tissue draped on polite enquiries about health, schooling, literary activities. It had hardly ever happened that he was her lone guest. But, as always, she had a slender stream of solicitous questions and comments on family and neutral matters.

'How are you managing alone at home? Does your girl cook? You must have proper meals. It's important for your health. Don't you want to take your jacket off? It's a hot day. But at least it's not like the khamseen in Israel. That kind of heat I found unbearable. I could hardly breathe. But if that was the only trouble they had there I would be grateful. Oh, those fedayeen! Shooting at a school on a kibbutz, injuring children. It breaks my heart to think of poor Israel. The trouble never seems to end . . .' (Her surviving son lived there.) They listened in to the broadcast news together and she tutted apprehensively or deploringly at the various dangers and wickednesses at large in the world.

He was left to scan Uncle Lewis's knowledgeably chosen objets d'art (this watercolour was a Maris; could that tiny engraving actually be a Rembrandt?), the eclectic bookshelves (Nietzsche, Marx, Freud, Wells, Shakespeare . . .), the showcase with its two never-touched tea sets and its restrained assortment of somehow unaccountable ornaments (china shepherdess, meticulously dressed Geisha doll: could these have been his uncle's choices?); then to sprawl awhile on the anti-maccassared settee over a newspaper—while Aunt Sarah busied herself with her African maid in the faintly gassy kitchen, before presenting him the meal.

As they ate, her streamlet of talk flowed on: Did the chopped liver need more salt? The kitke was nice and fresh, and well-baked. Speier's. She dished up with a curiously hesitant hand, as though the food or the cutlery were alive, or as though the minutest difference in quantity given or withheld was of some particular import. She was sure he would like the chicken giblets soup. It was very tasty soup. A pity, some of the miniature parogen that went with it were a little burnt. The girl turned the stove up too high. Such a pity. But here was another one that wasn't burnt that he should have. Have! Have! They were very small. Made with very nice chicken fat . . .

After the meal she read him a letter from her son, to whom, last year, for the sake of being in a rounded family, the orphaned grandchild she had been rearing had been sent. It was amusing to see, when she went out, she told him, how many Africans in the streets recognised her and greeted her as 'Martin's grannie!' After such a long time they still remembered, and asked how Martin was.

When the maid had washed up and left the kitchen with her own meal to eat in the servants' quarters, Auntie Sarah told him about the black woman's troubles. 'She has to share a room with two others. It's very unpleasant. No privacy. And one of the others is a drunkard. There was such trouble there the other night. Fighting and screaming. The police came. But they are always so ready to hit and arrest. So cruel. That is the way she has to live. I feel so sorry for her. Her husband has been trying for seven years to get a bus driver's license so that he can improve himself. He got it at last a few months ago and she was overjoyed. But now he has lost his job because they found that he is an alcoholic. Isn't it heartbreaking? And now I'm so worried about her daughter. She is fourteen and she wants to leave school and take a job in a factory. I say she should stay in school at least until she is sixteen and try to become a nurse or a teacher. There is so little for them. If she goes to a factory she'll mix with bad types and become a loafer. Goodness knows what will become of her. It worries me so. But what can they do? They are so poor, so poor!'

And her 'they' was general: she was bearing a weight for all the underprivileged in the land. Felix wondered if she would feel any lightening of heart when she made her proposed move to Israel, to be with her son and Martin and the other grandchildren. It was to be, instead of the nearness of these African poor, the oppressions of the khamseen and the obstinate ferocity of el Fatah. The cares of the world were not escapable, and acknowledging them was part of Auntie Sarah's respectability. This was different from revealing the broken edges left by the clouts of her personal disasters—and Felix felt himself, during the two or three hours of his visit, to be enclosed in a clean well-padded nest, or washed over by resistless ripples of orderliness (resistless, since even his presence did not disrupt their rhythm).

He was putting on his jacket in preparation for leaving, and speaking with some animation about a project of his that Auntie Sarah had asked about, when the accident took place. For emphasis he flung out a hand, and over went a vase. It was an elaborate item of cut-glass and it shattered. In his contrition he futilely reached to pick up one of the pieces and caught the ball of his thumb on a blade-fine edge. Then he stood upright, burning with apologies— but expecting to exchange them with his aunt for reassurances, dismissals of guilt, phrases of comfort.

Instead, she was as though stricken by the loss. 'Oh dear, oh! The cut-glass. Oh, you should be careful. It was an accident, but, oh dear, oh dear! One of a pair . . .' She looked at its double at the other end of the sideboard, as though it had been damaged by the destruction of the first. 'Cut-glass . . . I don't think they make this kind of thing anymore . . .'

It was a minute or two before the accident began to leave her feelings at rest. It had plainly borne her a shock that went deeper than it seemed to warrant. She was soon to move, to break up her home. There was one awkward item the fewer to be transported or disposed of (who, in this generation, would want this style of ornament?). But to her, it must have been a crystal of silenced memory, an intended heirloom for Martin perhaps, an emblem of the fragile continuity that made it matter to be respectable, to go on being respectable, to go on . . .

At last she noticed the blood on his thumb. It was really the second injury that he had sustained during the visit. The sharp prongs of the dainty fork with which he was eating a rissole had caught him under the tongue and broken the skin, but he had said nothing about it. There was much that it was preferable to remain silent about.

He wondered, as, with her composure still not all restored, she dressed his thumb, what else in her world would fall to pieces if she were made to know all that was in him, the sought and bought besmirchment of only yesterday, the dark red disorderliness that seemed to have burst a first tiny crevice for itself at the mercurochrome-smeared nick on the adjacent forefinger.

Maja Kriel

Number 1-4642443-0

Lying in bed in the morning, she could see him through the lace curtains, moving about the garden. He would always begin in the same way, by sweeping the front veranda and the paving in front of the bedrooms. She liked the rhythmical sound of the broom, very faint to begin with as he started on the far end of the house, and getting slowly closer to her bedroom with each stroke. He was patient and careful, never rushing the job even though the paving stretched away in front of him. It was almost like a warming up of the muscles in his arms and back. He would be smoking his early morning cigarette, flattened between his lips. She would know that it was eight o'clock sharp. She enjoyed the confidence of knowing that it was eight o'clock on Saturday morning and Amos had started. The bed became warmer and more comfortable when she saw him outside through the curtains. After all, the world was made up of people who had little privileges that were unavailable to others. She loved the feeling of order and tidiness: she could lie in bed unharassed, while the world still carried on in a proper way, with everyone knowing the time and the place.

But there were other times when that steady sound of sweeping compelled her to get up. Something insistent and determined about it as it drew closer to her bedroom. He would go on, shamelessly, past her room, so that she could see his shape behind the curtain, and he knew that he could be seen. Then she would get up and busy herself around the house; pull down the bathroom blind and let in the bath water, aware that he was only a short distance away and could hear all the activity and sounds of splashing. Then she would wrap herself in a towel and run through to the bedroom hoping he would not see her through the gaps in the curtain. Why did he work around the bedrooms so early in the morning?

She would dress and have breakfast in the kitchen. Sometimes he came into the yard through the side gate. She could see him through the kitchen window going into the toilet. She could not help noticing whether it was a long time or a short time; coming out of that little room with its cement floor and the bath that stood on four arched feet and was only big enough for a grown man if he sat upright against the back with his legs bent in front of him. But if he went into his room, then she would tell herself that it was only nine o'clock and he had to wait until his breakfast at half past ten. He was wasting time deliberately.

Often she would rush out of the house after breakfast, pleased that she could be seen to be busy with important activities outside of the house. At other times she stretched out on the *chaise-longue* next to the window and read a book, looking up every now and then to watch him in the garden. She liked him to work where she could watch him. She could see the strength in his arms when he raked the leaves with that same steady rhythm, and he easily touched the ground without bending his knees to pick up the garden debris and put it on the wheelbarrow. He was master of his movement and knew how much energy to spend without tiring himself; like an athlete who paces his performances, steady and not stopping.

When he was not working for her, he was employed as a builder. She could visualize his muscles labouring under the weight of a wheelbarrow loaded with bricks, or his chest expanded and straining as he carried a heavy wooden beam over his head. Then he was a man among men, working with all the dangers of a building site, taking his orders from a rough white builder and collecting his pay on Fridays. She had noticed that he was missing a joint on his index finger, perhaps from one of those fearful building accidents. His body was hard and his skin was dry and cracked from exposure to the sun and from working with hard materials. He did not wear the khaki overalls she had given him for work in the garden. He wore his own clothes and the shape and definition of his body stretched his flimsy T-shirt.

In the middle of the morning, after his breakfast, she would walk down to him in the garden. If she could not see him from her window, she would suspect him of sleeping under a tree behind the hedge near the compost. But he was always raking or watering. She felt it was important to appear in the garden at least once a day to show him that she was firmly in control and expecting a full day's work. As she walked to him directly across the grass she was conscious of something stiff and military in her stride, her arms swinging forward in time with the opposite leg. She would give him his tasks for the day, pointing with an outstretched arm to a flower bed that needed weeding or grass that had to be cut. She wanted to impress him with her keen eye and her high standards. She felt there was a surliness about the way he looked at her and answered. He never smiled showing white teeth like the other gardeners. He looked as though he was thinking about something else and only pretending to work. But she could not fault him.

In the afternoon, when she lay down to rest, she had that same feeling of both confidence and discomfort. She would be sure that everything was proceeding in an orderly way. But when she closed the curtains he would know that she was lying on her bed. From where he worked he could see her shadow behind the curtain, moving from the bedroom to the living room. When he used the tap he would be standing right outside her bedroom.

At five o'clock, when he was finished, she walked around the garden deliberately to see that everything had been done.

'Very good work. The garden looks nice and clean.'

He made no answer, not even the echoing 'nice and clean' they sometimes said.

What was he thinking when he looked at her face? She tried to ignore her high heels sinking deep into the damp earth where he had been watering and her sudden drop in height. Perhaps he wanted to ask her about his pass book which she had been carrying in her bag: Amos Selepe. Ethnic group: Tswana. Number: 1-4642443-0. The paper is dirty and warped from having fallen into water. It has the slightly rancid smell of his pockets. It is curved from being worn inside his jacket and pressed against his chest. The corners of the pages are bent and discoloured from his fingers. His face looks out from the photograph in an expression of fixed surprise, taken in a kiosk, two for seventy-five cents. He carried it in his pocket with a box of matches and his half-smoked cigarettes. And now it lies in her bag, next to her scented handkerchief and entangled with the hairs of her brush. But he will not speak to her about it. She knows that he will wait as long as she can wait.

Once, she called him into the house to help her move the bedroom carpet. She felt strange about having him inside, allowing him to see her room from the other side of the window. He walked in quietly, first taking off his shoes, with an exaggerated softness in his step. He looked shabby standing there, surrounded by polished furniture and fragile ornaments, shamed by the wealth, his knees bending with politeness and his hands clutching each other across his stomach. He got onto his knees and began to shift the carpet with tenderness, privileged. And she stood over him directing his movements: "More to that side and then a bit more to the corner."

He smoothed out each crease and wrinkle, his hands bearing down as the weight of his whole body stretched to the outer edges of the carpet. She looked at his flat feet and gnarled blue toe-nails, his thick hair matted and caught with little twigs in the tightly sprung coils.

She was always standing up when she spoke to him, and he was always on his knees. But now when he worked in the garden he would know the secrets of her room, the feel of her carpet under his feet and the touch of the velvet upholstery; he had seen her bed.

One Sunday morning, while she was sitting in the kitchen, she saw his door open. The room was dark inside, with a wedge of sunlight across the floor. Two young women walked out and left quickly through the yard gate. She thought of the dark little cell and the narrow bed, more for a child than a grown man. She thought of the sweaty debris of tangled sheets and clothes; a pot in the corner with dry mealie meal clinging to the sides, perhaps an encrusted frying pan with congealed fat, a pair of shapeless trousers hanging from a nail on the wall, a gummy comb lying on a table. He was still in his room, belonging to its darkness and dirt, while the two girls had disappeared into the street still carrying his smell. So this is what was happening in the yard? While the front overlooked trees and shrubberies with scented herbs and honeysuckle creepers trailing around the doors and windows to allow perfume to drift into the house, the back was polluted with vice and vermin; every wretch could find her way to his door. She would not speak to him now. She could see him still tired and limp, lost in the dimness of his room. She thought about him all day. Her mind kept returning to the sight of the two black girls coming out of his room like two beetles crawling out of a dark hole.

The next day, she waited for him to return from work, and knocked on his door. It opened immediately. He looked so black standing there barefoot with only the whites of his eyes catching the light through the opened door. She looked past him and into the room. Slowly outlines began to become clear. There was the bed, in the corner and against the wall. It was covered with a starched white cloth embroidered with blue thread, puffed up on one end by pillows and standing on bricks, each one wrapped in newspaper sharply folded along the edges. There was a table with a primus stove and two shiny pots on the shelf under the table. He had improvised a cupboard by hanging a piece of printed cloth across one wall and he had built some shelves into a corner of the room which had pictures and photographs. The walls were freshly whitewashed. She remembered the room as she had given it to him, still dirty from the previous occupant, with the ceiling gaping from an old leak. He had said that he would repair it with a piece of boarding from one of his house jobs. Then he had moved in silently one night without her even noticing.

'Listen Amos, I saw two girls coming out of your room yesterday morning and I told you when you started that I am not having my yard full of strange people and girls in the rooms. Every time I look in the yard there is another girl walking around. I told you that I want the outside gate locked and nobody in the rooms.'

She was pleased with the clear-cut statement and the assertive tone of her voice. It had that high-pitched unwavering sound which she had heard her neighbour use when she spoke to her servants. It was just right and she felt herself to be convincing as an indignant householder pleading for rightness and decency. This time she was facing him directly and he was on his feet. He would not give her a feeling of doubt and confusion. He would be the defensive one, stooped with shame and guilt. He turned around and reached for a framed photograph on the shelf. He stood in the picture with the same expression of fixed surprise, wearing a hat and a dark suit. Next to him was a young woman in a white dress, stiffly facing the camera and holding a bouquet of flowers in front of her.

'The one girl is my wife who come to Johannesburg with her sister for weekend. They sleep one night in my room for go to father's funeral.'

She looked at the photograph again. She had always thought of Amos as alone in his room, living in her yard. It was Amos, and it was his life. The photograph was a pretence. He was not the bridegroom in an expensive suit. And inside the shiny shoes were his blue toenails, and under the hat, the matted hair. The young bride in her frilly dress was a doll kept as an ornament on his shelf.

She became aware of the smell of French perfume rising up from her body. She wanted to wash it off and get it out of her nostrils. She held her polished fingernails behind her and she shifted away from him and walked back into the house.

Lilian Simon

God Help Us

People in Krugersdorp called my father a 'gentleman.' Even his mother-in-law used to say, 'Chaim is a gentleman' because he wrote receipts for her whenever the tenant in the little old house she owned, paid the rent. My father was very patient with her although he usually had to repeat everything he said to her at least three times. She never admitted that she was deaf—indeed, she heard everything she wasn't supposed to—and she couldn't read or write in English so communication between them was difficult.

'You mustn't make a fuss,' my father would say to my brothers and me. 'Don't complain. You must have patience.'

I never saw him eat without putting on his jacket, go through a doorway ahead of my mother, enter a building without taking off his hat, or step into a lift before all the women were inside. When my brother was taking him to hospital just before he died of a coronary, he stood aside to let a young woman into the lift, his face bluish-white, his breath coming in short gasps and his eyes already glazed. The nurses prayed for him the night before he died.

'He never complains,' they said. 'He is so good. He doesn't want to give us any trouble.'

'I have to go now,' I told him three hours before he died. I wanted to get away from the sight of him lying helpless in his oxygen tent, from the hospital smell, the sister who kept looking in and frowning at his chart, and his old friend, the superintendant of the hospital, who kept saying we'd neglected my father.

'You were always worried about your mother. You forgot about him.'

My father didn't utter a word of protest when I left, but I saw his lips twist into what tried to be a smile but turned into a grimace. I never saw him again.

'Don't make a fuss,' he'd said. I translated that into 'Don't make a scene. Don't look for trouble,' as well as 'Don't complain.'

I didn't complain when my mother said there wasn't enough money to buy the pink and white ice-cream dress in the window that I'd set my heart on for the Jewish New Year. But I cried into my pillow the night after I saw my friend wearing the dress in Shul and my mother sitting up in the gallery dressed in a new outfit from the same shop.

I left Krugersdorp to get married. During the first few years of our married life, Leslie and I lived in an upstairs flat next-door to the Yeoville police station. We hadn't been in the flat very long when, one morning, I heard screams coming from the courtyard of the police-station.

I joined two other tenants on the fire-escape and we peered down into the courtyard. Evidently a black policeman had been instructed to hold down a prisoner under a tap, while a young white constable turned on the water to let it jet down into the prisoner's mouth and nose. The prisoner screamed in between spluttering, gasping, choking, and whooping for breath. The constable showed no mercy while we looked on.

'It's terrible!' I exclaimed. 'Horrible.'

'We've got to do something,' one of the other two women said. 'We must go down there and stop him.'

I looked down at the young policeman, at the way he'd flung his head back to look at us with his lips squared away from long, sharp-looking teeth—like an animal guarding his kill. I couldn't move. I couldn't say anything. We didn't go down; we didn't complain, not even to his superior afterwards. But somebody else probably did because we never saw the young constable again.

I never forgave myself for not interfering, for being too afraid to do so. Looking back now, I don't think I can put it down entirely to not wanting to make a scene or not looking for trouble. I think it also had to do with fears that started in early childhood.

'If you don't eat all your food, I'll call a policeman,' my mother used to say. 'Go to bed now or the policeman will come and get you.'

I suffered from all kinds of fears. I was afraid of the dark, at first without any real reason. I would wake up in the middle of the night, listen to the creaking in the old house and forget that the sound came from rotting floors and crumbling roof timber. I would pull the bedclothes over my head, draw my body in so stiffly that the joints would click in protest, and wait for the sweat to gather under my pyjama collar, to bead across my forehead, and trickle down into my eyes. I hardly dared to breathe while I waited for a burglar to come into my room, to grab my throat with his big, black hands. When he didn't come and the creaking died down, I would call: 'Daddy, I'm frightened.'

I would lie back then and listen for the sound of my father getting out of bed in his room, fumbling for his slippers, then shuffling down the passage with his weight coming down more heavily on his good leg. He didn't grumble when he came, just sat down on my bed, put his arm around my shoulders and told me a story, or sang Jewish folk songs softly till he felt the tension go out of my body.

One night I woke up to find him searching around my room with a torch. He wouldn't tell me what he was looking for, just kept on shining his torch. I watched the beam going down, under the bed, heard my father's sharp intake of breath followed by a very faint whistle as someone expelled air very softly.

A man leaped out from under my bed just as my father sprang. My fists clenched, my whole body contracted while I listened to grunting, snorting, scuffling. My father yelled as the burglar broke loose, rushed to the open window and dived out into the darkness. My father chased him but couldn't keep up because of his gammy leg.

The burglar may have disappeared into the pass office opposite our house. Nobody ever understood why a pass office had been built in a residential area. I don't know if the spate of attempted burglaries in our neighbourhood was due to the proximity of the pass office; they certainly occurred much more frequently in our part of town than anywhere else.

As a result of them, I was afraid to stay alone in the house even as a teenager, but I didn't object when my parents sometimes went out at night, leaving me by myself in an empty house. I was ashamed of my fears. They grew even stronger after I woke up one night to hear someone trying to get in through my bedroom window.

When I jumped out of bed, the man outside the window called, 'Wat is dit, miesie?' and I realised that he knew this was my room and that I was alone in it. I screamed and screamed.

Nowadays, if the light begins to fail while I'm walking beside Emmarentia Dam, I quicken my step when I see a black man approaching, and I look round, hoping to see a car coming past. Sometimes I hear screams from outside my house at night, and I immediately think of rape. I will not open my door, although I really would like to help the person being attacked.

Even in the daytime, when a black man tries to hitch a lift from me, I lock the car doors and drive on. I feel guilty about not stopping but in the midst of my guilt, I hear that voice at my window.

My mother was always shouting at the servants. I used to watch my father cringe as she went on and on at dinner, then he'd finally leave the table saying, 'I'm not hungry, thank you.' I cringed too.

She shouted because they mixed up the milk and meat utensils in her kosher kitchen, because they came late for work or simply because she was in a bad mood.

'Leave them alone,' my father would say. 'Let them get on with their work. If they're no good, tell them to go.'

He had Gert working for him in his shop for thirty years, and when Gert was run over in the township and died two days later, he could hardly eat or sleep for a week.

Whenever my own servants break a plate, I hear my mother shouting and my father saying: 'Leave them alone.' I keep quiet.

My mother was always ill. As a little girl I remember going with her from doctor to doctor, sitting in overheated waitingrooms where the flowers wilted quickly, paging through old magazines and comics, and listening to patients talking about their symptoms and operations till I wanted to run away—out into the fresh air.

I had to learn not to do things that displeased her—like nagging to go to a party where I would be the only Jewish guest. At sixteen I fell in love with an ex-R.A.F. pilot, who wasn't Jewish, and after I told her about it, she stayed in bed for three days—too ill to get up. I learned to discard people and things she didn't want. I think that is one of the reasons why I hardly ever fight now, why I find it difficult to protest, why I just let things go on and on.

'God will help us,' my father always said.

When I was a child I used to wonder how God, sitting way up there in the sky and busy with very important affairs, could find the time to come down and let my mother have the money to pay for my brother's matric exam or help my father find the money to pay merchants on time. However, my father was so sure that God wouldn't let him down that he convinced me too. And somehow, help did come. Rich Uncle Louis sometimes sent a substantial sum of money as a new year present or my mother's cousins lent her a fiver here and there.

'God will help,' my father reiterated when my mother had a brain operation. Her personality changed but that didn't affect his faith. She lived. That was enough.

I still have a picture of an old-man God sitting up in His sky with too much work to do. Perhaps that is why He couldn't save the six million Jews. I still pray to Him for help but now I ask questions. Is He too busy to stop a Biko from being tortured to death, members of an Olympic team from being massacred, and his own protesting ministers from being arrested? My father's black and white pictures are blurring.

Sandra Braude

Behind God's Back

The Sabbath is an island in time, a day of rest, when one is required to emulate God. For six days He laboured and, on the seventh day, He rested. He made all the things and creatures of the earth, culminating on the sixth day. Then He was entitled to rest. And so is the ultimate of His creations — man.

On Saturday, 10 April 1993, little groups of worshippers were returning home after the Sabbath service. They were walking slowly, and chatting amongst themselves, as befits pious Jews. To the synagogue you run, with joy and alacrity; when you leave, you dawdle, as though held back by ties to the house of God.

'It's amazing,' said one. 'Do you know that ours must be the only shul in the world where they give a *bracha* on *Pesach*?'

'And what a *bracha*!' said another, smacking his lips. 'Three different kinds of herrings. And that cake — did you taste that chocolate cake?'

'I did,' said his friend. 'I wonder where it came from?'

'Must have been Vered's,' interpolated a third. 'Only Vered could have made a cake like that.'

For a moment there was an appreciative silence. When God made the world, He, in his wisdom, did not neglect the possibility of chocolate cake.

The intellectual in the group piped up. A thin, ageing man, he always had something to contribute.

'The *sedra* today was very interesting,' he said. 'You see, Moses wanted to see God. But of course he couldn't. It would be too much. No man could survive that. The Almighty told him that outright. "You can't see my face," he said, "but I'll allow you to see my back as I pass." Now, what do you think that means?'

The group passed down the street, arguing the point vehemently.

A couple were still stuck on the idea of the chocolate cake, but those we shall disregard as of little importance.

At the corner the group split. Some went to the south, others to the east, where they had to cross a bridge over the highway. Cars whizzed past underneath, hurrying to their destinations. A slip street marked the exit from the highway. Here cars had to stop and allow pedestrians to cross over. The thin man crossed first.

Several cars had stopped. In the first sat a plump, yellow-haired woman. She shouted loudly at the man, and gesticulated wildly.

'These bloody drivers,' commented one of the pious. 'She's clearly Jewish. What does she have to drive for anyway on the Sabbath? She should be in shul like the rest of us. And why does she have to behave so badly, making a spectacle of herself like that? Does she have to shout and wave her arms around like a mad woman? Why doesn't she just sit quietly and let pedestrians have the right of way? I suppose she thinks because she's sitting behind the wheel that she owns everything. I've got a good mind to tell her what I think of her!'

He walked quickly up to the car with this intention in mind. But as he approached, the words he heard did not make sense. Instead of the woman warning pedestrians to keep out of her way, as he would have expected, she was shouting excitedly,

'He's been killed! They shot him! They shot him through the head! He's dead!'

'Hey! What's that you're saying? He's dead! Who's dead?'

'Hani!' she shouted, 'Hani! Chris Hani! He's dead!'

'Hani? Head of the Communist Party? He's dead, you say? How's that? When? Who killed him? Who shot him?

The yellow-haired woman was weeping. 'I don't know,' she said. 'I just heard it on the news. They said he was dead. That someone had shot him through the head. I don't know . . . this is terrible . . . terrible . . . terrible . . .' She revved her car and disappeared in a haze of exhaust smoke down the road.

The thin man whistled between his teeth. 'Whew. This is bad. Oy vay, this is bad. This is what we need in our lives? Hani, the head of the Communist Party shot dead?' He shook his head.

'So? He was a communist,' said one.

'So? So he was a communist? So what?' asked the thin man.

'Wasn't he a human being? Wasn't he one of God's creatures? And so what if he was a communist? Do you remember how many of us were communists in the old country? And isn't a man entitled to his beliefs, whatever they are?'

'So what's going to happen now?'

'*Freg mir*,' said the thin man, 'ask me another. Who knows? But whatever happens, we know it won't be good for the Jews. We remember the deaths and the pogroms in the old country. One madman starts something, and who knows where it ends?' He shook his head again, and sighed.

Then he continued. 'In the *sedra* it says that God would not let Moses see His face. He passed by, and let Moses see His back. What does this mean?' He paused. 'It means,' he said, 'that one cannot see what is going to happen in the future. One can only look at things that have already happened and then judge them.' His eyes looked into space. 'Who knows,' he said, 'what the death of this Hani will bring about?'

The next week began to show what the death of Hani would bring about. Anger began to rumble about the country. This had been a leader. Even those who had not realized it before, realized it now. He was loved and revered by many, and held as a figurehead, a symbol of freedom by many more.

The name 'Hani' was on everyone's lips.

The President appeared on the television screen. His face, normally totally controlled and devoid of emotion, was sombre. 'We regret this dramatic event,' he said. Only dramatic? Not lamentable? Not tragic?

But drama was indeed in the air. Within a week there would be a funeral, the likes of which the country had never seen before. Then, seventy-five thousand people would converge in ordered formation, would cram every inch of space of the massive stadium in Soweto, the great, black, shadow city of Johannesburg, would show their fists to the sky, and raise their voices in protest. 'We are the people,' they would cry, 'we, the legitimate. We will no longer tolerate injustice. We will prevail.'

Their leaders would arrive on the scene in stately fashion, driving in the newest model Mercedes. Statesmen from all over the world would be there, declaring solidarity. In sobre mood they would stand, awaiting the funeral cortège. This would wind, in stately fashion, onto the stadium-grounds. The ornate coffin would be unloaded, huge bouquets of flowers adorning the white hearse. Freedom soldiers would carry the coffin, with great care, to a dais, followed by a satin cushion, bearing the Cap of Freedom. Then, to the solemn music, the soldiers would perform the funeral march around the stadium, slow and measured, arms swinging, legs rising. Round the stadium, slowly and rhythmically they would march, while the people shouted and saluted. Soon they would be back at the dais where the coffin lay in state, under a yellow canopy, on which the words 'City Funerals' were embellished, and next to which stood a man, naked from the waist up, except for the symbolic chains which enclosed him.

Then the leaders would rise, one after another, and speak to the people. The leaders of the tripartite alliance—the ANC, the SACP, and COSATU. Their messages, although the words differed, were all the same.

'Amandla! Power! We shall prevail! We, the people, shall prevail! We have suffered! We have lived under injustice! We shall rise! The future is ours!

'Viva! Viva! Viva the ANC! Viva the SACP! Viva COSATU! Viva the memory of Chris Hani! His body is dead, but his spirit shall live! Viva! Viva! Viva Chris Hani! Long live! Long live!'

And the people would reply, 'Viva! Viva! Long live! Long live!'

They would rise and spontaneously began to toyi-toyi, that wonderful, energetic dance, that must surely make revolution in South Africa the most rhythmic revolution in history?

The speeches that would follow would rouse the people into a spiritual frenzy. 'We are the people! The land is ours! We are the legitimate! Our leaders are the legitimate leaders! The present government is not legitimate! On to the future! Viva! Amandla!' The cause was righteous, timeous, supported by messages from the whole world.

'I have not time to read you all the messages,' one speaker would say, 'but the world is with us, with our cause. I would like to read you just one—from Fidel Castro.'

And the people would shout, 'Viva Castro! Viva Castro!'

On the outer wall outside the stadium, where the words CHRIST DIED FOR OUR SINS were scrawled, someone would put a stroke through the T:

CHRIS DIED FOR OUR SINS.

But all this was afterwards, a sort of culmination of the event. A funeral is a rite of passage, a requisite killing of one's dead. For the week before there was only anger, and the expression of anger.

It did not take long to apprehend the assassin. A woman who had been passing heard the shots, saw a car skid away, took down the number and gave it to the police and, within hours, a man had been arrested.

The newspapers commented on his origin. A Pole, in the country for only a few years. Was his anger against the Communists, who had taken away his family's possessions—before he was born, in fact? Was there a mental aberration? Someone mentioned that Verwoerd's assassin had also been a foreigner. Was there some sort of subtle connection between the two events? The newspapers also spoke of his personality. 'We cannot believe it,' said his colleagues. 'Such a gentle man—loved animals, would not hurt a fly.' Should one add, in passing, that Hitler had been known to kiss babies? And that murder is always murder?

The period of mourning started almost immediately. A day of marches and demonstrations was called for.

The silent people were silent no more, the invisible ones invisible no more. South Africa was alive, moving. People joined together in masses. They moved, in solidarity, chanting and toyi-toying. Being denied the right to put a cross on ballot-paper in expression of their desires, they marched.

White fears, supported by military might, responded. Police stood by, their guns at the ready. Helicopters buzzed overhead, drowning out the chanting. Television cameras showed people like swarms of ants, of bees.

Throughout the world viewers sat in front of their television sets, watching, while mobs swarmed down city streets, rioting, looting, destroying. A captivating shot of a youth, running up the side of a shop-window and kicking it in. Strength, virility, beauty. A flower of evil. Grabbing and running, and shots from waiting police guns.

Scampering away with goods, fighting over a clothes-dummy. The loss of reason.

In another scene a young, Afrikaans man stands, bewildered, stammering his response to the camera. 'Man, I was standing in my lounge, and suddenly this group of people breaks in. Quick-quick, everything in my house is gone. I runs down to the gate to call the police, and it's all gone!' Around him is chaos and emptiness—broken lamps, smashed furniture, smashed dreams.

Fifty thousand people close in on a police-station in Soweto, and the police open fire. Two marchers are killed, shot in the back as they are running away. More anger. Anger precipitates anger. 'What right had the police to shoot on peaceful marchers?'

Memories of Sharpeville, when so many died, shot in the back with dum-dum bullets.

And fear? Families, predominantly Afrikaans, say, 'If the police will not protect us, then we will protect ourselves.' And the sale of firearms soars.

The youth-leader stands. His hand movements are specifically expressive: 'de Klerk—No!' he shouts, his thumb pointing down, and, 'Kill the Boers!' He begins to toyi-toyi and, round about, the toyi-toying starts.

As the mob mood takes hold, anger and fear predominate.

The Sabbath has come around once again. The island in time. So much trouble in the world, but here is a haven of peace. It is inevitable that this should be, unless the world is to end, and we are not there yet. We still have to wait for Moshiach, and he will only come when either utter goodness or indefatigable evil prevail.

The little synagogue emanates an atmosphere of calm and quiet joy. The congregation is intent on reciting the amidah, the standing prayer, ancient and beautiful. Eyes close, bodies sway, lips mouth silently.

Then the chazan begins the chant. 'Kadosh, kadosh, kadosh—'Holy, holy, holy . . . ,' and all rise to their toes, in emulation of the seraphim and the need to reach towards the Almighty.

The strains of song are taken up by the congregants. 'Who is like God? There is none like God,' 'Lord of the universe, you are with me, and I shall not fear.'

As the service ends, the women kiss the covers of their prayer books, which are tenderly laid on the shelves. Then they walk out, chatting, and wishing their friends a '*shabbat shalom*,' a sabbath of peace, and join the menfolk for the after-service *bracha*. A blessed meal, for the more observant of the worshippers have not yet eaten, and they look forward eagerly to breaking their fast.

The tables are, as usual, well-laden, for this is an affluent community. Cakes, biscuits, herring, and little balls of *gefilte* fish are spread out on the long tables. Cold drinks and tea are there, and one member carries round a bottle of whiskey, which he liberally pours into proffered glasses. There is laughter, and sounds of clinking cutlery, and then a fork is rapped sharply against a bottle.

'Please, please. It is time for the rabbi to talk.'

'Nu—so who's stopping him?' More laughter.

The rabbi stands behind the dais. As he leans on it, he sways forward and back.

'Good *shabbes*, everyone. It is good to see you all here, and I am looking forward to this opportunity of speaking to you.'

He pauses and takes off his glasses to clean. The lenses are thick, and his weak eyes look distorted behind them.

'I have something very important to say. You know that I do not hold back when I feel strongly about things. There are some of you who get upset, but this I must take the chance of. So, please bear with me.' He pauses, and puts his glasses back on, better to see his community.

'Tomorrow,' he said, 'is Yom ha-Shoah—the Day of the Holocaust. Now who has made this *Yom ha-Shoah*? That is what I want to know. Who has set the date for this? I will tell you—it is a secular date. It is secular people who have decided on it. Where did they get the date from? That is what I want to know.'

One of the congregants sitting at the main table bites his thumb.

'Rabbi,' he says, 'tomorrow is the anniversary of the uprising of the Warsaw Ghetto. That is what the date is.'

'And so?' asks the rabbi rhetorically. 'Firstly, it is not the date of the uprising of the Warsaw Ghetto and, secondly, what if it is? What has that to do with the Holocaust?'

'Rabbi,' says the same man patiently, 'the president of Israel will be present at the Warsaw Ghetto tomorrow to participate in its uprising. Is he wrong?'

'I'm sorry,' says the rabbi, throwing up his hands, 'but he is wrong. It is not the right date. And in any case, I ask you again, what has that to do with the Holocaust?'

The man tries again. 'It's a symbol, Rabbi,' he says. 'Six million of our people died, nameless. They simply walked into the gas ovens. At least in the Warsaw Ghetto they fought. They died, but they fought.'

The rabbi shakes his head.

'That is exactly what I am saying,' he said. 'They fought. They took up arms. Who told them to take up arms? Is this what God wanted? If God saw fit to cut off so many Jews, perhaps there was a reason for his doing so. Who can say? Is it up to me? Is it up to you?

'But I tell you this, that God did not want his people to act like the animal that slew them. If Hitler, may his name be blotted out, was the instrument of destruction, then maybe there was a reason for it.'

Now his audience is listening intently.

'What I am saying, is that it is not right that a secular date should have been set for the commemoration of the Holocaust. Do you realize that now is the month of Nissan? That there may be no *hazkorim* during this period.

'The secular may not take it upon themselves to determine God's will. I shall not be present at the memorial services for Holocaust victims at the cemetery tomorrow, and I call upon you, my congregants, not to be there either.'

There is some mumbling, but general silence, as grace is said, and the community disperses. They begin walking towards their homes, in little groups.

Suddenly from the bottom of the synagogue garden a noise is heard—voices raised in song. It is the voice of Africa. Some take no notice, simply shrug their shoulders, and walk away. But some prick up their ears, and hurry down the garden slope.

The lower lawn of the synagogue verges on the wide, multi-laned highway. Usually traffic swishes past at great speed, but today there is no traffic. Instead there are people, masses and masses of people, walking arm-in-arm, towards the city. Some are singing, but most are silent, intent on the march. They look tired, but there is a spirit that emanates tangibly from them.

'My God,' says the thin man, who is standing at the front, watching. 'These are the marchers. They have come all the way from Alexandra, and are going into the city. D'you know, that must be at least twenty kilometres? And nowhere to stop, and nothing to drink on the way. What spirit these people have!'

The marchers go by, rank after rank after rank. They stare at the onlookers standing on the verge above them. Some smile. If there has been anger, it has long since worn away.

One of the marchers raises his fist in salute. 'Peace,' he shouts, and the cry is taken up by the marching crowd. 'Peace! Khotso!' cry the marchers, amidst a forest of fists. And the thin man responds, 'Shalom!'

'Peace! Peace!'

A Jewish woman, a survivor of the Holocaust, is weeping. 'Peace!' she cries, and thrusts her hand in salute through the rows of razor wire that surround the synagogue property. The sharp little blades catch and cut her arm, and huge gouts of blood drip onto the highway below.

'Peace! Peace!'

The marchers trudge past. A contingent of military vehicles bearing soldiers, their guns at the ready, rolls along behind them.

The thin man shrugs.

'God never shows his face,' he said. 'You can only see his back, from behind.'

Tony Eprile

Letters from Doreen

Let us begin this story where it ends. Mark Spiegelman is visiting
his parents in San Diego one summer—he is out on the West Coast
for a friend's wedding—and, as always, he asks about the news
from South Africa.

At the time, he and his mother are in the kitchen putting away the
dishes. She does not answer him immediately, but instead hands
him the gravy boat and says, 'Here, you're tall. You put it away.'
Mark stretches to slide the gravy boat, still hot from the dishwash-
ing machine, onto the topmost shelf. Its warmth—as if the dish is
some living thing—is transferred to his hand.

'We think Doreen passed away,' his mother says. Mark knew his
parents had been worried about Doreen because this past year there
had been no Christmas card from her and no response to the eighty
rand they'd sent as a Christmas present.

'We got a letter from Irmgard,' his mother continues. 'She called
the Gillins, who said that they hadn't heard from Doreen and that
she must have died.'

The Gillins were the people who moved into the Spiegelmans'
flat when they left the country. 'We could use a decent girl,' Mrs.
Gillin had said. 'Can you recommend Doreen?' So Doreen went to
work for them and stayed with them until about a year ago. Since
she worked for his family for nine years and Mark had been eleven
when they left the country, he calculated that Doreen must have
worked almost twice as long for the Gillins. Still, in a recent letter
to his mother she had voiced her old complaint about Mrs. Gillin:
'She never talks to me like you used to. . . .'

'Did Irmgard say anything else?' Mark asks.

'Just the usual—prices are going up because of all the boycotts—
especially food. It's not so easy for someone living on a pension

anymore. Now that Max is dead, Irmgard really doesn't have much reason to stay in South Africa. She thinks she'll probably move back to Baden-Baden.'

A number of his mother's contemporaries, German Jews who fled to South Africa at more or less the same time she did, have been going back to the fatherland to live. Many of them get a generous pension from the German government, as well as money to simply come and visit. The German word for reparation is *Wiedergut-machung*, which translated literally means 'making good again.' Mark finds this term absurd, a bit of linguistic black humor. There are some things that can not be made good again. They become part of the past, and the world is forever changed by them.

Dearest Mam and Master:

I am keeping fine and family. I got the money at last now they tell me the money is dollars so this end is less in S.A. they gave me R36.59 that's what they gave me. So I say thanks again Sorry I could not send you a card for Pasach I could not even go to town to get one. . . . I don't know how long I will still be with the Gillin's as the work is too much for me now as they are trying to decrease the staff the days they don't come in the servants must do the flat they just to sweep do the bath-room windows. You must do the stove wash doors walls, This is what I am doing washing daily ironing, baking biscuits once a week silver (you didn't have a lot of silver) there's no lunch hour you must be ready when they get home with supper, cook for the daughter she eats here whenever they want to come. My thumb does not come right from the soap pad all the other fingers are alright. I hope you are well and family.

Love Dor.

Lately Mark has found himself asking the young white South Africans whom he meets everywhere these days, in New York, the Midwest, Washington DC: 'What happened to your nanny?' It is safe to assume that they all had one.

The usual response is to dismiss the question. It is one of those things of childhood that have been set aside.

Some of his South African peers classify themselves as Marxists and try earnestly to convince him that the real issue in South Africa is not race but capitalism, rule by elites. Late one night, Mark is standing on a street corner in Manhattan's Upper West Side talking to one of them, Peter—whom Mark likes mainly because he has the same squarish head and mole on the left cheek as Nigel Asheroff, a childhood friend.

'Of course there were some excesses in the Cultural Revolution, but that's not the point,' Peter expostulates. 'The revolution had been subverted by the intellectuals, and they had to be dealt with somehow. You shouldn't swallow everything in the capitalist press . . . all those crocodile tears about violinists planting rice.'

While they are talking, they are constantly approached by beggars. 'D'you want me to starve, is that it? You want me to starve!' says one lurching drunk who has just been dismissed by Peter with a wave of the hand. The drunk is beginning to get belligerent, but he sees other prospects and staggers off in their direction. Mark asks Peter about the black woman who brought him up: Where is she now? How long was she with them? The question annoys Peter. 'I don't know,' he responds. 'We had one woman, Bertha, who took care of us as kids, but she's gone back to the homelands now. Everyone had servants growing up; that's not the problem.'

A ragged-looking man approaches them. He fits the category of beggars to whom Mark usually tries to give money: his shoes are much worse than Mark's trodden-down sneakers. They are a size too small and he has worn down the backs with the heel of his foot. 'Go away,' Peter says. 'We're not giving you money.' But the beggar had noticed the barely perceptible motion of Mark's hand toward his pocket and says to him. 'You would have given me money, man. Come on.'

'No,' Mark responds.

'You're letting him control you,' the beggar cries, pointing toward Peter. 'He's stronger than you.'

Dearest Madam,

My self & family are keeping well. How are you & the family hope you are all fine. Wishing you all a Happy New Year & well over the fast. I last time wrote to you that I dont know how long will I still be here at Gardens I am still hanging on as times are so bad. Food, clothing are so expensive that you hardly have enough for a second helping for the kids I mean Lenora's kids they only have one meal a day, and thats in the evening when she comes home from work. She's divorced last year, her husband left his job 2 years back, does not even support the kids the law does not do anything they keep telling her to hang on. The Mainzers are on holiday oversea but I dont know where, they left the end of August I think they went for 3 or 2 moths. Shes stooping since she had the operation . . .

When, at the age of sixteen, Mark returned to South Africa after four years' absence, he immediately got in touch with Doreen. 'Hullo, Mutt,' he says in their first phone conversation. 'When am I going to see you?'

As a child, Mark was always a slow eater, often forgetting the food on his plate while he immersed himself in reverie. Doreen would sit with him, as his mother did not have the patience to watch him toy with his food. As if to make up for his lack of progress in nourishing himself, Mark had learned to read very early on, and he would read aloud to Doreen from some comic book while she periodically interjected: 'Ag, man, just eat a little of that pineapple.' Doreen's favorite was *Mutt and Jeff*, and she never got tired of the way little aggressive Jeff would lure his tall friend into some new misadventure. They came to call each other Mutt or Jeff interchangeably; sometimes Doreen was Mutt, sometimes Mark.

. . . I have been home for the holiday Johburg is hot but out there is boiling you open the windows at 4 A.M. but still its the same by 6. you open the doors you are perspiring you are wet.

I am glad you found a nice apartment, I didn't know how to write to you as I thought you moved knowing you were looking for a place Mrs. Mainzer had an op. she's much better now She's swimming daily only she stoops a little. there's nothing happening at Eden Gardens it's all quiet My family is keeping very well the 2 kids are at school, only the little at home because he's only 4. Mutt must be a good cook you know he used to ask whats that you are adding now only he must not add too much salt & swear. . . .

What amazed him in retrospect was the warmth with which African adults, almost any African adult, would respond to him as a child. Walking past throngs of black men and women in the late afternoon, his overstuffed schoolbag banging against his bare calves, Mark never felt any trace of fear . . . even when these same adults were waiting patiently, handcuffed, in line to be pushed into the next available kwela-kwela wagon for some pass infraction. There would invariably be friendly comments about any new possessions or items of clothing. 'Very nice, little master.' 'Siyakubona, mFaan.' 'You give me that bag, yesss?' Doreen, on the other hand, would mock all new acquisitions with the Afrikaans phrase, *Skilpad het a nuwe doek*. Tortoise has a new hat.

Although Doreen was officially classified as a Coloured and so was exempt from carrying a pass, it was not safe for her to leave the apartment building without some form of identification. When Mark was five she disappeared without warning for an entire weekend, returning on Monday morning sour and subdued. She had gone across the road to talk to a friend and had been picked up by policemen who did not believe she was Coloured; they thoughtfully kept her from disturbing her employers with a phone call on the weekend.

Even the African gangsters were friendly. A group of them used to regularly play dice in the back seat of an old and commodious car parked in the quiet culvert below Eden Gardens. The gamblers would give Mark and his friend from the apartment building, Lenny Mainzer, each a tickey—the thin, sensual 2 ½-penny coins of that era—to go play elsewhere and not draw attention by staring at them. Bribery had its drawbacks, however, for whenever the sharp-eyed Lenny spotted the car in the distance he wanted to go by and claim his tickey, and it was only with difficulty that Mark could draw him away.

One day they saw the police break up a similar group of gamblers who were playing excitedly beneath an oak tree beside an empty lot. A car slowed down and suddenly all four doors were flung open and athletic young policemen were upon the gamblers, who scattered in all directions. They watched as one policeman chased after a wiry African who was running 'hell for leather' still clutching several pound notes. The policeman caught up with him near where the boys were standing, grabbed him by the scruff of the neck, and doubled him up with a quick blow to the solar plexus. 'Hell,' Lenny had said, 'I want to join the police when I'm grown up.' Mark had seen the smiling policeman give the handcuffed gambler an additional sharp punch to the neck.

In the brown cardboard accordion file where Mrs. Spiegelman keeps her correspondence, Doreen's letters are easily recognizable. She always wrote on official blue aerograms, with their prominent injunctions against *insluitings* and the customary reproduction of

the Provincial Buildings in Pretoria. On his last visit to his homeland, Mark had visited these buildings, where enormous tapestries
depict the conquering of Southern Africa by the white man, and
where a sculpture of a man wrestling a bull gives rise in the accompanying free catalogue to eloquent musings on 'Liberty Curbed.' It
was odd to think of an elderly coloured woman spending one percent of a week's income on such stationery.

   . . . *we don't have a caretaker any more that old Missus Vogel she got killed
a boy hit her on the head with an axe she was taking money from all the boy's
pay-packet, and Efroom too was doing it. The police caught the boy who
killed her it was 6:30 in the morning. You remember how Voggie used to shout
at the children when they played near the flowerbeds she was always cross but
it was not nice to die like that. Shame . . .*

Mark remembers telling his mother one day how he hated Mrs.
Vogel. 'She's a lonely old woman,' his mother had said. 'She
doesn't have a husband or any children.' What about Efroom, he
had asked, isn't he her husband? Efroom was the black bossboy, a
ramrod-straight older man with a gray mustache and steel-wool
hair. He had the military bearing of a pukka Englishman and had
been 'up North' during the Second World War. He issued harsh,
peremptory orders to the servants employed by the apartment
building, punctuating his commands with a wave of the stout
wooden cane that he always carried. One day when the family was
chatting in the kitchen, the evening paper was thrust through the
partially open door leaving a bloody smear on the stove and landing
on the floor with a thud. Mrs. Spiegelman pulled open the door and
the newsboy half tumbled in, apologizing profusely. He had ridden
upstairs in the elevator instead of taking the back stairs and Efroom
had hit him on the head to teach him a lesson. Mark's mother
washed his head with a cloth that she dipped in an enamel basin
filled with warm water and Dettol. The water turned red and had to
be emptied twice. She finally located the cut—'A tiny cut, really. But
there's always so much blood from the head.'—and closed the
wound with a sticking paster.

   . . . *you remember Grace who used to work upstairs for Mrs. Mainzer she's
left now also the Harmon's girl left there's mainly young ones now they drink
and go out with tsotsis they don't like me because I don't drink with them they*

poured water under my door. Why don't you come to our parties they ask, There a lot of rubbish they cut up my uniforms when I was out, make noise all night I can't sleep I have a headache the next day. . . .

Christmas. Africans shuffle along, singing, spitting as they yell filthy imprecations that make Mark and his younger brother giggle from their hiding place on the balcony. The doorbell rings constantly as Africans arrive to claim their 'Christmas Box.' They know his mother to be a soft touch, and Africans from as far away as the pharmacy in Rosebank somehow find themselves at the Spiegelmans' door. Years later Mark can always make his parents laugh with his imitation of an African his mother doesn't recognize demanding a present. 'Hau, missis. I'm the boy for carry-it the groceries. Is me, Esteban, misses, for putting-it the food inna car. How you don't know me?'

Whenever I think of the kids I take out my Album and I have a look at the pictures I do miss you a lot but you are faraway I cant even come & visit, money's the problem. The Mainzers also went on a holiday they left the end of October. Its only the 2 of them at home here, Johnny lives in Isreal, Lenny is also still aboard its only Roy who still lives here. Did I send you a recipe of cabbage white and red with nuts? The family are all well Lenora always asks after you she got a job at last. She's by herself & the kids the husband left he's really useless he drinks too much does not see to the kids she's saving to get a divorce. Mam please when you write to Joel give him my regards.

Tell Jeff I will write to him soon.

Love to all the family.

ps I will be visiting you someday

When they used to go to the seaside, Doreen would ask the children to bring her back some ocean water in a jar. When they asked her why, Doreen told them that she liked to drink it. 'It keeps her regular,' Mrs. Spiegelman explained.

Mark would neglect to fill the empty mayonnaise jar until the last day of the holiday, remembering it only occasionally as he peered into the mesmerizing depths of tidepools, butterfly net near at hand. The closing ritual of the holiday was always that before-breakfast dash down the cliffside past the narrow-gauge railway to the beach. There he would take off his shoes and wade knee-deep into the surf to fill the jar, being careful not to get too much sand along with the seawater. Then Mark would climb slowly up the footpath back to the hotel, pausing to dig his bare feet deep into the cool red dust. When he held the jar to the sun he would see tiny particles floating in the clear water, some of them minute living creatures that propelled themselves to and fro.

They went to the same hotel every year. The first year, when Mark was seven and Joel five, was the only time Doreen had gone away with them. The first few days had been miserable, Mark and his brother having to eat in the Children's Diningroom, which was crowded and noisy with squalling children barely contained by their African nannies who simply raised their voices to converse about the appalling din. Mr. Spiegelman talked to the Indian head-waiter who said the children could eat in the adult dining room provided they 'behaved like grownups.' It meant dressing properly for each meal: tight shirt collars and wet hair brushed hard down on sensitive scalps, but the rewards were real food and the affec-tionate admiration of the waiters. Bobbie, the Indian headwaiter, would come by at each meal, raise three fingers to his lips with a smacking sound, and say, 'Good eating, yes?' while the children tried to suppress their giggles.

When they came home from holiday they would regale Doreen with the tales of their adventures. Mrs. Spiegelman would tell her how, when told that a favorite waiter had been fired because he drank, little Joel responded: 'Well, maybe he was thirsty.'

'I remember that boy,' Doreen had laughed. 'He used to always tell the children dirty stories.'

Mark would tell her all about the multicolored fish he had seen in the tide pools and how he almost stepped on a brown mamba while walking on the river path.

'Why doesn't Doreen come with us? We miss her,' he had asked his mother during their holiday. 'Because sometimes Doreen likes to see her own family,' his mother had replied.

Mark vaguely remembered meeting Doreen's daughter, Lenora. She was lanky and thin and bore little resemblance to her mother. In her arms she had carried a small child with a running nose, his head shaved against ringworm.

On his first return visit to South Africa, Mark stayed with his older sister, who lived in a Spanish-style house in the suburb of

Melrose with her husband and two children. One Thursday, the two of them went to pick up Doreen on her 'day off.' Mark, now a gangly teenager, towered over Doreen. 'Now we're really Mutt and Jeff, hey, Dor?' he said. Doreen seemed embarrassed and uneasy in his presence. She seemed even more so when they sat and had tea under his sister's pleasantly shaded verandah by the swimming pool. 'Yes, missis. Thank you, missis,' Doreen said to Eileen's offer of another biscuit with her tea. The ensuing silence was broken only by the sound of the birds thrashing among the branches of the mulberry tree. As far as Mark could remember, Doreen had always called his sister by the pet name he had given her: Dixie.

Mark told Doreen all about his job working on a bus survey for a market-research firm. Basically, the job consisted of standing on the street all day, stopping buses, and counting the number of people on each of the two decks. 'When I got the job,' he said. 'They told me that if there are coloureds on the back of the bus, I should count them as people.'

'That's nice,' Doreen said. She stood up and began to stack the dishes neatly on the tray.

'Leave it, Dor—' Dixie started to say, but her attention was distracted by her two-year-old, who was waddling toward them foaming at the mouth. She reached her fingers into his mouth and disgustedly pulled out a partially masticated garden snail, which she flicked into the bushes. The child began to wail with great heartbroken sobs, while Mark ineffectually tried to wash out its mouth with cold tea. 'He's like you, Mutt,' Doreen said happily. 'You was always putting everything in your mouth.'

Mark and Dixie took the tea things into the kitchen, Mark almost dropping the full tray as his eyes adjusted from the bright sunlight of the garden to the cool darkness of the house's interior. 'Yuck, a snail,' Dixie said as she ran hot water over the dishes in the sink. When they returned outside, Avi was sitting on Doreen's capacious lap staring at her with wondering eyes as she sang softly to him in Afrikaans.

While in college in the United States, Mark studies Modern Poetry with the thought that someday he would like to be a poet. The first poem he ever memorized was a ditty in 'Kitchen Dutch' and was taught to him by Doreen. It goes like this:

Ouma en Oupa sit op die stoep,
Oupa let off a helluva poep,
Ouma se: Wat makeer?
Oupa se: My maag is seer.

This ditty about Oupa's stomach ailments resurfaces at inappropriate times in Mark's life—during an exam, in the middle of a serious conversation, while making love. For no reason at all, he will find himself waking up in the middle of the night chortling, '*My maag is seer*.' (My stomach hurts.) He remembers how when he would come home tearful from a fall, knees badly scraped from crashing his bike in some daredevil game, Doreen would start him laughing by asking in Afrikaans what was wrong: *Wat makeer?*

. . . *I have to wash doors, walls, do washing. the boy only does the stove, windows and sweep.* . . . *I really enjoyed my holiday at Potch even though it was so hot. Here in Joburg it rain now & again even now its raining. Killarney is no more save, too many muggings, Robbery & Killings going on, nearly all the flats are & buildings are fenced with guards during the day & night they are busy here now.*

. . . *tell Dixie I am happy she's well and about again. I am earning R90 now but things clothing, food is too expensive plus tax. Hope the family Master you and the Boys are all fine.*

Good night
Love to all the family
Love also from the family.

Mark is watching television in his apartment in New York City. On the news there is a brief feature on a demonstration at the University of Cape Town. The censors have been forced to temporarily let up, thanks to a court order, and this is the first live footage in a while. We see some students shouting slogans, marching around with banners. Suddenly we see the police firing tear gas, running forward. A young girl drops her banner and starts to run. A policeman quickly catches up with her and begins to beat her in that near-comic slow motion of real violence. We see the whip rise and fall, rise and fall. The girl is slim and blond. She sits down, hugs herself as if she is cold. The policeman runs on. The scene changes to another riot in a township. Small black children dart out from between shacks and toss stones with the accuracy of champion cricketers. Howzat! A policeman crumples to the ground and is hustled into a truck. A spiderweb appears across the windshield of the photographers' van. End of footage.

I dont know will I be able to move back to Potch when I leave the Gillins the government says you are too dark you have to live in the bantustan. I went to see your friend Mr Bernstein you know the one whose a lawyer his brother is in the same office. He said Doreen its nonsense you can live there if you want they cant stop you. I don't know what it means I can live with Lenora but she has the kids her place is too small. . . .

Mark goes to visit his former roommate, Saul, on 95th Street, where, coincidentally another South African has moved into the room Mark vacated. 'Give these South African Jews a foothold and you can't get rid of them,' Saul joked.

'Hey, how's it?' Danny, the replacement South African, says. 'You've got to see this book. A friend of mine at Ravan just sent it to me.'

The book is a collection of drawings done by children in Soweto. Like most children's drawings, these are crude: stick figures, the perspective misjudged so that people are larger than houses. And what are the children of Soweto drawing today? Look, this is a policeman shooting at your brother. Here are children crying from tear gas. Here some children play with the nice police dog. See how sharp his teeth are. Here is a policeman being 'throwed on with stones.' Here is a Casspir armored vehicle in the schoolyard. Here is a funeral. Here is a funeral. Here is a funeral.

Dearest Madam & fam.

Thanks very much for the letter and contents which is 20 rand thanks again it came in very handy I am going to buy myself something very nice. The weather is very hot its really boiling you can hardly sleep at night. I had a lovely Xmas & a very happy New Year only it was too short, I didn't see everybody I wanted to see but I enjoyed it anyhow. I am alright now, you know the doctor was wrong I havent got heart trouble thats what the doctor said at the hospital he's a German. What I really have is high blood pressure I go to the hospital once a month for tablets. I am happy that you are nearer to Dixie. The kids must be big. Eden Mews the Mews, Gardens are all sold out only some of the old tenants move out, but nearly everyone bought his own flat. I am happy that you're all still well especially Master. . . .

Mark's sister, Dixie, also lives in San Diego now. Mark is visiting her when some other South Africans come over to spend the afternoon. One who is just visiting the area is Beryl, Dixie's childhood friend, who has children the same age as her own. Beryl is slim and attractive, though her skin is a little dry and taut across her face and lines crinkle outward from the corners of her eyes, the legacy of years of playing tennis in the sun. Avi, who is now nine, always liked Beryl's maid, and he asks: 'How is Selma?'

'I've got another Selma now,' Beryl replies, turning to arrange food on a tray. Mark winks at his nephew who is looking nonplussed and twists his index finger in the direction of his forehead. The child grins, understanding now.

Mark joins his parents out on the verandah where they are telling his brother-in-law, Arthur, about Doreen.

'I don't know,' Arthur muses. 'I'd hate to think people assumed I was dead every time I haven't written to them for a while. Maybe she just got tired of writing to her old master and missis. Maybe her daughter told her to stop. Lots of things could have happened.'

His parents are indignant at this idea. After all, they have been corresponding with her for almost twenty years and this is the first time she has failed to send a Christmas card or acknowledge the money they have sent her. 'And besides,' his mother says, 'we sent her a fair amount of money every year. I'm sure it came in very handy. How can we go on sending her money if she doesn't write back to us?'

. . . Master must be happy with the swimming pool as he likes to swim you know that old lady at Eden Mansions remember the one who looks like she's got a hunch I dont know if shes German or Hollander she always talked to you at the swimming pool she died 2 weeks back the husband died a year ago. Love to Dixie and the family. . . .

There is quite a community of South Africans living in this part of Southern California. In the manner of immigrants everywhere, all it takes is for a couple of families to establish a foothold for others to quickly follow. And then, the weather is almost identical to that of Johannesburg, allowing for a lifestyle in which swimming and tennis playing feature prominently. Dixie invites Mark to a 'citizenship party' held at the home of one such resident, Beryl's sister, Shareen.

'You've never been to the Sillimans' place, have you?' Dixie asks. 'Well, there'll be a little surprise for you there.'

The surprise turns out to be that the Sillimans have brought their coloured servant Sofi with them to America. Sitting on the attractive outdoor patio with its swimming pool and view of a sagebrush- and scrub-filled canyon, Mark watches Sofi move among the guests with a tray of hors d'oeuvres. 'It's *déjà vu* all over again,' he says to his father. As if on cue, the hostess calls out: 'Sofi, my girl, just bring me one of those cold drinks, quick now.'

Mark wonders where Sofi stays. Does she have a little room to herself in the house or are there some servants' quarters on the grounds? Does she perhaps live in the Mexican neighborhood and ride a bus to her missis' house?

He remembers how he and Lenny had once gone over to the servants' quarters in The Mews, the oldest section of flats in the Eden complex. They had noticed an open window in one of the rooms and had climbed up the drainpipe to peer inside. The interior of the servant's room was disappointing; it smelled musty and stale and there was no mystery to the cramped space with its iron bedstead, humble bedside table, and ancient radio. Their expedition was not a complete failure, though. A maid from the Mews spotted them and she chased them several hundred yards, swatting at them with a rolled-up magazine and calling them cockroaches.

Mark finds himself in conversation with a pasty-faced South African girl of about his own age who works in advertising. She tells him she is not really worried about events in South Africa.

'You see, my parents have a flat in London. So if things get really bad they can always move there.' She confides that she herself left because 'you just can't make money there anymore.' Luckily the host is calling everybody to gather around him, and Mark is able to extricate himself from having to make further polite conversation. The party is in honor of the fact that the Sillimans have just been granted U.S. citizenship, and now an enormous three-tier cake in the colors of the American flag is brought out. The guests' doubts as to whether to salute the cake or eat it is quickly dispelled by the host carving triangular shaped wedges in it with a large knife. Mark takes a piece of what turns out to be mainly vanilla ice cream and goes to sit with his mother, who is deep in conversation with Sofi.

'I'm saving money so's I can buy one of those little houses in

Dube,' Sofi is saying. 'But it's lonely here, missis. I wish I could leave tomorrow.'

Later, Sofi shows Lena Spiegelman some black-and-white snapshots of her grandchildren. Mark glances over their shoulders to get a glimpse of a tall, thin African child looking shyly to the right of the camera, his hand resting on his smaller brother's shoulder. 'And this one must be Vusi?' his mother is saying, while Sofi beams with pleasure.

Mark's father is amused. The previous night he and his wife had argued for a long time over the fact that a friend of theirs was extremely upset that her son had married a Zulu woman. Charles had remarked that the woman was just being prejudiced; as long as the son's wife was a decent person, what did it matter what color she was? Mark's mother had disagreed. She felt that there were always problems when people of different backgrounds married.

'You know,' Charles says now, 'your mother is the only person I know who can spend the afternoon talking to the maid without making it seem like condescension.'

'I think she can get away with it,' he adds, after some thought, 'because she's really not a liberal.'

Dearest Mam & Master,

I hope this letter to find you in good health. Wishing you a very happy holiday over the week and a happy Easter. Sorry for having delayed so long to write and say thanks for what you are doing for me. Its because I have been in hospital for 3 weeks I went for a check up and they kept me there saying my high blood was too low they kept me from the 27 March I only got discharged on Saturday 14th April They gave me tablets for my high blood. I was alright all of a sudden the nurses gave me different tablets till I left. They gave the right ones and the other 2 kinds which they gave me there which I dont know I know which is the right ones, on arriving home they phoned I must throw the other 2 pks away as they are the wrong ones. I went to hosp. again I went to the physiartricist yesterday I still do not feel right. I only hope for the best. Please thank Joel, Mark, Master not forgetting yourself for everything you are doing for me. Mrs Gillin got me the money from the Standard Bank. Thanks also to master for the note he enclosed for me. When phoning to Dixie, Joel give them my regards. . . .

Mark's parents are told about a low-priced package tour and they make their first trip back to South Africa in fifteen years. On their first night back in the States, Mark talks to them on the telephone. They sound hoarse and exhausted, the tour was 'an absolute whirlwind, no time to even catch our breath,' they tell him.

'I'd forgotten how beautiful the country is,' his father says. 'And we saw the most magnificent game at Kruger. You would have loved it.'

'We went back to Eden Gardens,' his mother chimes in from another extension. 'It was very different, everything was locked up and you had to ring a bell at the main entrance just to get in. So we rang the bell and this huge African with a bald head opened it and says: "What do you want?" Then he looks at us and yells "One-Oh-Five," and he throws his arms around your father.'

'It was Suleiman,' Mr. Spiegelman says. This was the day watchman who used to shout at Mark for riding a bicycle in the parking garage, back when they lived in 105 Eden Gardens. 'Oh, he was so happy to see us. He kept asking "How's Mark? How's Joel?" It was quite touching.'

'I asked him about Doreen,' Mark's mother adds. 'He also thought she must have died. He said she went funny in the head toward the end, but I'm not sure I believe him. Suleiman was always such a liar.'

. . . *Winter is closing in we only get rain now some days its hot some days cold The kids are wearing jerseys to school already coming home tying them around their waists. They are all keeping well. I am going to buy myself warm underwear and a coat with my present you know I am always cold in winter although I like winter because in summer I always get those hot flashes.*

Thank you for all you are doing for me love to master not forgetting yourself tell Mutt to not be so lazy and write the money was R89.60.

Love Dor.

Pieter-Dirk Uys

Evita—the Legend

'Drop Evita Bezuidenhout or we'll kill you!'

This was on my answering machine the morning after the night I had carelessly spoken of my plans to write her biography. Someone stuck her indiscretion into the evening newspaper as a bit of fluff at the rear end of other woolly rubbish that passed for 'nonpolitical news.' The rest of the still smugly self-censored paper was full of blood-curdling facts and graphic images of 'democratically bound and gagged' South Africa, at the end of 1988.

The guttural threat was not the first I had received and I was sure it wouldn't be the last. The recent revelations that even the City Council of Johannesburg secretly spied on people like myself, whom they regarded as 'subversive' ratepayers, made it even more clear that anything was possible in my country. I had already taken to flushing the toilet twice before use, just in case the ablutions inspector had a periscope up the poo-poo pipe.

So they would kill me if I didn't drop Evita Bezuidenhout! I remembered how that was often the reaction from some prissy critics when I started impersonating this national monument on stage. 'Kill her off or she'll take over,' they clucked, patting me patronisingly on the arm while wondering whether I went to bed wearing what I imagined the real Evita would sleep in.

And when they managed to kill me, if I didn't 'drop Evita Bezuidenhout,' who would come to my funeral? Those critics, to affirm that they were right after all? Would she herself find a moment in her busy schedule to come to the graveyard and say thanks for the interest I had shown in her life? It actually goes beyond mere interest, this involvement of mine in the life of an extraordinary Afrikaans woman from a tribe of remarkable people, who are either loved or hated, but cannot be ignored. Somehow we'd become quite deeply involved through the years, as she rose to prominence, perfumed and proud, prejudiced and powered, her high-heels puncturing the rotting flesh of the victims lining the granite under her feet.

Evita Bezuidenhout, darling of the nation!

Evita, the Lorelei of the National Party!

Evita, the Bitch Goddess that made soap-opera queens look like humble nuns in the slums of India's cities.

Evita (whose name was difficult at birth), avid supporter of charities and politics she didn't really care about. A woman of many parts, all of them working overtime and each more dangerous than the other. As someone bluntly put it: a woman with balls.

Was she worth dying for?

She'd always been the most tempting figure to send up on stage with her large hats and gloves and church bazaar clothes, her lilting Afrikaans accent pushing every sentence into an upward inflection, her sweet quasi–Vivien Leigh smile, her icy Darth Vader disdain, her thinly camouflaged involvement with the lethal inner circle of South African politics.

Could someone called Evita in the 80's be far from the blueprint passed down from one Mrs. Peron to the next?

Since 1981, her character became for me a convenient mouth-piece for saying what people in the audience expected but, in the sa-tirical context of theatre, heard with a different ear. She became my clown with Reality her purple hair and Familiarity her large red nose.

She said factual things, not funny things, because apartheid is the most unamusing thing in the world, coming a close second to the grim experience of Auschwitz. The day that Jews produce a musical about the death camps and call it *What a Gas* is the day that apartheid can venture a little 'knock-knock' joke.

But the absurd horror of an 'intelligent,' 'Christian,' and 'civi-lized' white society living with apartheid as their umbrella is terri-bly, hideously, repulsively funny. When a Group Areas Act enforces racially determined living space and this becomes 'normal,' bad, bad jokes and sick, sick gags are the only medicine to fight the deadly virus.

But is it worth dying merely to expose—through her costume, hairstyle, and familiar wholesome 'holiness'—a minor chink in the decaying armour of Afrikaner Nationalism? I could lose an eye, half a mind or a life half-lived.

How would they kill me? Recent Security Force death-squad members, with quaint names like 'Peaches' and 'Slang,' bragged about their dubious achievements which included hanging a dead baboon fetus at the front door of Archbishop Desmond Tutu's home. Was I in for an aardvark's afterbirth? Or would they stop pulling the wool over the public's eyes and get down to what they did so well?

Shoot me from a passing stolen car?

Poison my box of colourful Smarties?

And then, sweet heaven and my last will and testament forbid, will Mrs. Evita Bezuidenhout turn up at my funeral, dressed to kill in basic black with hat, bag, gloves, and just enough pretty white pearls to remind us who was in charge of the masses? Will she leave her bodyguard at the car and come and stand just close enough to the open grave so that I can see her half smile through the thin veil over her face? Will she say 'Only I get away with murder, *skattie*,' as the first clods crash over my face, blocking the view of the orange, white, and blue sky?

Is that her laugh?

I can't make it out. A taunting whisper enters the space left by my fleeting soul. 'Goodbye *skattie*,' she chuckles, 'but remember that I'm still here!'

As I'm finally buried and gone, she turns to the waiting media and weeps ever so slightly, keeping the sun—her least favourite keylight—up to the right where it glows to her advantage. She bids a noble farewell to the notorious assassin of her character and the polluter of the great Afrikaner dream.

She has learnt to conjure up compassion for page one for the colour supplements. Her black outfit contrasts sharply with the ice-white of her large Cadillac convertible, the limp South African flag hanging post-coitally from the silver bonnet pole. 'Yes,' she purrs, loudly enough for the soundman from NBC to get a clean reading, 'I suppose I will miss him. He tried to make a fool of me and my family, by dressing up and copying me on the stages of our country and abroad. Of course it hurt. I'm human after all. He was very vicious and cruel and yet strangely, even for a third-rate comedian, not at all funny.'

She lets 'that smile,' so treasured by photographers, flit slowly across her sad face, the cameras click-click-clicking a hungry rumba on her cheekbones.

'But then is it not the final proof of our freedom of speech here in South Africa that this Pieter-Dirk Uys was allowed to go so far with so little? Believe me, if our jails weren't so full, he would've been locked up years ago.'

She glances back at my rapidly filling grave.

'Well, at least he had nice legs . . .'

Even living as I did so far away from the centre of the European world, growing up in a sleepy garden suburb nestled in a forest on the edge of the Cape Flats, I always had an awareness of something dark and unmentionable in the past. My mother was from Berlin. There was a cluster of elegant photo-albums in one of our bookshelves and I'd often carefully page through them. The sepia photos had laminated edges, stuck into elaborate corner-mountings, and between each page was a thin sheet of moulded tissuepaper, sometimes with spiderwebs embossed across it, other times covered in the wisps of roses and leaves. And there would be a young woman who became my mother, posed at the Brandenburg Gate, elegant and laughing in her twenties fashion, cloche hat and furcollar protecting her against the winter. And while all was in severe monochrome, I could always see the colour of her eyes. She grew up during that period of madness and mayhem, the time of Cabaret and Mar-lene, until the Nazi authorities started insisting that before she could call herself a concert pianist, she was first and foremost a Jew. So her Aryan friends drove her to Bremenhaven and she got on a boat and came to Cape Town where her parents had already settled. 'It would all blow over within a few months,' they told her in Germany. She left her life in Europe with ten shillings in her pocket and a Berlin telephone book in her hand. It took me years to work out why? It's now so obvious: so that she had the addresses of all her friends at home. She never went home again. She found a new home. That telephone book is still on our piano. The only damage to it is what my mother herself did. She carved a hole out of the thick cardboard cover and threw away the swastika that squatted in the centre like a spider of death.

You are now leaving the Republic of South Africa
You are entering the Republic of Bapetikosweti

I passed this black-on-yellow sign four times during my drive to the South African Embassy in the independent homeland Republic of

Bapetikosweti. There were eight pieces of this barren, dusty former bantustan scattered over the lushness of white South Africa. A ninth piece was rumoured to have been washed out to sea during one swift and unexpected flood, probably the divine answer to some sweaty prayer meeting in the local Dutch Reformed Church:

'Dear God, send another great flood to rid us of all these Kaffirs. The Ark is ready with two of everything. Two microwaves, two washing-machines, two BMWs, two PCs, two Swiss bank accounts.'

I never believed that we Afrikaners had a private hot-line to heaven. Outside of my relatively normal home life (my mother was a Jewish refugee from Nazi Germany and had tasted racism like blood in her mouth), I was brought up like all other Afrikaans kids in that decayed Christian 'Much Deformed Church' that propagated apartheid as an eleventh commandment. Having thus successfully been molested as a child by both Christian Nationalist Education and politically organized religion, the shocking idea of a God with a sense of humour frightened me even more than the blasphemy of a Goddess with a black skin.

God Almighty had chosen our Afrikaner forefathers that art now in heaven, hallowed be their names: Founder Jan van Riebeeck, Voortrekkers Piet Retief and Andries Pretorius, President Paul Kruger, General Hertzog, to mention but a few from the official history books. Then came the Gods of our *boere* Olympus, the holy leaders of the Afrikaner Empire: Premiers D. F. Malan, J. G. Strydom, Hendrik F. Verwoerd, and Balthazar John Vorster; and State Presidents P. W. Botha and F. W. de Klerk. The six horsemen of the *Boerewors* Apocalypse, foster fathers each of their own new enlightened brand of apartheid, and leaders of the chosen few that made up our democracy of less than one million voters out of thirty million souls. Democracy and Christianity: two simple words that have never enjoyed their honest meaning in South Africa.

South Africa.

It is the most beautiful country in the world. The nicest people live here and I know them; the jokes are the funniest and I steal them. The food tastes the best, the flowers bloom the longest, the sun is the safest, the air the cleanest (or used to be). The maids are the cheapest, the garden-boys the best, the education is the easiest, the Afrikaans language the greatest. The rhythm of the black dancers is the most exportable. The past is the most interesting, the future the most exciting, and the politics the most appalling in the world.

We never spoke about that past. We often asked her about the other life and she would briefly talk about it as if it belonged to another era, another world, another person. I was too young and frankly being brought up in an Afrikaans school, the only confusion I felt was from the names I was called by others. Because I spoke English some called me a 'Rooinek'; because my mother was German some called me a 'Nazi.' And when I played with the English-speaking kids, because of my Afrikaans background I was a 'boer'!

The Bezuidenhouts never liked Jews.

Aalwyn and Bettie had for years simply tolerated those rich Cohens and loud Bernsteins down in Laagerfontein because they so successfully ran the banking section of the town's business centre, and imported most of the best clothes from Johannesburg. Money and material—that was allowed them, and a cordial relationship was maintained between the overlords at Liefdesbodem and the Jews of Laagerfontein, although within memory no Jew had visited the estate by invitation.

Ouma Ossewania Poggenpoel had a very simple philosophy which she drummed into her daughters from an early age: 'Remember, the English are your arch-enemies, the Catholics are the anti-Christ and the Jews are all thieves.'

She never mentioned blacks.

In fact, the Bezuidenhouts never mentioned the blacks either. The blacks seemed to have been accepted by all as just part of the scenery which, apart from the occasional flood or drought, would always stay the same. Evangelie and Baby had been brought up to carefully avoid Jews as one of those groups of non-Afrikaans people that would only bring trouble with them if they were taken into the bosom of the family, the school, or—God forbid—the Church.

Their teacher had explained to them once how the Jews had killed Jesus, and had said that a man called Hitler had almost managed to do the job properly. Evangelie had never found what job that was, but from the films of the day, she realized that whatever it was that those Germans had done, it was not liked by the Jewish people in Hollywood. She would cut out all the pictures from

The Ten Commandments that appeared weekly in the *Stage and Cinema* and paste them in her Bible Study Book. She couldn't help noticing that Charlton Heston, who played Moses, looked Jewish. So did all the princesses of Egypt and Sodom and Gomorrah. Gina Lollobrigida as the Queen of Sheba and Yul Brynner as Solomon also looked Jewish.

It was part of the Zionist conspiracy, the dominee had once told them down in Laagerfontein at a fund-raising tea-party for the D.R. Church. He had to speak softly because the Bernsteins were donating a lot of goods to be sold that day. One didn't want to hurt their feelings. Evita and Hasie kept their distance from the merchants and bankers of the district, although Mrs Bezuidenhout secretly envied Mrs Cohen her wonderful, thick black hair and those nails she always seemed to keep so perfectly groomed.

'She's probably half-coloured,' Ossewania snorted when her daughter pointed out the attractive shopkeeper's wife in Neethling Street. 'They are all mixed up from Turks and negroes and Arabs. Sis!'

It didn't really matter that Mrs Cohen was from Cape Town, born and bred under the watchful eye of Christian Nationalist Education, and had never been to Israel. The fact that the Cohens and the Bernsteins were strong supporters of the National Party in their annual donations and their unquestioned vote, election after election, never seemed to count in their favour.

Hymie Bernstein decided to stand as the N P candidate in Laagerfontein. It was a great shock to everyone to see an English-speaker and, worse than that, a Jew, standing for the N P. But Mr Bernstein told the constituents at a meeting that he knew what it was like to be repressed. His own family had not been allowed to own land because they were Jews, and had been forced to wear yellow stars and carry special passes because of their religion. Some of them had been exterminated in the concentration camps. Never would the world succeed in doing to him what Hitler had done to his family. He was a very good Nationalist.

'He won the election in Laagerfontein for the N P. Of course Hasie was very sarcastic about the Bernstein victory. I remember him saying: "How can a Jew who escaped the Nazis support apartheid?", but I don't think Hasie was being serious as we all knew that none of us Nationalists were supporting apartheid any longer. 'We gave the Bernsteins a celebration party at Liefdesbodem. Now that they represented the Party in Parliament, it didn't seem to matter that they were Jewish. Why, they even ate some of the pork ribs that Oom Aalwyn had specially braai'd for them, which just shows how the newspapers can tell lies about Jews not eating pork.'

She only went back to Germany in 1957, because her then-fiancé had met a younger woman and married her. He'd survived the War. His wife became one of my sister and my great friends. She only died a couple of years ago, in Wiesbaden. The most extraordinary link. Through her we found out an enormous amount about the secret personality behind what we thought was mother; of the letters she wrote back to Germany in which she said how disgusted she was by the 'Whites Only' signs and how upset she was to be part of something that she fled and suddenly—a victim of that terrible anti-semitism becomes exactly the sort of person who sits on a 'Whites Only' bench. She was completely aware of it in the letters. Never to us. We never spoke about it.

She had a close circle of friends in Cape Town, many from Germany, most of them also refugees, or as one would always say, 'new South Africans.' 'We didn't run away from Hitler,' he told me once. 'We ran towards Table Mountain!'

As kids we were never told when to go to bed or how to behave when guests came to dinner. The unbroken rule was: you can listen as long as you like, but you don't join into the adult conversation. Often I'd scamper up to my room above to listen to Mark Saxon on Springbok Radio, with one ear strained to hear the wonderful stories below about the former life in that clouded universe called Europe. Sometimes I'd even fall asleep on the wooden floorboards, my ear pressed against the crack between the planks listening to the treasures of their anecdotes and experiences.

I was about twelve when a woman arrived to visit my mother and to meet for the first time my father. I could sense that this was something very special. It frightened me to feel so much emotion, and only many years later in my forties, have I understood for the first time that passion and the pain. This woman, Freda, had been a close friend of my mother's in Berlin. She'd disappeared one day and no one could find her. They eventually wrote to my mother that Freda had been sent to a concentration camp because she was a

Jew. That was the end of that. Then in the early 1960s, Freda came to find her best friend in Cape Town and show her that life had won the terrible battle against Nazi death. She then visited often, usually in the morning when my mother didn't have piano pupils or recital broadcasts. I'd try and bunk school whenever I could and was there when Freda arrived one teatime and sat in the musicroom. I came in to say hello and she laughed at my feeble attempt to pretend that I had a cold.

It was then that I saw the numbers tattoo'ed on her wrist.

'Is that a phone number?' I asked.

I remember my mother getting up and leaving the room very upset, possibly angry at me for asking, but Freda didn't seem to mind. She looked at the number on her wrist. She laughed and said, 'if I phone now, there'll be nobody there to answer.' Then she told me about the deathcamps. I'd never heard about that detail of the war. I'd never realised that my mother had escaped with her life to give me life, and had lost so many of her family and friends.

I don't know what a spoilt twelve-year-old Afrikaans Calvinist child looks like when faced with such true stories of horror. I remember Freda taking my finger and tracing over the terrible numbers. Then she smiled and said: 'And do you know what I remember the clearest from those times? How we laughed! How we made jokes, terrible shocking jokes about terrible unspeakable things that were being done to us and there was no one to save us, or help us, except ourselves. The terrible jokes made us brave . . .'

It's taken forty years for me to understand what she meant. And although you can't see it, I know as I rub my fingertips along my wrist that Freda's number is still there, ready for me to dial whenever I'm frightened.

Ironically, it was Evita and Hasie who saw the Wailing Wall in Jerusalem before Mrs Cohen did. 'As true as God, I just don't believe it,' Mrs Cohen said, clasping her manicured, beringed hands together. 'You are going to Israel. Oi, to die for!'

Evita smiled 'that smile' and tried to make sense of her nasal accent and strange, outlandish phrases. Israel? All she knew about it was what Paul Newman had showed her in Exodus. She had liked the music from that film, but did not find all the dust and ruins and Arabs and Jews very appealing. The idea of a sea that was dead quite revolted her. Mrs Cohen was just too happy to fill in the gaps in her knowledge of the Holy Land. She actually phoned Evita at Liefdesbodem on Tuesday and invited her to meet her and Mrs Bernstein at the Nuwe Koffiehuis in Neethling Street, where they could have a chat about 'things.'

Mrs Bernstein had lost most of her family in those Nazi concentration camps and was very supportive of Israel. Mrs Cohen gave Evita two books and a copy of her itinerary for a trip to the Holy Land that had never come off. It was quite fascinating. Evita suddenly realized that she would actually be walking the paths that Jesus Christ had trodden all those centuries before. He and a few million tourists. She would see the Wailing Wall, the site of the Temple, the Mount where the sermon had taken place, and the desert where He had spent those forty days and nights. It was Hollywood come true, and she would be Mary Magdalene.

'You must swim in the Dead Sea,' Golda Meir said to Evita while stirring furiously at the large pot on her crowded stove. 'You will not sink. I promise you, dahlink, you will stay afloat no matter what happens.'

She lifted the spoon out of the pot carefully, sniffed at the content, and then held it out to Evita.

'Here dahlink, taste.'

Evita tasted. It was delicious.

'I must have this recipe, Mrs Meir, it's wonderful. What is it?'

'I call it Golda's Surprise. Every time it turns out slightly different. I'm glad this time we've been lucky.'

She poured the liquid into three earthenware bowls and served them on the kitchen table. Hasie, Evita's husband, was in the other room with General Moshe Dayan. Mrs Meir called through in Hebrew. 'Dayan, come eat. Leave the problems till after dinner.'

General Dayan strode into the small kitchen. Evita's heart jumped. Kirk Douglas in *Spartacus*?

Kirk Douglas fixed her with his one good eye.

'I've been explaining our problem to your husband,' he said with a smile. 'He said it was similar to yours. I didn't realize you Afrikaners also have an Arab problem.'

'Don't tease the girl, Dayan!' muttered Golda.

'I'm teasing you, Mrs Bezoodn . . .'

He gave up.

'Ag, just call me Evita,' she said graciously.

'Oi, please, one Evita this century is enough. We'll call you something else,' laughed Golda. 'From now on you are Dahlink! When in doubt, always say dahlink.'

Dahlink laughed too.

'In Afrikaans that's *skattie*,' she said.

'*Skattie*?' tried Golda Meir. 'Say no more, *Skattie* it is.'

And so two small-town Afrikaans anti-Semitic bigots spent the most wonderful evening of their year, if not their decade, in the crowded kitchen of one of the most remarkable women in history. They laughed at each other's countries and jokes, and they told endless stories. They sang melancholy songs and they pondered imponderable problems. And somewhere along the line, during that evening of grand détente, the square, brown, unmarked envelope that John Vorster had placed in the diplomatic pouch and handed to Hasie to guard with his life, changed hands without any fuss. The nuclear secrets that had been tested and proved in laboratories deep under the rock of the Transvaal eventually ended up in laboratories deep under the Sinai Desert, and South Africa and Israel were a little step closer in their common aim.

A bomb to end all bombs!

'A bomb? What nonsense!' scoffed the Ambassador when I showed her the clipping from the *New York Times* alleging South Africa's collaboration with Israel in this very matter.

'It was 1967. If they had had the bomb then, would there have been all that loss of Israeli life during those wars with Egypt? I remember telling Mrs Meir that there was only one way to handle the problems of a rebellious majority.'

She paused.

I waited.

She thought.

I wondered.

She spoke.

'Negotiation and dialogue,' she said.

She lied.

'A six-day war. There was a lesson to be learnt somewhere, but I don't know quite what. A handful of brave Jews against millions of

barbaric Arabs, protecting the Land of God against the Moham-
medan invaders. It just shows what you can do with your back
against the wall,' Evita Bezuidenhout said twenty-three years later.
The problems which had caused that Middle Eastern war had multi-
plied by the 90s and had been met with tried-and-true brutality.

Golda was gone, and so was Dayan.

Ironically the Jews of Israel had inherited the blood-soaked man-
tle of oppression so slyly dropped by F. W. de Klerk when he became
the new King of the Boers. Throughout the civilized world posters
previously screaming 'FREE MANDELA' now read 'Free Palestine.'

Evita ignored the battle scars of both chosen peoples. 'Anything
is possible if you have the Will. Even God can be convinced. Once
that Will is gone, you find yourself sinking, even in the Dead Sea.
And God will drown with you.'

She got up and looked at her watch.

'I can't talk more today. Here is the diary you asked for. 1967?'
She handed me the small book tied with a pink civil service ribbon.

'It starts after our return from Israel. John Vorster went back to
Koffiefontein, where the Brits had locked him up during the war
years because of his sympathies with Hitler's Germany. What an
irony. After visiting an Israeli museum which described what happened to Mrs Bernstein's family at Auschwitz, there we were celebrating the memories of an internment camp in our own land.'

The sound of motor bikes revving loudly made her part the lace
curtains. Outside, in the courtyard, a couple of young men in khaki
uniforms were straddling their motor bikes. Izan Bezuidenhout
had brought his friends home to watch a video of AWB leader
Eugene Terre'blanche's most recent speech, again ironically at the
site of the Koffiefontein Campe.

There Terre'blanche had called for an all-out war against the
enemies of the Boer state—the ruling National Party and the major
pretender to the throne of the land, the ANC. The crippled swastika
of the AWB fluttered on the mudguards of the bikes.

Evita Bezuidenhout watched her son lead the motley collection of
young fascists out of the paged square and across the border into
South Africa proper to roar off into the afternoon. She sighed like
so many millions of mothers throughout history.

Golda Meir would weep if she saw this. But I know she's not
looking, wherever she is. Probably washing her hair . . .

Albie Sachs

EXCERPT FROM Soft Vengeance
of a Freedom Fighter

I

Oh shit. Everything has abruptly gone dark, I am feeling strange and cannot see anything. The beach, I am going to the beach, I packed a frosty beer for after my run, something is wrong. Oh shit, I must have banged my head, like I used to do when climbing Table Mountain in Cape Town, dreaming of the struggle, and cracking my cranium against an overhang. It will go away, I must just be calm and wait. Watered the tropical pot-plants, stared at the ten heads on the giant African sculpture in my beautiful apartment. Oh shit, how can I be so careless? The darkness is not clearing, this is something serious, a terrible thing is happening to me, I am swirling, I cannot steady myself as I wait for consciousness and light to return. I feel a shuddering punch against the back of my neck, and then what seems like another one. The sense of threat gets stronger and stronger, I am being dominated, overwhelmed. I have to fight, I have to resist. I can feel arms coming from behind me, pulling at me under my shoulders. I am being kidnapped, they have come from Pretoria to drag me over the border and interrogate me and lock me up. This is the moment we have all been waiting for, the few ANC members still working in Mozambique, with dread and yet with a weird kind of eagerness.

'Leave me,' I yell out. 'Leave me.'

I jerk my shoulders and thrash my arms as violently as I can. I always wondered how I would react, whether I would fight physically, risking death, or whether I would go quietly and rely on my brain and what moral courage I had to see me through.

'Leave me alone, leave me alone,' I demand violently, aware that I am shouting in both English and Portuguese, the official language of this newly independent state where I have been living for a decade. I've forgotten my Afrikaans after twenty years in exile, I'm screaming for my life yet with some control, some politeness, since after all I am a middle-aged lawyer in a public place.

'I would rather die here, leave me, I'd rather die here.'

I feel a sudden surge of elation and strength as I struggle, making an immense muscular effort to pull myself free. I might be an intellectual but at this critical moment without time to plan or think I am fighting bravely and with the courage of the youth of Soweto even though the only physical violence I have personally known in my life was as a schoolboy being tackled carrying a rugby ball. I hear voices coming from behind me, urgent, nervous voices not talking but issuing and accepting commands, and they are referring to me.

The darkness is total, but still I hear tense staccato speech.

'Lift him up, put him there.'

I am not a him, I am me, you cannot just cart me around like a suitcase. But I am unable to struggle any more, I just have to go along and accept what happens, my will has gone.

We are travelling fast, the way is bumpy, how can they leave me in such discomfort, if they are going to kidnap me at least they could use a vehicle with better springs. I have no volition, I cannot decide anything or even move any part of me. But I have awareness, I think, therefore I am. The consciousness fades and returns, swirls away and comes back, I am lying down like a bundle, there is a point in my head that is thinking, and then oblivion and then awareness again, no thought related to action, but passive acknowledgement that my body is being transported somewhere, that I exist, even if without self-determination of any sort. I wonder if we have reached the South African border yet, I wonder who my captors are, what their faces look like, do they have names? This darkness is so confusing.

More urgent voices, speaking with rapid energy, treating me as an object, to be lifted and carried and moved this way and that . . . I feel the muscles and movements of people all around me, above me, at my side, behind me. Nobody engages me as a person, speaks with head directed towards me, communicates with me. I exist as a mass, I have physicality, but no personality, I am simply the object of other people's decision. They point their mouths to each other, never towards my head, I am totally present, the centre of all the energetic talking, but I am never included in the discussion, my will, my existence is being violated, I am banished even while in the group.

All is very still and calm and without movement or voices or muscular activity. I am wrapped in complete darkness and tranquillity. If I am dead I am not aware of it, if I am alive I am not aware of it, I have no awareness at all, not of myself, not of my surroundings, not of anyone or of anything.

'Albie . . .' through the darkness a voice, speaking not about me but to me, and using my name and without that terrible urgency of all those other voices '. . . Albie, this is Ivo Garrido speaking to you . . .' the voice is sympathetic and affectionate, I know Ivo, he is an outstanding young surgeon and a friend '. . . you are in the Maputo Central Hospital . . . your arm is in a lamentable condition . . .' he uses a delicate Portuguese word to describe my arm, how tactful the Mozambican culture is compared to the English one, I must ask him later what that word is '. . . we are going to operate and you must face the future with courage.'

A glow of joy of complete satisfaction and peace envelops me, I am in the hands of Frelimo, of the Mozambican Government, I am safe.

'What happened?' I am asking the question into the darkness, my will has been activated in response to hearing Ivo's voice, I have a social existence once more, I am an alive part of humanity.

A voice answers, close to my ears, I think it is a woman's, '. . . a car bomb . . .' and I drift back, smiling inside, into nothingness.

2

I am elsewhere and other. There is a cool crisp sheet on me, I am lying on a couch, aware that I have a body and that I can feel and think and even laugh to myself, and everything seems light and clean and I have a great sense of happiness and curiosity. This is the time to explore and rediscover myself. What has happened to me, what is left of me, what is the damage? I am feeling wonderful and thinking easily in word thoughts and not just sensations, but maybe there is internal destruction . . .

Let me see . . . A joke comes back to me, a Jewish joke from the days when we Jews still told jokes to ward off the pains of oppres-

sion and humiliation, from when I was still a young student and my
mountain-climbing friend had a new joke for me each week, and I
smile to myself as I tell myself the joke, and feel happy and alive
because I am telling myself a joke, the one about Himie Cohen
falling off a bus, and as he gets up he makes what appears to be a
large sign of the cross over his body.

A friend is watching in astonishment. 'Himie,' he says, 'I didn't
know you were a Catholic.'

'What do you mean, Catholic?' Himie answers. 'Spectacles . . .
testicles . . . wallet and watch.'

My arm is free and mobile and ready to respond to my will. It is
on the left side and I decide to alter the order a little, I am sure
Himie would not mind in the circumstances. Testicles . . . My hand
goes down. I am wearing nothing under the sheet, it is easy to feel
my body. My penis is all there, my good old cock (I'm alone with
myself and can say the word) that has involved me in so much
happiness and so much despair and will no doubt lead me up hill
and down dale in the future as well, and my balls, one, two, both in
place, perhaps I should call them testes since I am in hospital. I
bend my elbow, how lovely it is to be able to want again, and then
be able to do what I want; I move my hand up my chest, what
delicious self-determination, what a noble work of art is man . . .
Wallet . . . My heart is there, my ribs over it seem intact, the blood
will pump, the centre of my physical being, the part you take for
granted is okay, I am fine, I will live and live robustly. Spectacles . . .
I range my fingers over my forehead, and cannot feel any craters or
jagged pieces, and I know I am thinking clearly, the darkness is now
feather-light and clean, unlike the heavy, opaque blackness of before. Watch . . . my hand creeps over my shoulder and slides down
my upper arm, and suddenly there is nothing there . . . so I have lost
an arm, Ivo did not say which one, or even that they were going to
cut it off, though I suppose it was implicit in his words, and it's the
right one, since it is my left arm that is doing all the feeling . . . So I
have lost an arm, that's all, I've lost an arm, that's all. They tried to
kill me, to extinguish me completely, but I have only lost an arm.
Spectacles, testicles, wallet, and watch. I joke, therefore I am.

Zuma was laughing as he received me into his arms at the front
door, while comrade John had grave, sad eyes despite my exclama-

tion of pleasure on greeting them; I have become quite expert at embraces, at welcoming with my left arm and giving a little twist to my body so as to protect the injured right side. Leaders, friends, comrades, I do not know which comes first, I am happy to have them with me, and it will also give me the chance to ask them directly about something that, if I was not sick already, I would say has been driving me sick with worry.

My question can wait, now is the moment for me to describe 'what happened.' Often when African comrades are telling a story I feel very 'white' and inhibited, lacking in laughter and impatient to hear the story's end, as if what matters is the piece of factual information being conveyed and not the savour of the telling and the rich personal interactions involved in the narrative. Yet today I know that I will relate the story well, African-style, no hurry, emphasis on the concrete little episodes that illuminate the multi-faceted relationships involved, detailing the humour, irony, and human quirks, a slow progression building up the narrative so that its denouement is fully prepared and yet filled with interest and surprise. There are times for solemnity, times for earnestness, times for passionate calls to battle, and times for laughter. This is a time for laughter, the listener participating in the story by means of almost continuous and celebratory laughter. I will enjoy doing the narration and Zuma will get pleasure from egging me on to even richer and more comic concreteness, counterpointing my reportage with a melodic accompaniment of rising and falling laughter. Zuma's smile and good humour are famous, he even claims that a police spy gave himself up when he saw Zuma smiling at him. John Nkadimeng, trade unionist since my father's day, he has known me since I was a child, I want him to celebrate my survival with me, the arm is a detail, not the main thing, though I must remember that he himself lost one of his sons to a similar bomb blast, and perhaps I remind him of his slain child.

As I launch into my story, Zuma sits close by and watches me intently, ready to respond with warm chuckles and vigorous swings and shakes of his body to each statement I make. When I describe how, lying on the ground in Julius Nyerere Avenue, I shouted ('but politely') in English and Portuguese he almost falls off the chair. He knows that area well, for ten years he was one of our leaders in

Maputo, most of the time he was our 'Chief Rep' there, and the discussions we had over the years were extremely rewarding, and always filled with humour; the bomb that got me could well have been introduced into the country to kill him, only he was withdrawn just over a year ago and I stayed on. I start describing the part when I thought I was fighting for my life against kidnappers from Pretoria when really I was making a few feeble flaps with my shoulders against my Mozambican rescuers, and he lets out roars of supportive laughter, not waiting to the end of the sentence but, as if to underline and share with me the poignant hilarity of the situation, accompanying the climax of my words with happy explosive gurgles. I look across at comrade John, trying to force him with my vivacity to join in the mirth, but he stares back at me with sad, moist eyes. I cannot require him to laugh, and yet in my soul I agree with Zuma; the situation was truly comic, we human beings really get up to the most astonishing things. Wait till I reach the Himie Cohen falling off the bus part, surely comrade John will respond then, and if Zuma is collapsing off his chair with laughter now, what will he be like when I actually tell the joke within a joke part?

Slowly I take Zuma through the hospital portion of the story, of hearing Ivo Garrido's voice and his exquisitely polite word for the state of my arm (huge laughter) and then his statement about operating and my having to face the future with courage (quieter laughter this time), and my comment at the relief I felt at being in the hands of Frelimo (appreciative laughter, high marks for being a good comrade at all times and for telling the story in a gracious and non-boastful way).

I pause so as to give space for the Himie Cohen joke, where the story will resolve itself in genuine euphoric comedy. I wonder if Zuma has heard it already, I suspect that it has done the rounds in ANC circles, though in the rather reduced form of: 'And the first thing comrade Albie did in the hospital was feel for his balls.' People have difficulty remembering the spectacles, testicles part; even Wolfie, whose cultural background is the same as mine, asked me to repeat it three times so that he could write it down correctly.

Looking directly at Zuma's smiling face, and swinging round from time to time to confront comrade John with the humour of my story, I launch into the final portion. '. . . what do you mean,

Catholic? . . . spectacles, testicles, wallet, and watch.' Zuma doubles up and yells with laughter, his mouth wide open, his head rolling back and then coming down again, his eyes full of sympathetic mirth. I feel moved by the situation, by the intense interaction between us. This is what the ANC is, we do not wipe out our personalities and cultures when we become members, rather we bring in and share what we have, Zuma's African-ness, his Zulu appreciation of conversation and humour is mingling with my Jewish joke, enriching it, prolonging and intensifying the pleasure. We are comrades and we are close, yet we do not have to become like each other, erase our personal tastes and ways of seeing and doing things, but rather contribute our different cultural inputs so as to give more texture to the whole. This is how one day we will rebuild South Africa, not by pushing a steamroller over the national cultures, but by bringing them together, seeing them as the many roots of a single tree, some more substantial than others, but all contributing to the tree's strength and beauty.

How many times have I not been asked why I, a white, am in a black movement, or, put another way, why I am fighting for the blacks. For years I knew there was something wrong with the question, but did not know precisely what, and it took a fortuitous statement by a teenage boy at a meeting in the USA to unlock the puzzle for me—he said his friends were arguing that the trouble with people like me was that we were always fighting to liberate others, never to liberate ourselves, was that true? I knew what he was getting at, that we should concentrate on opening up our own heads instead of running away from our personal oppression (spiritual, psychological) and becoming surrogate liberators of others. Maybe that was true of some of the middle-class protestors in the USA, though I preferred to take people at face value and not always look for hidden motives; even reactionaries could be just that, reactionaries. The fact was that it simply did not correspond to the kind of people we were in the South African struggle, where the issues were so real and entered directly into our lives—would one say that the resistance fighters against the Nazi occupation (to take the heroes of my childhood) were simply acting out their own problems? But this young guy had a point and it was a fundamental one: we were not fighting to free someone else, we were in fact fighting for ourselves, we were struggling for our own rights, the right to be free citizens of a free country, that was the answer, and the only way we could achieve our own true freedom was by helping to destroy the system of white domination that was crushing the whole country and denying us all our humanity, black and white.

Graeme Friedman

The Demobbing

Usually I have some idea who is waiting for me but today I have rushed in, breathless, the file unopened under my arm.[1]

The patient leans forward, his elbows on his knees, his gnarled hands holding onto each other. His clothes are grubby. I settle into my seat, glance at the identifying details on the cover of the hospital file, and introduce myself to him. His face is familiar. *Kobus Venter*. I have a feeling that I should recognise his name.

He doesn't make eye-contact. This is the time that I would normally explain to the patient what the initial session is about: that we will discuss his problem and elements of his background—family relationships and so forth—and then we will decide upon a course of action. But I feel thrown, and sit in silence before finding my voice.

'Do you recognise me?'

He looks up slowly. 'What did you say your name was, doctor?'

'Rosenthal,' I say. 'Leonard Rosenthal. And I'm not a doctor. I'm a psychologist.'

He studies my face. I sit remembering.

Coming down to breakfast that morning over a decade ago I'd had a queasy feeling in my stomach. This was my first trial. I was in my mid-twenties, I'd been qualified for barely a year, and there I was doing doggy paddle in the deepest of ends: *The Weipe Trial*. Abraham Molefe, MK cadre, stood accused of a spate of landmine explosions that had taken place in the farming district of Weipe during late

---

1. This story is based upon actual events that took place during *The Messina Trial*. Some of the trial evidence is taken verbatim from the court record. However, the characters of the story are products of the writer's imagination and do not resemble any actual individuals.

1985. The region was known as the Soutpansberg military area, on the border of Zimbabwe. The farmers were all members of the local commando, were armed and in twenty-four-hour radio contact with the security forces. They formed a human Maginot line, a buffer for the guerrillas coming over the border.

The trial had entered its fifth month by the time I was called to the witness box. Defense advocate Yunus Hussein and myself travelled to the border town by small aeroplane, usually a four-seater, a bearable flight in the morning when the weather was generally good, but nightmarish in the afternoon when the summer's thunderstorms threw us around in the sky. We stayed at the Royal Hotel, a run-down establishment that—in its ornate, yellowing ceilings and faded portraits of a royal visit—showed signs of a grander former life. Hussein was just light-skinned and confident enough to confuse the management. I was giving expert evidence in the trial-within-a-trial to determine the admissibility of Molefe's confession. The defense claimed the confession had been forced. The prosecution said it was freely and voluntarily given. My evidence concerned the accused's state of mind during the weeks of interrogation preceding his confession.

I finished my evidence-in-chief. Now I would be facing cross-examination. At the breakfast table, waiting for Hussein to join me, I went over the prosecutor's possible line of attack. It was unlikely that he would focus on the methodological or clinical aspects of my assessment. No, I thought, he'll try to undermine my credibility.

Some ants had launched an attack on the bottle of honey, and got crushed between the threads of the screw-on top. My grandfather taught me to use a clean utensil when extracting food from a communal container. Not everyone who passed through the Royal had a grandfather like mine: suspended in the honey were bits of toast and butter. I dipped my teaspoon in anyway. My concentration seemed shot, other thoughts kept intruding. My mind returned to an event of the previous night, the hotel's white bartender showing us the unusual artifact of which he was the proud custodian. He kept it in the storeroom behind the bar counter—in case, he told us conspiratorially, any ladies should come into the bar. And then he showed it to us. It took a while for me to figure it out, but there it was: a stuffed elephant's penis.

We arrived at the courthouse. Security was as tight as usual. Road blocks to be negotiated, police dogs standing obediently or growling on command of their handlers, over thirty riot policemen stationed in and around the barricaded courthouse, metal detectors and body searches invading privacy, and the occasional helicopter passing overhead.

Abraham Molefe was kept in leg irons, even in court. Hussein had earlier in the proceedings requested that the chains be removed. 'My client is presumably innocent until proven guilty. I don't think he should suffer the indignity of wearing irons in court.'

The judge had turned him down. In his pleasing red robes, with his wavy white hair and soft, craggy face, the judge was a gentle looking man, one could picture him appearing as a guest on a children's television programme. 'The seriousness of the charges,' said Judge Malan, 'makes the removal of the leg irons a risk. And besides, if the Security Police believe there is a risk, I have no reason to doubt their judgment.'

The patient unhooks his hands from their embrace and looks at me quizzically. He is unshaven but that's not what has thrown my memory off. It's that he has aged way beyond the twelve or so years that have passed since last I saw him. His cheeks are lined and sallow, the bones of his face press against the skin.

'Rosenthal. . . .' He repeats my name a few times. 'Rosenthal. . . .'

'Yes, Rosenthal. Leonard Rosenthal.'

The furrow between his eyebrows deepens. 'Should I know you?'

'Perhaps you don't remember me, Mr. Venter. I gave evidence in the Weipe Trial. . . . expert evidence, during the trial-within-a-trial.' I hesitate before adding, 'For the defense.'

He breaks off contact, his eyes look out the window. From where he sits there is nothing to see but blue Jo'burg sky.

The Weipe allegations were indeed serious. There were a total of forty-seven charges, including nine of murder and twenty-six of attempted murder, terrorism, and an alternative charge of treason, the longest charge sheet in the history of South African criminal law. More whites had been killed than in any other case to date.

Molefe had been captured in the bush after an extensive land and air chase. His comrades were executed on the spot. He was beaten almost senseless, hands tied behind his back with a shoelace (one police witness later said this was all that was available), and thrown, with the captured weapons of his unit, in the back of a bakkie driven by two security cops. The policemen underestimated his resilience: he broke free and shot them. A week later he was recaptured. He'd wandered around in the bush under an overcast sky from which he could not get his bearings and, finally on the right path, had been betrayed by a farm labourer a couple of kilometres from the border. A sturdy, well-built, handsome man, the photographs of Abraham Molefe from his recapture show an emaciated skeleton, scratched and bruised, wearing only underpants. He was assaulted by ten men, handcuffed, kicked, hit with a stick, and thrown violently about; a Sgt. Steenkamp stamped his foot on Molefe's stomach until he defecated and lost consciousness for a minute or so. Molefe was placed on a chair. Some excrement escaped his underpants, messing the seat. He was made to eat it, and lick the seat clean.

Venter starts to speak, but his words disappear like vapour exhaled on a cold day. He seems to be thinking about it, about whether he can talk to me.

Finally he says, 'It doesn't matter.'

And then he turns to the window again, his thoughts thrown somewhere outside, perhaps into the clouds that are gathering out there.

'Are you sure? I can make an appointment for you with somebody else.' I want to say that I am not at all certain of my ethical responsibility in this situation, but I don't press this case too strongly. I feel reluctant to say goodbye to him.

He doesn't answer me. Someone laughs in the corridor just outside the room. I have to suppress an urge to yank the door open and tell them to shut up. I am aware of time slipping away, and that I have a five o'clock appointment back at my rooms. But I can't bring myself to hurry him.

That first morning of my cross-examination I made for the toilet, where I managed to close the door of the cubicle before vomiting into the bowl. Overwhelming anxiety did that to me. I suppose the same thing would happen now, if I ever again had reason to feel that scared.

Jan van der Vyver, the prosecutor, leant forward and posed his first question. I remember diagnosing chronic alcohol abuse in his case. The flabby, vein-mapped face gave him away.

'Mr. Rosenthal, are you a South African citizen?'

'Yes, I am,' I said.

'Were you born in this country?'

'I was, M'Lord.' I'd been coached to address my answers to the judge. Look the prosecutor in the eye, think about your answer, turn to the judge, and speak. Keep it brief. The less you give them, the less they have to attack you on. Never say anything you can't back up with evidence. If you're not sure of something, say so. Don't stick your neck out, you're there as an impartial witness, a professional.

'Rosenthal. That's Jewish isn't it? Are you a Jew?'

I remember staring at the prosecutor's pile of folders, and then at his mouth, looking for reassurance that I had heard correctly. Was I a Jew? What kind of question was that?

Of course Rosenthal was a Jewish name but was I a Jew? I hadn't been inside a synagogue since a cousin's barmitzvah years before. At the reception I had refused to stand for the singing of *Die Stem*, and had remained sitting when the band rolled its way into the first bars of *Hatikvah*. Bar the rare brave Rabbi, South African Jews did not speak out. Most were like the devoutly Jewish Percy Yutar, prosecutor of the *Rivonia Trial*, trying his best to prove that Jews were good patriots. They referred to their black servants as 'the girl,' or 'the boy,' even if these men and women were old enough to be their parents. I wanted no part of it.

So when van der Vyver glared across the courtroom at me, asking me if I was Jewish, he was posing a complex question.

'Answer the question, Mr. Rosenthal.'

'Yes,' I said. 'I am a Jew.'

Van der Vyver seemed dissatisfied with my answer. 'To which faith do you belong?'

'I am Jewish.'

'Do you consider the oath you have taken, on the Holy Bible, to swear to tell the truth. . . . do you consider this oath to be binding on your conscience?'

'Yes, M'Lord.' As green and anxious as I then was, I knew what he was doing. Yunus Hussein also knew.

'What, M'Lord,' he asked, jumping to his feet, 'has it got to do with an expert what his religion is?'

The judge stared down at him. 'He is an expert and if the State has reason for asking the questions I am certainly not stopping the State at this stage. You object far too easily, Mr. Hussein, kindly think before opening your mouth again.'

A few minutes later, during an unrelated exchange with Judge Malan, Van der Vyver let something slip. 'The line of cross-examination,' said the prosecutor, 'is to show bias on behalf of the witness.'

I remember thinking again of the bartender's stuffed elephant penis. Of his beaming face in the room behind his bar, of him gesturing like a triumphant child over the dismembered elephant part.

'Rosenthal,' says Kobus Venter, '. . . . that's Jewish, isn't it?'

I can barely nod in reply.

He stares down at his hands. 'Jews,' he says, as if to himself, 'make the best doctors. You are a clever race. Maybe you'll be able to help me.'

Exhibit H of the State's evidence included photographs of the deceased. They were shocking, atrocious images of guerrilla warfare. Men, women, two seven-year-old girls, a couple of toddlers. The one I remember most was that of a young white woman. She could have been sleeping as she lay in her dress, the top of which gaped open to show her cleavage. She seemed to have been pretty in life. The other pictures showed bodies—incomplete bodies—that could not by the wildest stretch of the imagination appear as if they were sleeping.

I could hardly look at those pictures, or think about those children, or those surviving family members. It was inadvisable to feel compassion for the enemy during war, it rendered you impotent. And it threatened to evoke complicated feelings towards comrades who had perpetrated the killings. I liked Abraham Molefe. I felt his support as he sat in the dock while I underwent days of cross-examination, shaking his head, sometimes a private grimace on his face, at other times smiling sympathetically at me.

We governed our world by a simple rule of apportionment: bad things did not reside inside our own skins, but in theirs.

Kobus Venter, who had been one of the border farmers, one of those human buffers, told the Weipe Court about a game-viewing outing he had gone on with his family when their bakkie hit a landmine. 'I heard my wife calling, "I'm burning, I'm burning!"' he said. 'She was two metres behind the bakkie. Her foot had been stuck between mopane trees and we tried to smother the flames.' A flap of flesh from Venter's deeply cut forehead had hung over his eye. Jacob, Venter's four-year-old son, was lying a metre from the burning trees. 'I turned him on his back to extinguish the flames. He was badly wounded and I could see he wouldn't live.' The farmer's son did not survive, nor did his wife and daughter. Venter broke down in the witness box and sobbed.

We turned away.

The defense led evidence. But it was, from a legal point of view, a lost cause. After hearing evidence in mitigation, Judge Japie Malan sentenced Abraham Molefe to death.

He is back in the room now, smiling. An odd sort of smile, skew, not begrudging, but reticent.

'Some wars,' Kobus says, '. . . . turn ordinary people into soldiers.'

'Ordinary people like us,' I say.

He is looking intently into my face now. There are sounds in the corridor outside. A trolley scrapes against the wall, a snippet of muffled conversation, the lift's alarm bell—someone has got stuck in there again. I am aware of the shortage of time.

'Are you ready to tell me what has brought you to the hospital?' I'm not going to take notes; there is no need, I will not forget anything he says to me.

'I'm frightened,' he blurts out. 'All the time. I'm shaking, look!' He lifts one trembling hand. 'I can't sleep. My wife says I scream in my sleep.'

'What are you frightened of?'

'O-of. . . . I. . . . you know, ach!' He shakes his head as he begins to cry. '. . . . It's the baby.'

It gradually emerges that he has recently married, and his wife is pregnant. I wonder, absurdly, whether she is white or black. He is still crying and I am trying to find some way of communicating empathy. I will have to say something, because he has his face in his hands.

'You are worried about the baby.' My comment feels hopelessly inadequate. He falls silent again.

The sky outside the consulting room window has turned dark and heavy. I picture him in the witness box weeping for his lost family. I picture his first wife and their children, burnt and broken, and him with blood and skin and smoke and heat in his eyes, trying to put out the flames that spring from their bodies. I picture them dead. I think about my own wife and little boy, who is almost the age little Jacob Venter was when he died.

I think about Kobus' new, pregnant wife, and wonder aloud whether this new life has not given birth to his old nightmare. He looks up from his cracked farmer's hands.

The sky opens up. Johannesburg's thunderstorm has begun for the day. I will have to fly in it again.

Matthew Krouse

The Mythological Structure of Time

Purimshpiel

A ray of light shines through the synagogue portal. It's the same old ray of light, the one you probably saw in every synagogue you went to, in just about every corny Yiddish film you saw, in every photo or portrait of Jewish life ever pictured on earth. The difference is that I am looking at the ray of light. That's God's Light, I reckon, standing in the back row davening away among the whole community. We're all swaying and nodding, like neurotic partners doing a barn dance in a mental asylum. The men that is. Downstairs we're all draped in taleisim so my new yomtov clothes don't show because I've got a big talis covering me, falling to the ground, like ones the pious Jews wear. Not a shiney fake little one with blue stripes, but a convincing cotton special. Status in the eyes of God.

The cantor sings: 'Haman!' And we all go wild, stamping our feet and shouting back, 'Haman! Haman!'

It's Purim of course. Haman, as we know, was a previous Hitler. He also hated us, and it's obvious why. It's because we behave like a herd of cattle, and we look like moneylending, baby blood drinkers. We can't seem to change. History never worked the stinky-herring-look out of our genes.

Who Haman really was I honestly don't know. They say he wore a three-cornered hat. So, on Purim we eat sweet poppy seed cakes apparently the same shape. In our sad gluttony all we can do is to devour what he wore on his head.

On Purim we even write Haman's name under our shoes. Then when the cantor sings, 'Haman,' straight from the Megilah Esther, we stamp on his name until a gabai bangs his flat hand loudly on his desk, and goes, 'Shht!' and we all shut up and wait for Haman's name again.

We hold up Homen dreidels, clappers of plastic; some old people have ones made of wood. These we wave in the air when the cantor sings: 'Haman! Haman! Haman!' Until the gabai hits his hand on his desk and we shut up again. Our response is contrived to liberate us from our hatred, when we hear that terrible name. And as we make complete idiots of ourselves we also realise, emphatically, that we're all miserably the same.

On Purim we also dress up. They say it's the only time of the year when a Jewish man may wear a woman's dress. But this I've never seen. I've seen hundreds of girls dressed as Queen Esther, but never a man dressed as her. I'd like to make up as Queen Esther though, but in a real crown, with jewelled earrings, and not just a paper crown painted a shoddy gold.

The light shines through the synagogue portal. Old men drop their reading glasses and fall asleep before their books.

Jesus

At fourteen, about a year after my Barmitzvah I decided to confront God. Perhaps I was just acting out what I pictured to be a scene from *Fiddler on the Roof*, playing Tevieh the Milkman, challenging Him. I looked up to the sky and asked some fundamental question, I forget—no answer. Then I grabbed my best friend after cheder, when the shul stood empty and dark. We sneaked off behind the curtain of the ark where we stood in front of the torahs, and we ceremonially chanted the name, 'Jesus! Jesus! Jesus!'

No response, just silence, and the eery red light of the oil lamp, and the creaking of the wooden beams of the roof.

Troimen

I dream of my parents' wedding. The old home movie shows that, in the era of rock-and-roll when they stood beneath the chupah, there was no carpet in the shul, just a bare wooden floor. But the fake marble pillars were there, and the lions, and the big chandelier in the shape of the Magen Dovid, and the embroidery on everything donated in the name of a Zeida, nobody should ever forget.

For five minutes we sit in the lounge watching as a family—a silent film in and out of focus, filmed by a friend. The projector sounds like a steam train. A steam train shunting through the lounge. For a second I fiddle with a projector button and the retinue moves backwards. Back into Auntie Sylvia's house, then forward again, everybody prancing out the front door. Each family member kisses the mezuzah. In the garden they all pose formally around my mother, the radiant bride. Bobba can't stop talking, but the film is silent and her words are lost. They're all gathered in front of a fishpond, complete with a concrete elfen, pouring water from a little urn.

Later, at the shul, everybody is leaving—and there is no carpet, just the bare wooden floor. They all kiss the shul's mezuzah, again. Bobba's still talking. The projector sounds like a steam train, clattering through time, through the lounge. And my parents name all the faded faces, framed, smiling, tottering abruptly as figures in historical films.

'There's so-and-so,' whispers mommy, 'shame, she's gone now.'

And, 'there's so-and-so,' they whisper to each other, 'and shame, he's gone now too.'

So many links are broken, I realise as I write. So many guests departed, as though marriage is just a funeral, and love affirmed only for the purposes of the dead.

Yiskor

The empty shul. An old black cleaner, Eddie, shuffles up and down the rows of wooden seats. Brass name plaques confirm which members have paid their fees. Eddie picks up some kid's crumpled sweet papers, then gathers up the prayer books for the library shelf. And somewhere in the third row, where a negligent old Jew removed a hanky from his pocket, Eddie finds a ten rand note, one that had fallen mistakenly to the floor. The rules have been broken, but Eddie wouldn't know—that we're not supposed to bring money into shul.

Eddie locks the main doors, and shuffles off to the adjoining community hall. In the hall Eddie packs away a film projector, and

puts a precious reel of film into a brown cardboard case. The film is
burning. The film, an historical shard. It was community propaganda, shown after one memorable shabbes—Holocaust was its
frightening name.

Naked men and women line up to be shot. Then, dead, just fall
into a trench. Their grave, like an inverted shul, inside out and
upside down. And we all cried out aloud, drowning the din of the
projector, just as we cried when the Rabbi got up in the heat of
the fast, and in anger announced the Yom Kippur war. Eddie packs
the film into its coffin. Eddie is the chevrah kadishah of our film.

To cry, the adults send the children outside, to play in the garden,
while they dutifully recite Yiskor, communal memorials to the dead.
I kissed a boy during Yiskor, it left me feeling guilty and proud.
Once I fought and hit a bully during Yiskor, then felt that mixture of
guilt and pride too.

Cakes

The Oriental style is domed, and pillared, almost like a wedding
cake. Inside there is lots of fake marble and red velvet, and bal-
ustrades, and the facsimile of the ten commandments supported by
two lions above the ark. To get everything just right the architects
must have consulted the Rabbi, and the Chazen, and the shul's
President, and the Women's Committee, and the Beth Din, and the
Hebrew teacher.

Old pictures of the shul's unveiling show only the backs of posh
Yiden hovering about the engraved dedication stone, outside in the
garden of the new shul. Chief Rabbi J. L. Landau is busy doing
something official in the photographs, at the stone engraved in
Hebrew and English, he's in a long black clergical robe, complete
with rabinical kipeh and talis. That was in 1930, and you can see the
women dressed like flapper girls from the previous decade, wearing
what was fashionably called the cloche hat, beneath which must
have been cute bobbed hairstyles, with their shoulders tucked dain-
tily under fox fur collared coats. It must have been winter.

The gabaim were wearing the essential top hats and tails. The
main players were standing before the Union Jack. And the shul, in
the Oriental style was a virgin, pure white like a new wedding cake.

Whereas today, almost seventy years later, it's like the crumbling cake of a marriage that, perhaps, never was.

Allah

'The shul will have to close, they say,' comments mother in passing, over one shabbes lunch.

'No Jews left here,' moans father, wolfing down a slice of pickled tongue. 'We don't even get a minyan on Yom Kippur,' he groans playing on my guilt.

'What'll they do?' I ask, my question born more out of curiosity than concern.

'Well, we could join services with the next town. But walking's a problem on shabbes so we could meet at the Rabbi's down the road.'

'What'll happen to the shul itself?' I ask, thinking of the big chandelier and how it would look hanging in my lounge.

'The Jewish Board of Deputies may sell the place.'

'They're already putting out feelers. And guess who's put in the first bid?' Mother's eager to reveal the shocking truth.

'Who?'

'The Muslims, from the centre of town,' mother's voice says, trembling a bit.

'And where do they pray now?' I'm very interested to know.

'In an empty shop,' father blandly reports. 'But there are too many of them now, and they're looking for a mosque.'

'It's going to cause trouble,' mother warns. In the tone of her voice there's a tinge of resentment, I detect.

'Pity Yitzchak Rabin's not around to draft the Peace Accord,' I joke, but the parents aren't impressed.

And for dessert there's pareve ice cream—suitably cold.

Treyf

Bobba found treyf in the kitchen. Like a General preparing for war she commanded the maid, and mother, to stack all the milk pots and ordered them outdoors. In a dignified procession the three hefty women marched to the garden to bury the utensils in a flower-bed. The appropriate spot, among the azaleas, was chosen by Bobba, after a barrage of Yiddish debate. The grave was to be dug by Bobba herself, while the gardener laughed and Nona, the Maid, clucked angrily to herself.

Bobba was on her knees digging, the sand was flying in the air. I watched from my bedroom window, she was wearing floral gardening gloves, scooping out sand with a trowel. For 24 hours the pots stayed buried, a brief death for such a ceremonious funeral. Then, having been reincarnated, Bobba was satisfied they were kosher again. The disgraced Nona was sent outside to dig them up.

Perhaps Nona was scolded for cooking her meat in the milchikeh pots. Perhaps she was dismissed—I can't recall. Yet because of what happened, when we next ate milchikeh my stomach turned. How it emphasised the division in the home.

My darling parents,

I have news. Important news I daren't share, about which there is a despairing silence.

I have fallen in love with a poor, uneducated Muslim. I don't know how to tell you so I'm writing this letter. But this is a letter I hope you never read, because it's really my acknowledgement, intended only for myself. On the other hand, perhaps it'll be published—who can tell?—you know my ambition's to be a writer, so I'm committed to paper. Bluntly, I'm proclaiming by this, that I now offer whatever soul I might have to the love I've found.

If you were to meet him, which I'll spare you, or merely glance at him crossing a familiar road, you'd think nothing. He's not an oil painting, but I desire him all the same. However, you'd probably note, unconsciously, that there goes the child of an immigrant home. Their history isn't dissimilar to ours. And these old misfortunes are not the only things we share. I think, with a sense of irreconcilable irony, of our dietary laws, resembling theirs in certain ways. Where we have treyf they have haram—forbidden things one may not devour. Only yesterday I had the disturbing thought that, since our love is between men from two conflicting groups, it could be called a treyf love, or a love that is haram. Our forbidden gluttony.

This caused me to remember the day Bobba caught Nona cooking her meat in the milchikeh pots. Remember how furiously she buried them, in the flower bed until they were clean? I think of my love—If only the rules were the same!—if we could bury our love for a night and a day. We'd sleep underground, in each other's arms, emerging good and pure, proudly, sanctioned by God.

This is impossible, and such an absurd suggestion makes a mockery of the law. So, all I can ask is your forgiveness, and all I can wish for is your warmth.

Your beloved Bubbeleh

P.S. Mom, your week at the health farm did you the world of good. This Pesach you looked ten years younger than the glamorous Shula Berr.

Friends

When Bobba was dying, in her final days the community performed an ancient rite. In the synagogue they renamed her. Why this ceremony occurs I haven't properly found out. I've been told that the ritual's origins can be found in the Kabalah though. They say, too, that with a different name the Angel of Death won't recognise you, he'll pass you by and you'll be saved.

And what was the new name they gave her, as she lay in a cancerous coma, on the brink of an untimely death? I'll never know, but it didn't save her. If there is indeed a God he still chose that moment to take her away.

Fifteen years later my Lithuanian Zeida, in hospital dying of emphysema, softly called my mother to his side.

'Temma, Temma where are all my friends?' he asked his daughter in Yiddish.

'Dead, your friends are dead, go to them!' she told him weeping. This she did with encouragement, to give him the courage he needed to die.

In our local cemetery, in the ugliest part of town, lies my whole family. Beside my grandfather—to the east—is the grave of a young Jewish boy killed in 1985, shot by Cubans in the Angolan war.

Beside my grandmother—to the west—lies the body of another Jewish boy, one who died in 1993. The cause of his death was AIDS.

For years we all stood together, now we all lie together, while the sound of passing traffic seems to murmur our families' names.

Acknowledgments

Excerpt from Rose Zwi, *Another Year in Africa* (Johannesburg: Bateleur, 1980). Reprinted by permission of the author.

Nadine Gordimer, 'My Father Leaves Home' in *Jump and Other Stories* (New York: Farrar, Straus & Giroux, 1991). Copyright © 1991 by Felix Licensing B.V. Reprinted by permission of Farrar, Straus & Giroux, Inc.

Dan Jacobson, 'The Zulu and the Zeide' in *A Long Way from London* (Boston: Little, Brown & Company, 1959). Reprinted by the permission of Russell & Volkening, as agents for the author. Copyright © 1959 by Jacobson, renewed © 1987 by Dan Jacobson.

Sarah Gertrude Millin, 'Esther's Daughter' in *Two Bucks Without Hair and Other Stories* (London: Faber & Faber, 1957).

Barney Simon, 'Our War' in *Joburg, Sis!* (Johannesburg: Bateleur, 1974). Reprinted by permission of the estate of Barney Simon.

Nehemiah Levinsky, 'In the Shadow of Nuremberg' is a translation of 'In Sotn fun Nirnberg' in *Der Regn hot Farshpetikt* (The rains came late) (Johannesburg: Mishpacha, 1959). Translated from the Yiddish by Joe Podbrey. First published in English translation in *Jewish Affairs* 51, no. 3 (spring 1996): 60–71.

Excerpts from Dov Fedler, 'Gagman' are printed from the manuscript version by permission of the author.

Lionel Abrahams, 'Cut Glass' in *The Celibacy of Felix Greenspan* (Johannesburg: Bateleur, 1977). Reprinted by permission of the author.

Maja Kriel,' 'Number 1-4642443-0' in *Original Sin and Other Stories* (Cape Town: Carrefour, 1993). Reprinted by permission of the author.

Lilian Simon, 'God Help Us.' Reprinted by permission of the author.

Sandra Braude, 'Behind God's Back,' *Staffrider* 11, nos. 1–4 (1993). Reprinted by permission of the author.

Tony Eprile, 'Letters from Doreen' in *Temporary Sojourner and Other South African Stories* (New York: Simon & Schuster, 1989). Reprinted by permission of the author.

Pieter-Dirk Uys, 'Evita—the Legend' is adapted from 'A Part Hate, a Part Love' and is printed from the manuscript version by permission of the author.

Excerpt from Albie Sachs, *Soft Vengeance of a Freedom Fighter* (London: Grafton Books, 1990). Reprinted by permission of the author.

Graeme Friedman, 'The Demobbing' is printed from the manuscript version by permission of the author.

Matthew Krouse, 'The Mythological Structure of Time' is printed from the manuscript version by permission of the author.